THE NOTBOOK
OF KABIR

Advance praise for *The Notbook of Kabir*

To read Anand writing about Kabir, to read Kabir's words through Anand's rendering—this is a book (sorry, a notbook) that keeps on giving. It is history and politics, it is poetry and philosophy, it is prose at its most precise, it is simultaneously tender and savage. Anand's rendition establishes Kabir as a living testament to life itself.

Meena Kandasamy, poet, novelist, translator

Drawing on the rich experience of hearing Kabir and singing Kabir, Anand has brought us the rare gift of a set of translations that have been mined in the heart and refined in the head.

Jerry Pinto, poet, writer, translator

Kabir is mysterious, unknowable, playful, intimate, ubiquitous. Anand's remarkable collection does everything a translation should: it invites the reader to revel in the mysteries of Kabir by whatever means necessary. There is something for everyone: the nagari version, the transliteration, the joyous English translation, and notes which connect us to other avenues to the poet, to the versions of performers, the opinings of scholars and the interpretations of thinkers.

Daisy Rockwell, Booker Prize–winning translator

The Notbook of Kabir embodies the dialectic of one becoming many and many becoming one, capturing the universe's whispers in an embrace of uncertainty. It merges Anand— singer, poet, thief, translator, editor, madman, woman—into a singularity that implodes outward.

A/nil, author of *The Absent Color*

Playful, deep, beautiful, strange. The poet-musician Anand has taken Kabir and been taken by Kabir to places that are utterly different, unexpected, *nyaaraa*. I went a little crazy at first trying to compare the English to the original. 'That's not what it says in Hindi,' I grumbled. But then I just gave up and read the poems, swam, strolled, rolled, was startled, delighted, bemused. These are songs made of words by a person who hears the music. Kabir and Anand have inspired each other. As they say together, 'Such a large lock jangles on your heart/ Who but a poet can pick it apart?'

Linda Hess, translator-scholar of Kabir

Another iteration in the inspiring lineages of Kabir transmission and translation. Welcome once again to the essentials and particulars of this unique poetry of devotion and endurance.And may it continue to resound in the prodigious work of Anand.

Anne Waldman, poet

The idea of "Kabir" becomes an opportunity for Anand to free himself from writerly convention and create a new kind of text, one that refuses to accept demarcations between commentary, glossary, translation and poetry.

Amit Chaudhuri, writer and musician

Kabir's timeless wisdom is vibrantly brought to life in this *Notbook*, offering a fresh perspective through the lens of a vocalist. The masterful English rendering of Kabir's song-poetry, paired with insightful commentary on their aesthetic nuances, will captivate and thrill readers.

Anand Teltumbde, writer and scholar

Anand offers us an exquisite treasure, an eclectic, intelligent, sometimes maverick, even playful curation of Kabir's poetry. The Kabir Anand seeks out in the pages of this *Notbook* is the poet who is astride a song, not trapped in books of learning. Anand's is a compilation into which the reader can dip and find new meaning at every turn of her life. In lyrical and iridescent prose Anand describes why Kabir, in every age, spreads amongst those 'hungry for love and equality'. Kabir's poetry for Anand is 'a realization of fraternity among strangers' across centuries. He describes Kabir's sung-and-heard writing as Kabiri, a boundless community of poetry, a fabric without stitches, wear and tear, woven together by the poet, the singer and the listener into a 'warm blanket of words'. *The Notbook* of Kabir is a book that will not age.

Harsh Mandar, writer and activist

It is almost impossible to capture *The Notbook's* essence. Its seductive fragrance lingers on like the sound of silence after the drone of the tanpura fades out. Kabir is a tune that you can't get out of your head, which takes over your life. He has been hummed for centuries without pause. See what happened to Anand. 'Kabir had gone to his head, and he's full of emptiness.' Kabir had fun with god and now Anand has fun with Kabir. He invites us to join him on an unending journey to musically encounter Kabir the legendary master weaver who wrought his loom to produce a simmering tapestry—ethereal and durable at the same time. What resonates powerfully in *Thinner than Water, Fiercer than Fire* is the cry against injustice and inequality that pierces the deafness that surrounds us. There remains only bliss that is experienced when the ego is a extinguished. *The Notbook of Kabir* is a life-altering masterpiece.

Pushpesh Pant, historian and writer

Anand's extraordinary book embraces the ethereal space that surrounds Kabir's name, turning the material that many scholars dismiss as spurious and inauthentic into a powerful poetry of the present. Rather than a quixotic search for the 'historical Kabir', *The Notbook* presents Kabir as he lives amidst us now. Anand builds a bridge across time, language, genre and expectation, drawing on his formidable skills as a poet to render Kabir in English poetry as something truly beautiful and new.

Christian Lee Novetzke, author of *Religion and Public Memory: A Cultural History of Saint Namdev in India*

THE NOTBOOK OF KABIR

OF KABIR

Thinner than Water, Fiercer than Fire

ANAND

PENGUIN
VIKING

An imprint of Penguin Random House

VIKING

Viking is an imprint of the Penguin Random House group of companies
whose addresses can be found at global.penguinrandomhouse.com

Published by Penguin Random House India Pvt. Ltd
4th Floor, Capital Tower 1, MG Road,
Gurugram 122 002, Haryana, India

Penguin
Random House
India

First published in Viking by Penguin Random House India 2024

ISBN 9780143467670

Typeset in Bembo, ITF Devnagari, Neo Sans Pro
Printed at Thomson Press India Ltd, New Delhi

www.penguin.co.in

Two birds on a tree, one real, the other its desire
In walks Kabir, and sets the tree of meaning afire
What survives is a darkness that makes all equal
The sun falls on all—no one's untouchable

Contents

Language matters
भासा और लहजा

In this *Notbook*, the Nagari version of each song is given first, followed by its Roman transliteration. The translation comes last. The Nagari script conforms to the many accents in which the songs are sung, spoken and heard, and does not offer standardized spellings. The transliteration eschews diacritics to make it reader-friendly. Since Indian languages do not have the concept of capitalization of first words or nouns, the transliterations have none. In the transliterations, Kabir becomes 'kabeer'. While the anglicized Brahmin is capitalized (like Muslim, Dalit), brahman and its variants are not. English, unlike subcontinental languages, is not phonetic. Among other sounds common to subcontinental tongues, English lacks the voiced velar nasal or the voiced retroflex flap. The upper-case *T* in *kuTamb* (for family) is to be pronounced like the *t* in *tomb*. There's no dental *ta* in English. The lower-case *t* in *teer* (arrow) comes close to the sound of *thin* but think more to *Roberto* in Spanish. The *th* in *thaaro* (yours) aligns with *thick*. The *e* in *kahe* and *kare* and such is read as in *cliché*. In words that can be misread as English, such as with *mile, mare* and *bole*, the *é* are rendered as *miley, marey* and *boley*. The use of *D* in *chiDiya* (bird) is like the *d* in *dog*. In *gaDh* (fort), try American *birdhouse*; and the *gh* in *ghar* (home) is as in *loghouse*. For the *chh* in *chhoD* (leave), follow *achoo*. The lower-cased *d* in *dekh* (see) sounds like the *th* in *the* and *they*. The capitalized N in *maakhaN* (butter) is like in *burn*. Use these keys and figure the rest by giving in to eye–ear coordination. Even better, tune in to a select playlist of these songs I've curated on my YouTube channel, Raga N Bhim, https://t.ly/-VNS2. Italicization is used only for titles of works, for the first-time use of non-English words in the prose passages and for emphasis. The works of writers and sources I cite are highlighted in their first occurrence in **semibold**, and information on them is given at the end under "Notes on Sources" (where the corresponding page numbers are given to loop back to the main text).

The Nagari–Roman textual exercise is necessary since this is the first time all these songs are being bound in one book. Like much of old poetry, they do not have titles. Often first lines or refrains are given as titles in the Nagari script; with the English, I take liberties. The romanization is directed at the many who often hear and follow but do not necessarily speak, read or write what is called Hindustani (earlier Hindwi—that of the Hind). Given its propensity to mix and blend, this tongue was known during the Mughal period as Rekhta (literally that which is scattered and gets mixed), giving birth to the urbane Urdu, that eventually evolved into the polycentric modern language of Bombay movies. Like Kabir's shape-shifting songs, Hindwi/ Hindustani/ Rekhta/ Urdu/ Hindi too is a shape-shifting group of mutually intelligible languages and dialects spoken across swathes of northern India. Since I have tried to capture something that is sung, it helps to have some idea of how it all *sounds*. If Hindustani and its many scents and accents are mere impediments, simply jump to the translations.

An interjection
बीच में एक बात

Of all the dead poets, Kabir is the most alive. He comes to us with a song in his step and a dance on his lips. His songs change shape and course like a river. His words are mutable, not fixated on fixity.

Kabir is a disembodied spectre from the fifteenth–sixteenth century. One can broadly claim that he is from north and central India, though there's a grave for him far in the east in Odisha, besides the official one in Magahar, one hundred miles from Benares where he is said to have made a living as a weaver. One book says he was born in 1398, another says 1594. A colonial gazetteer says a mausoleum for Kabir 'Shah', the King of the Word, was built in 1450 by Bijli Khan (the adopted son of Pahar Khan, a Mughal faujdar or military commander of Ghazipur and Patna) in Magahar, on the right bank of the Ami river. Some believe Kabir visited the pilgrim centre of Pandharpur in present-day Maharashtra, the epicentre of the Marathi *abhang* song-making tradition, and even made it to Gujarat. Others say he travelled as far as Samarkand and Baghdad. The Sikhs believe he undertook a pilgrimage to the Gomti riverbank (near Pilibhit, in present-day Uttar Pradesh). Their sacred book, *Adi Granth*, has this verse in the raga Asa: 'Haj hamari gomti teer/ Jaha baseh pitambar peer'. (To the

Gomti bank I pilgrim/ To my yellow-clad master this hymn.) The Persian work *Khulasat-ut-Tawarikh* (Epitome of History, c.1695 CE), a history written during the Mughal emperor Aurangzeb's reign, says Kabir visited Ratnapur in Chhattisgarh, home to a major Kabir ashram for about four hundred years now.

Everyone wants a piece of Kabir. He was born in many places and died in many ways in still more places. He belongs everywhere and no-place.

Kabir is more of a mystery than a mystic, more a persona than a person. Kabir is a sign. A sign that the signature can be a shared consciousness, a collective way of being. In much of South Asian poetry, the poet's signature is embedded into each poem, often at the end of a verse. It is known as तख़ल्लुस/ *takhallus*, an Arabic word used in Urdu, Punjabi and Persian, and as भणित/ *bhanita* or *bhanita chaap*/ भणित छाप in languages affiliated to Pali and Sanskrit. **Takhallus** means to be liberated, be secure; **bhanita** means what is spoken or uttered. The signature 'Kabir'—meaning humongous, great, grand, illustrious—is at once democratic and demotic. Simply, 'of or belonging to the people'. Kabir is a signature that can and must be forged time and again, and forged so well as to merge with the Unseen Unseeable Unknowable Untraceable Original. It is what Mirza Ghalib, among the most aristocratic and singular of poets, calls in one ghazal 'being one with what you see'—*chashm ko chaahiye har rang mein vaa ho jaanaa*. It means opening the eye to every aspect of colour.

The Notbook of Kabir is an invitation to two kinds of readers: those who have never encountered Kabir either in song or in books, and those who have already read him and heard him in many versions, and consider themselves adepts, and yet can find him anew.

Kabir, first-most, is an invitation to play with words. Kabir is an invitation to listen, then sing along, and perhaps dance a bit. Kabir is an invitation to be in song, be in tune. First, with oneself. Kabir is an invitation to take joy in the delicious—and free—pleasures of language threaded to the abstract thought of music.

Kabir is an invitation to witness the formless take form. Kabir is an invitation to think the unthought.

Like many must have, I first encountered Kabir in school. I was perhaps eleven. His *dohas*, couplets, were a fixture in Hindi textbooks. Kabir's language did not sound like the Hindi we read in other texts, nor did it resemble the Hindustani of Bollywood movies, nor what we encountered on the streets and in everyday conversations in Hyderabad, where I grew up, which was more a Dakkhani (southern) variant with a smattering of Telangana Telugu flowing into Urdu. Yet Kabir spoke to me, like he did to many of my mates. He made us feel we could speak to him if we answered in verse.

Let me re-cite a doha I was taught. It is notoriously famous and is often cited by smug teachers, parents and elders to goad children to do homework, chores and such *on time*.

काल करे सो आज कर आज करे सो अब
पल में प्रलय होएगी बहुरि करेगा कब

kaal kare so aaj kar aaj kare so ab
pal mein pralay hoegee bahuri karegaa kab

Why wait till tomorrow, why not now
If there's doing to be done, do it now

If I must stake sweat-of-brow claims on Kabir, it could be:

Come, sweat on time's brow, do it now
Could be apocalypse next, you never know

I had parodied the 'original' and shared it with my classmates.

आज करे सो काल कर काल न आवे अब
पल में प्रलय होएगी काहे करे कछु अब

aaj kare so kaal kar kaal na aave ab
pal mein pralay hoegee kaahe kare kachhu ab

The world could come undone before you do
What good will doing have you do?

Why seize the day, save it for another day
If it all comes to nothing, why not delay?

Why rush now, there's tomorrow, there's day after
If the end of days is nigh, why even bother?

My friends too riffed on Kabir. It took me years to realize that there are Kabir poems that say the exact opposite of the values espoused in the revered couplets taught in textbooks. When I shared this with Alex George, my colleague, a lapsed Malayali from Mumbai, he proffered this recreation from his childhood, saying, *we* did it like this:

आज करे सो काल कर काल करे सो परसों
जल्दी बाज़ी काहेकू जीना है जो बरसों

aaj kare so kaal kar kaal kare so parson
jaldee baazee kaahekoo jeenaa hai jo barson

What needs doing now can always be put away
Why rush about when there's a life to live away

Kabir was and is an invitation to join a community of poetry, weaving ourselves into a warm blanket of words. Kabir is a fabric without stitches. No centres, no edges. No beginnings, no endings. While claiming that no one could weave like him, he invites everyone in:

The cloth Kabir bears knows no wear and tear
He holds the warp of love with the weft of care

Kabir equally says—as sung by Mahesha Ram, the contemporary Dalit singer from Chhatangarh village in Jaisalmer, Rajasthan, who like Kabir is a weaver—that words aren't what we must stake our pride on. For the Word can visit a blessing upon anyone:

It is not just Kabir who can see all this
    There's love in every heart, a poem in everyone
Mahesha Ram sings it, Anand dances to this
    Love is in every heart, a poem in everyone

This school of making poetry believes that poetry makes us, that it is our refuge, that we can each arrive at the boundless no-place of awareness in poetry. Even the accursed Brahmin may cease to be a Brahmin in this blessed no-place.

Raised as a middle-class Tamil Brahmin with little idea of Tamil, I have lived in a soup of languages, knowing not any one of them well. I was born in the Deccan, in the town of Raichur in Karnataka, where Kannada and Dakkhani are the predominant languages. I did my schooling and college across the state of Andhra Pradesh in the 1980s and 1990s, mostly in Hyderabad, amidst Telugu and Dakkhani. At home, an ossified variant of Tamil, my mother tongue (so to say), was spoken. English was the medium of instruction in the urban schools and colleges that I attended. I made a living as a journalist in Chennai for nine years, where I honed my spoken Tamil to a more generic accent, shedding the diglossic Brahmin variant I was raised in. I moved to Delhi in 2007. Since then, I've lived and worked in this city of thirty million people where variants of Hindi, Punjabi and Urdu are spoken. This is where I rediscovered and reconfigured Kabir as he was and is sung. A migrant in all languages, I am at home in even those I know little of. Those intrigued or piqued by the confluence of scents and accents I bear, often ask me in Hindi, आप कहाँ के हो? *Aap kahaan ke ho?* Where are you from? My ready reply is, अब तो कहीं का न रहा. *Ab toh kaheen kaa na rahaa.* Now, I've come to be from nowhere. Kabir makes me feel at home everywhere and nowhere, in language and in music.

Kabir did not leave behind any book. He is, however, found in many books. More often though, he is found outside of them.

The Notbook of Kabir is an effort to seek this absent Kabir. The unbound and boundless are bound here—this is the poet sung and heard. Not the one snared by definitions and pursuits of authenticity. This is both Kabir and Not.

Kabir today writes in English. He does not fear that the aural/ oratorical fluidity of this 'tradition' will suffer from such an appropriation. It has survived several such attempts on life. Kabir is the sign that the signature is a shared form of existence—the realization of fraternity amongst strangers.

The Kabir you will find here is how he is rendered by a range of artists: Prahlad Tipaniya, a Dalit from Luniyakhedi in the Malwa region of Madhya Pradesh who now performs across the world; the late Kumar Gandharva, a Brahmin from north Karnataka who discovered his Kabir while recovering from a phase of aphasia in Dewas, Madhya Pradesh; Mukhtiyar Ali of the Mirasi community, a Sufi singer from Pugal village in Rajasthan; Kaluram Bamaniya, a Dalit from Malwa who quarrelled with the Kabirpanthi establishment before finding his Kabir; Fariduddin Ayaz, Abu Mohammed and party, who trace their musical lineage to Delhi's Qawwal Bachchon ka Gharana and now make a living as *qawwal*s in Karachi, Pakistan; and many more. I heard several of these songs after I moved to Delhi in 2007 and found the multi-volume CD-and-book compendium produced by "The Kabir Project" anchored by the filmmaker-turned-singer Shabnam Virmani (hosted now on ajabshahar.com) and initiated in 2002. These have led me to more such songs. Most of the songs featured in *The Notbook* can now be found on YouTube if you search their first lines. Each singer who lights up Kabir is named and often discussed in the body of this book, interspersed by excursive exercises and *obiter dicta*.

The songs in *The Notbook* will not correspond with the lyrics printed in the posthumously published editions—the *Kabir Granthavali, Adi Granth, Bijak, Mahabijak, Kabir Parachai, Sakhi* and so forth, overseen mostly by 'pandit' scholars. This is not to say that these books contain a less (or more) authentic Kabir. It is just that binding Kabir in a book is like snaring the breeze in a box. Printed words do not breathe the way they do in shapeshifting songs that are renewed and regenerated each time they are sung and heard. Exercises at fixing Kabir also demonstrate modernism's urgent and compulsive need, however anachronistic, to celebrate individual genius and its refusal to see great poetry as anything but an expression of an absolutely unique mind. After all, like the French critic **Roland Barthes** said, 'The author is a modern figure, and the culmination of modernism is in the death of the author.' Kabir, whoever he was and whenever he was, felt no Ghalib-like existential need for originality—the need for a definitive *Divan-e-Ghalib*, of which he oversaw seven editions in his lifetime. We could say, Kabir had no need for such a need. He did not belong to such a time or class. Prahlad Tipaniya, Fariduddin Ayaz, Mahesha Ram, Kaluram Bamaniya or others in their performances pay no heed to and are unaware of these efforts at standardization: the Akademi/ academy-driven industry around Kabir.

Among the early efforts to take Kabir to the modern English-speaking world was the edition **Rabindranath Tagore** published in 1913 with Macmillan, London—*One Hundred Poems of Kabir*. Tagore made Kabir appear mystical and spiritual, and the introduction by the (now forgotten) Christian mystic and poet Evelyn Underhill compounded matters. Also, Tagore's was a translation of a translation, based on the 'printed Hindi text with Bengali translation of Mr Kshiti Mohan Sen'. Latter-day scholars, in their wisdom, regard only six of the hundred in this volume as 'authentic', an authenticity that is inherently inauthentic. There have been several translations and editions, invariably based on the Kabir bound and found in modern books. Bookstores in India stock very little poetry, but you'll invariably find a clutch of books on Kabir (alongside Rumi and Rupi Kaur).

Each singer and performer I have heard, each song featured here, is true only to itself—each quietly certain that the Original is but a distinctive and distinguished version.

Consider the etymology of the word *version* and the versions of its meaning:

> Noun. 1580s, 'a translation', from Middle French *version*, Medieval Latin *versionem* (nominative *versio*) 'a turning, a translation', from past participle stem of Latin *vertere* 'to turn, change, alter, translate'. Also with a Middle English sense of 'destruction'; the meaning 'particular form of a description' is first attested in 1788.

Kabir, like Ghalib, is totally aware of his genius and often praises himself. Many of his songs often speak of how he knows the path to the no-place, how he has seen the true light others can't see, and how he wears an unsullied seamless fabric. But he also betrays the humility that recognizes the need in every human to aspire for *equality* in the realm of thought. There's vanity here, perhaps even aporia. Kabir thus lives amongst us in an accretional corpus of words set free by an interconnected mode of authorship, where poems accrue to an ideographic signature—what the scholar **Christian Lee Novetzke** calls 'anamnetic' while discussing the work of the founder of the abhang form of song-poems in Marathi, Namdev (also called Namdeo) of the thirteenth century. The inauthentic Kabirs merely seem to enrich the genius of Kabir, making singularity a shared field of experience.

> I wrap your name in mine
>> I'm mixing weed with wine
> I'm the dot, you're the line
>> I'm the name, you're the sign

I weave myself into this associated mode of collective poem-making, Kabir emerging as a form of speech, as an utterance, as a phenomenon of language—in flesh and blood an unlettered *julaha*-weaver who bears a single name that means humongous–great–grand–illustrious, who lives in a ghetto and rails against every kind of god and sect, who sings of chopping off every pious beard and crushing every rosary but the rosary of breath, who pooh-poohs the mullah's piety, who mocks the Brahmin's tuft and thread, his twisted speech and decorated face, who denounces all sanctimonious humbug about god, who offers truths too bitter for the tastes of caste elites, but whose flesh-made-word-made-song strikes a chord in anyone wanting out of inequality and the unending tyrannies of unseeing non-existent gods.

In his time, Kabir was scorned by learned men as much as he heaped scorn on conventional learning.

पोथी पढ़ पढ़ जग मुआ पंडित भया न कोय
ढाई आखर प्रेम का पढ़े सो पंडित होय

pothee paDh paDh jag muaa panDit bhayaa na koy
Dhaaii aakhar prem kaa paDhe so panDit hoy

The rut of reading won't make a pandit
If you can't love, you just won't get it

But given Kabir's popularity, every sect and cult in desperate need of memorable poetry and the numbers required for congregations (Sufism, Sikhism, Vaishnavism, Advaita and of course, the often-Dalit Kabirpanthis to whom scholars are belatedly turning) recruited his spirit, which has spawned a million couplets. Each new and old tradition, seeking to bind him in religion, added him to their *books*, calling him god if not the one touched by god, for his words had spread like fire amongst those hungry for love and equality, amongst those for whom song and poetry and beauty were (and are) as pressing as shelter and food. Yet Kabir becomes a plurality, offering the delicious possibility of how each of us could get Kabired.

Deer, your heart is large, the forest small
The musk is within, in one and all

Kabir becomes in us a coded mode of speech—language in the condition of poetry, astride a song, away from inaccessible islands of book learning, the Buddha restated more memorably, with less pomp and without brave and noble origins, thought in the service of equality, the re-ordering of the world by a new order of words.

Walls of sand, pillars of breath—unfounded
Just look inside the shrine—you'll be astounded

There's much in Kabir's name that will not be allowed in holy books like the *Adi Granth*, that in its authorized edition, canonized in 1604, includes what are listed as 227 *padas* and 237 *slokas* by him, each assigned one of seventeen ragas in which it is to be sung, accentuating—from Latin *accentus*, 'song added to speech'—the song-worthiness of each spoken verse. In her 2015 work, *Bodies of Song: Kabir Oral Traditions and Performative Worlds in Northern India*, the scholar **Linda Hess** gives us some insight into what in Kabir's name was disallowed from the sacred book of the Sikhs:

> Two Kabir poems were written into the 1604 Kartarpur Pothis but then were crossed out and excluded from the [Adi] Granth forever after. Both were ulatbaamsi, 'upside-down language' poems with outrageous, nonsensical, sometimes shocking imagery. Ulatbaamsis appear everywhere that one finds oral and written Kabir traditions, east and west. They belong to a much older tradition of mystical poetry using such language in meaningful ways (Hess and Singh 2002, 135–61). One of the deleted poems from the Kartarpur manuscript seems to have been particularly offensive, drawing a picture of crazy mixed-up family relations, with the opening line, 'People, look at God's betrothal. The mother married her son and lived with her daughter.' Someone crossed it out and wrote 'useless' in the margin. The Sikh gurus apparently had a strong preference for plain language and domestic propriety. They also emphatically avoided anything that had even a whiff of tantric influence.

A couplet shines in a different light each time you hear it sung. Translations—and preceding it, the compulsion 'scholars' feel to bind Kabir's Hindified words to a book (scripted in what's called Devanagari, literally the script of the gods or *deva* of the *nagari* or city)—become exercises that seek a definitiveness that is constantly belied and eluded. Kabir was primarily a fine singer-composer, well-versed in a range of ragas. I reckon I'm a better singer of Kabir than a translator. I sing most of the songs featured here. Yet here I am, and not quite, in this fabricated book of songs: *The Notbook*.

The sung-and-heard Kabir often comes to us already translated, modified and altered—so much that the Original is nearly lost to sight—and yet its Structure remains. Kabir always comes to us with local inflexions and improvisations; couplets never coupled by one singer are medlied by another. Other poets walk themselves in, new words and phrases are imported, deleted, amended, invented—sometimes an entire song is faked. If the fakes can be so good, the Original ought to have been a fine fake. Other signatures also appear, and each song-maker says the song is an offering to their master and guru 'Kabir'. Some, more liberated, don't even show such courtesies. But the counterfeit has to earn its grace. Only then will it be repeated, passed on, picked up by others. Equally, many fine Kabiri songs may not circulate where commerce rules. We may call this emerging, expanding corpus 'Kabiri'—something said and done in the language of Kabir, and spoken–sung in Kabir's name and style, with or without his signature.

We see this happen in Prahlad Tipaniya's "Binaa chandaa re binaa bhaan"/ "No sun, no moon, but light" (p.94). Two signatures appear in the last stanza—Gulabi

Das is said to have spoken these words that open the locks to the heart, and Bhavani Nath who sings it signs in as well, saying he's flooded by light. Often, even the Kabir-signatured songs feature Kabir saying he's walking in a procession of dead poets, who lived for and lived in a house of words. He coaxes us to walk up to that sweet no-place even if the destination is always at our feet.

Most troubadours who perform Kabir are from oppressed-caste backgrounds. An other-worldliness for them is not possible unless they make it in this world, unless they work for their daily bread. A fruit-seller and Kabiri singer, **Kashi Ba** of Dewas (where 'Pandit' Kumar Gandharva got in touch with himself and his inner Kabir), does some plain-speaking in Shabnam Virmani's Ford Foundation–funded "**The Kabir Project**" that crisscrossed the subcontinent: 'If this body is a house that will soon be emptied, there's this belly here, the room that needs to be filled. Why else am I sitting here, selling fruit from a basket? And why is she here acting busy with her camera? We all run around to feed our bellies. We'll all fuck our mothers ...' She then breaks into a smile and a song. So it must have been for Kabir, the weaver, the most alive of dead poets in these parts of the world.

What follows this "Interjection"—where *the sky is bound and flung underground*—are fifty songs interspersed with annotations, reflections, dilations, digressions, meditations and illuminations often occasioned by a song, a phrase, a word or an idea. What does it mean to obsess over a guru? Why does conventional wisdom characterize Kabir as a Das, a slave or servant? How is breath hoarded in a poem? What does the word Brahmin or *baaman* mean and what baggage does it heave? What about the word

Ram, or Kaluram? How did the surname Bamaniya come about? What debt does Kabir owe to the Buddha? What does Babasaheb owe to Kabir? What do we owe them? Would Kabir sing 'Jai Bhim' today?

The songs in *The Notbook* are but a drop in the ocean of Kabir. There could be thousands like these found across the subcontinent, beyond our grasp. Yet, like Kaluram Bamaniya sings:

बूंद पड़ा दरियाब में सब कोई जानत हैं
समुंदर समान बूंद में जाने बिरला कोई

boond paDaa dariyaab mein sab koii jaanat hain
samundar samaan boond mein jaane biralaa koii

Everyone sees a drop fall into the sea
The rare one sees the drop that holds the sea

Most of the artists featured here—Dalits, Muslims, Brahmins, mostly men—sing the words of dead poets for a living. They profit from Kabir, unlike Kashi Ba and thousands like her who have the words of Kabir, Gorakh, Mira and other poetry sewn to their hearts and dancing on their lips. Offering us the same truth glistening in the light of new understanding from a near distance is Fariduddin Ayaz, the gregarious qawwal of Karachi. Ayaz says he was first wounded by Kabir as an eleven-year-old when a donkey-cart man made a winter bonfire by the street and sang as people huddled around. Feeling at home in his home, recounting this to the filmmaker Shabnam Virmani, Ayaz is sprawled on the floor along a bolster, his head at a tilt on his right shoulder, the fingers of his right hand tantalizingly holding a rolled paan (delivered dutifully by a child emerging from a curtained quarter of the house) meant to soften his hoarse voice with restorative juices, his left leg a gently waving triangle along the floor, his looming left hand all gestures. He entertains and enlightens Virmani and Prahlad Tipaniya, the Kabir singer from Malwa, with a song fragment:

ना कछु देखा राम भजन में
ना कछु देखा पोथी में
कहत कबीर सुनो भाई साधो
जो देखा दो रोटी में

naa kachhu dekhaa raam bhajan mein
naa kachhu dekhaa pothee mein
kahat kabeer suno bhaaii saadho
jo dekhaa do roTee mein

There's no enchantment in chanting the name
No enlightenment in the books of god
Says Kabir, and for this he earns fame:
It's the sight of bread that leaves me awed

Ayaz says a Kabir is born in each era in every region. 'Kabir' is the name of a symbol, a character. Kabir is a sign that can be assigned and reassigned.

Explaining a fragment of a song from which the subtitle of the book is taken ("Thinner than Water, Fiercer than Fire"), the singer Mahesha Ram says: 'Kabir koi bhagat tha, usne bhagwaan se mazaak karli.' Kabir was a devotee who had fun with god.

I see him more as a sceptic, and I have fun with Kabir. I began paying attention to Kabir in 2008. Since 2014, I have been both singing and translating his songs. In *The Notbook of Kabir*, I read, sing and weave my way into Kabir through the frames offered by Babasaheb Ambedkar and the Buddha. We hear Kabir singing himself in new light.

The songs you read as poems here—first in the Nagari script, followed by a transliteration, and then my English version—are a brazen effort to commit to the page words that never settle for meaning. It is like pressing a wisp of silk-cotton into a book only to see it fly away when the page is opened.

All this chant is cant, a good lyric is just a trick
Says Kabir, to know the lamp, lick the wick

If you're reading this in a book, Anand's notorious
Kabir's gone to his head, and he's full of emptiness

A thief prowls the town
जाग्रत रहना रे

आछे दिन पाछे गये किया ना गुरु से हेत
अब पछतावा क्या करे जब चिड़िया चुग गयी खेत

जाग्रत रहना रे नगर में चोर आवेगा
होशियार रहना रे नगर में चोर आवेगा
    चोर आवेगा एक दिन जम (काल) आवेगा
तीर तोप तलवार ना बरछी ना बंदूक चलायेगा
आवत जात नजर नहीं आवे भीतर घूम घुमावेगा
    होशियार रहना रे नगर में चोर आवेगा
गढ़ नहीं तोड़े किला नहीं फोड़े ना कोई रूप दिखावेगा
इस नगरी से कोई काम नहीं वो तुझे पकड़ ले जावेगा
    होशियार रहना रे नगर में चोर आवेगा
धन दौलत और माल खजीना यहीं धरा रह जाएगा
भाई बंधू और कुटंब कबीला खड़े देख रह जाएगा
    होशियार रहना रे नगर में चोर आवेगा
कहे कबीरया यह मुल्क वीराना कोई नहीं यहां अपना
मुट्ठी बांध कर आया है बंदे हाथ पसारे जाएगा
    होशियार रहना रे नगर में चोर आवेगा

aachhe din paachhe gaye kiyaa naa guru se het
ab pachhataavaa kyaa kare jab chiDiyaa chug gayee khet

jaagrat rahanaa re nagar mein chor aavegaa
hoshiyaar rahanaa re nagar mein chor aavegaa
    chor aavegaa ek din jam (kaal) aavegaa

teer top talavaar naa barachhee naa bandook chalaayegaa
aavat jaat najar naheen aave bheetar ghoom ghumaavegaa
    hoshiyaar rahanaa re nagar mein chor aavegaa

gaDh naheen tode kilaa naheen foDe naa koii roop dikhaavegaa
is nagaree se koii kaam naheen vo tujhe pakaD le jaavegaa
    hoshiyaar rahana re nagar mein chor aavegaa

dhan daulat aur maal khajeenaa yaheen dharaa rah jaaegaa
bhaaii bandhoo aur kuTamb kabeelaa khade dekh rah jaaegaa
    hoshiyaar rahanaa re nagar mein chor aavegaa

kahe kabeerayaa yah mulk veeraanaa koii naheen yahaan apanaa
muTThee baandh kar aayaa hai bande haath pasaare jaaegaa
    hoshiyaar rahanaa re nagar mein chor aavegaa

Your good days are past you
But you didn't seek your guru
What will this regret yield?
The birds have sacked your field

Awake! A thief prowls the town—alert
Hey, he's sneaking up like a speck of dirt
When the thief comes calling one day
He'll take your breath away

He won't swish swords nor rain arrows
He won't wield a gun nor decree cannon blows
You can't see him come, you can't see him go
He'll swirl inside you, he'll make you whirl
    Swoosh, this thief is not after pearls

He won't rubble a fort nor blast a castle
He won't show himself till the last tussle
He'll find your city's riches drab
It is you he wants to grab
    Look who the thief's out to nab

Your wealth and riches, your treasures and stash
They'll all be left behind, they're all trash
Your family and friends, your kith and kin
They'll shed some tears, raise a din
    Hey, this thief steals with a furtive grin

The world's a desert even to Kabir
He too will go alone on the bier
You come with a clenched fist
You'll go with palms outspread
    Look, the thief's out to steal your breath

Kaluram Bamaniya sings Kabiri songs, known in some
circles as Kabiru, in what's come to be known as the 'Malwa
tradition'. He lives in the Tonk Khurd village in Dewas
district, Madhya Pradesh. Malwa is a region in west-central
India spread across western and central Madhya Pradesh,
south-eastern Rajasthan and northern Maharashtra, and
comprises a hilly plateau fringed by the Vindhya mountains

and the Narmada river to the south. Malwa, which is older than modern states, is a good thousand kilometres from the city of Benares by the Ganga, associated with the historical Kabir. Bamaniya's "Jaagrat rahanaa re" features in a two-CD album called *Malwa Mein Kabir* (Kabir in Malwa) as part of Shabnam Virmani's "The Kabir Project".

Freeing freedom from itself
ऐवी ऐवी सेहण

ऐवी ऐवी सेहण बताई म्हारे सतगुरु
मुख पर कह्यो नहीं जाए है
    ऐवी ऐवी
हमारे रे देस मैं ना धरा नहीं गगना
नहीं कोई पवन नहीं पानी
    ऐवी ऐवी
हमारे रे देस मैं ना चंदा नहीं सूरज
नहीं कोई नौलख तारा
    ऐवी ऐवी
हमारे रे देस मैं ना ब्रह्मा नहीं विषनू
नहीं कोई शंकर देवा
    ऐवी ऐवी
हमारे रे देस मैं ना बाणी नहीं कोई खाणी
नहीं कोई वेद नहीं गीता
    ऐवी ऐवी
हमारे रे देस मैं ना मरे नहीं जनमे
नहीं कोई शबद ना साखिया
    ऐवी ऐवी
मंजले रे मंजले एक संत जाई पहुंच्या
कबीरा संत चढ़या निरवाना
    ऐवी ऐवी

aivee aivee sehaNa bataaii mhaare sataguru
mukh par kahyo naheen jaae hai
        aivee aivee

hamaare re des mein naa dharaa naheen gaganaa
naheen koii pavan naheen paanii
        aivee aivee

hamaare re des mein naa chandaa naheen sooraj
naheen koii naulakh taaraa
        aivee aivee

hamaare re des mein naa brahmaa naheen vishanoo
naheen koii shankar devaa
        aivee aivee

hamaare re des mein naa baaNii naheen koii khaaNii
naheen koii ved naheen geetaa
        aivee aivee

hamaare re des mein naa marey naheen janame
naheen koii shabad na saakhiyaa
        aivee aivee

manjale re manjale ek sant jaaii pahunchyaa
kabeeraa sant chaDhayaa niravaanaa
        aivee aivee

My true guru revealed to me such signs
I cannot utter them with this tongue of mine

In this world of mine
No space
No sky
No breeze
No water

In this world of mine
No sun
No moon
No star
No time

In this world of mine
No Brahma
No Vishnu
No Shankar
No god

In this world of mine
No Veda
No Gita
No text
No secret

In this world of mine
No death
No birth
No word
No song

Step by step by step, I reached this kingdom
My soul has climbed to its final freedom

My true love has revealed to me such signs
I cannot capture their truth with these lines

I

Kabir, and through him the singer of this song, Mahesha Ram, assert at the outset that the truth they witness cannot be captured in words. This is stated as an absolute truth, as a matter of fact, as a fact of nature, as a non-negotiable state of affairs, as a matter of existence, as an irrefutable first principle, as the fundamental premise. They then go on to disavow this truth, and offer five perspicuous and definitive ways in which this elusive truth can be actually uttered and sung, and thus be inhabited.

II

What Mahesha Ram presents in "Aivee aivee sehaNa"/ "Seeing light" (featured in "The Kabir Project") is the simultaneity of negation and affirmation. We're first presented the truth that the truth is indescribable, and then this truth is gloriously described in a series of negatives: neithers and nors. We're taken to a sunless, moonless world where even Kabir's words cease to exist. This is no-place, the real of nothing. We are offered a series of propositions whose assertions specifically deny the truth of the fundamental proposition of the opening lines. In doing all this, Kabir and those who listen to Kabir (for he goads us at the end of every song to heed, to *listen*, with the imperative call *suno*) seem to also listen to something passed on through Siddhartha Gautama, the Buddha, the Enlightened One (a word that was formerly written as *inlighten*, from Old English *inlīhtan* 'to shine', where you shine from within, are made luminous). Gautama proposes the theory of *anatta*, non-self or no-self. The existence of soul is denied. And truth inhabits the realm of *sunnya*—often misunderstood as emptiness, according to Ambedkar, who chooses to see the Buddha's idea of sunnya as 'a point which has substance but neither breadth nor length'. **Ambedkar goes on to say that *sunnya-vad*** (sunnya-ism) 'means the perpetual changes occurring at every moment in the phenomenal world'. He therefore says that it is 'on account of sunnyata that everything becomes possible; without it nothing in the world would be possible. It is on the impermanence of the nature of all things that the possibility of all other things depends.'

Like the Buddha, the tenth–twelfth century figure of Goraknath saw this too, and with him the Nathpanthis who were influenced by what scholars call Sahajiya Buddhism (that spread in eastern India and involves ritual sexual intercourse) and Tantric Buddhism (the Vajrayana or Thunderbolt school where esoteric symbolic language and mantras are used). In the twentieth century, Kumar Gandharva arrives at this gate in his own style (although he could not overcome his Brahminness, and, like many savarna musicians of post-independence India, was **prejudiced about the Islamic influence** on raga music), as do the various troubadours who have sung Gorakh, Kabir, Mira and other preceptors who have perceived this truth.

Ambedkar is part of this tradition, not only because he is born into a part-Kabirpanthi family, but because he, like Kabir, reaches this kingdom step by single step: 'To realize that every living being will die sometime or other is a very easy matter to understand. But it is not quite so easy to understand how a human being can go on changing—becoming—while he is alive.' He says this in 1956, for he has changed, he has become something else, he has evolved from his position in 1936 where he defined annihilation of caste as a rebirth. Ambedkar aspires, draws his breath, for annihilation of caste. He speaks of rebirth in this very life, not in another life.

III

While Mahesha Ram's Kabir arrives at the casteless utopia, the imperium of equality, bearing the ecstasy of song, Ambedkar arrives here in the sobriety of prose—issued as unambiguous declarations, without the equivocations of poetry. Consider the first four among the twenty-two oaths—'of his own devising', as his biographer **Eleanor Zelliot** says—he administered in Marathi to himself, his Brahmin wife Sharada Kabir (who changed her name to Savita), and to more than half a million people, almost all Untouchables, clad in white, on 14 October 1956 in Nagpur, Maharashtra:

1. I will not regard Brahma, Vishnu and Mahesh as Gods nor will I worship them.
2. I will not regard Rama and Krishna as Gods nor will I worship them.
3. I will not accept Hindu Deities like Gauri, Ganapati, etc., nor will I worship them.

4. I do not believe that God has taken birth or incarnated in any form.

The centrality of negation in these vows of a modern Buddhist echoes an old mode of disavowal—*via negativa* or apophatic theology, found equally in Greek, Buddhist, Islamic and Sufi thinking, and often in Kabir. In Linda Hess's *Singing Emptiness: Kumar Gandharva Performs the Poetry of Kabir*, we find a poem ("Spot less ness" in this book, p.282) that says as much:

Creator Preserver Destroyer—the trinity is nonsense
Eye shadow Krishna and his million girlfriends

Here even poetry comes to an end, the Vedas
                                        make no sense
All distinctions come to nothing, at once
                                        subtle and dense

All this greenery just colour, god just bestselling fiction
All worship is pretence, rituals are the doing of done

In the posthumously published **Riddles in Hinduism**, Ambedkar says: 'The Vedas are a worthless set of books. There is no reason either to call them sacred or infallible.' After affirming faith in the Buddha as an enlightened being, and not as a god, Ambedkar's oaths 9 and 10 hold the key:

9. I believe in the principle that all are equal.
10. I will try to establish equality.

The Buddha never says anything like this. No prophet or saint or god of the subcontinent has made such a disambiguated declaration and helmed the largest collective declaration of equality in human history. Should you return and listen to the song carefully, this is what Mahesha Ram, a Dalit born into a Kabirpanthi family (without necessarily being a follower of Ambedkar or the Buddha), is singing about in Maand, a raga that is ubiquitous in Malwa, Rajasthan. Kabir and Ambedkar arrive at the same no-place of sunnyata in their own ways. They negate the Veda and Gita, deny Brahma–Vishnu–Shankar, repudiate all priests and books of god, and all the entrapments of inequality. Ambedkar's nineteenth oath reads: 'I embrace today the Bauddha Dhamma discarding the Hindu Religion which is detrimental to the emancipation of human beings, and which believes in inequality and regards human beings other than brahmins as low born.' This is where, and this is how, we bear witness to the norm of equality and partake in it.

Scratching my head over the years, I realized that I had read something attributed to the Buddha that echoed both the words and sentiments of this Kabir song, and in turn Ambedkar's rather pointed train of thought. The Buddha here, of course, speaks in the voice of those who recorded his 'words' a good four to five hundred years after his passing away. These records or recordings, that become a part of the annals in coming to bear the stamp of official discourse, are far removed from the way things may have been said, if at all. Despite these caveats, they convey something close to home, appearing as they do here in the form of a poem at the end of the Bahiya Sutta attributed to the One-Well-Gone, the Tathagatha.

This **Thanissaro Bhikkhu** translation (1994), accessed from accesstoinsight.org, throws light:

Where water, earth,
fire & wind
have no footing:
There the stars don't shine,
the sun isn't visible.
There the moon doesn't appear.
There darkness is not found.
And when a sage,
a *brahman* through sagacity,
has realised [this] for himself,
then from form & formless,
from bliss & pain,
he is freed.

The Pali version reads like this:

यत्थ आपोच पत्थवी तेजो वायो न गाढ़ति
न तत्थ सुक्क जोतंती आदिच्चो न पकासति
न तत्थ चंदिमा भाती तमो तत्थ न विज्जति
यदाच अत्तना वेदी मुनि मोनेन ब्राह्मणे मानुसो
अत्थ रूप अरूपा च सुखदुःख पमुच्चति

yattha aapocha patthavee tejo vaayo na gaaDhati
na tattha sukka jotantee aadichcho na pakaasati
na tattha chandimaa bhaatee tamo tattha na vijjati
yadaacha attanaa vedi muni monena ~~braahmaNo~~ maanuso
attha roopa aroopaa cha sukhaduHkha pamuchchati

Mine (well, so to say):

Where water, earth, fire and wind have no footing:
Where the stars aren't shining, the sun isn't a bright thing
There's no moon waxing-waning, no darkness lurking
When a seeker reaches this state through understanding
Released from form, formlessness, bliss and pain,
finds sweet nothing

Whoever committed this and scores of such suttas to verse—and it is unlikely it was one person given the range, volume and the many recensions—must have had a keen ear, and an eye on the future. A *sutta* means both a thread and that which is heard, and it is the Buddhist–Pali equivalent of the Sanskrit *sutra*, a terse aphorism. The words of the Buddha, his discourses as heard and collected by his followers, take the form of a sutta. In canonical Buddhism, over ten thousand suttas are collected in the *Sutta Pitaka*, literally a basket of Buddha's suttas.

Read the Bahiya Sutta aloud in the Pali even if you don't know the language. Feel it on the tongue, heed to the many ways the *t* and *th* sounds resonate, alliterate and bounce off each other: It can be enjoyed even more when the words are strung to music. I wrapped the words of the sutta in the raga Bhairavi to the weft of the tevra taal.

This is the verse the Buddha speaks upon the death of Bahiya of the Bark-cloth, once a rich, sea-faring merchant from the place Bahiya (whence his toponym) who loses everything in a shipwreck and comes to be clad in tree bark. Bahiya (बाहिया), a word that also means foreigner or outsider and figures as *bahya* in Brahmanic literature, gains renown as someone close to enlightenment, but a wise man (in fact the god Brahma in tall stories) tells him that he is not as enlightened as he thinks, at which Bahiya leaves his lodgings in Supparaka, a town by the sea, and seeks out Gautama in Jetavana, a retreat-cum-park located to the south of the city of Savatti (or Sravasti in Sanskrit). (The Buddha of course was well provided for, unlike say Ambedkar or Kabir.) Three times the Buddha turns down Bahiya when he beseeches for the dhamma. The fourth time the Buddha tells him:

> You should train yourself thus: In reference to the seen, there will be only the seen. In reference to the heard, only the heard. In reference to the sensed, only the sensed. In reference to the thought, only the thought. … When there is no you in connection with that, there is no you there. When there is no you there, you are neither here nor yonder nor between the two. This, just this, is the end of stress.

After being given this discourse, Bahiya, glad to be accepted into the *sangha* (the monastic order), sets out to fetch a bowl and robe for his monkhood, but on his way, a cow (some versions say an ox) gores him to death. A death that the know-all Buddha claims he anyway knew would come thus and then, and then he speaks the words of the sutta. But how do we let pass the lines 'a sage, a brahman through sagacity…' in the Buddha's spoken poem? Canonical Buddhism of the suttas and the *jataka*s (birth stories of the previous incarnations of the Buddha) of course held that **a *bodhisatta* (an enlightened, awakened being) could be born only as a Brahmin or Kshatriya:** not a Meghwal-weaver like Mahesha Ram or a Mahar like Ambedkar nor a fruit-seller like Kashi Ba. Hence the reference to a wise sage as a 'brahman' in a Buddhism that came to adapt and appropriate some of the Brahmanical language and baggage in its course. Setting this Pali sutta to the all-encompassing raga Bhairavi, I amended and corrected the words attributed to the Buddha to make him walk in step with what I understood of Ambedkar and Kabir. One of the key concepts Ambedkar derives from Buddhism is *manuski*: translated as human-ness but more 'the reclamation of the human personality', in Ambedkar's words. In the last two lines of what's attributed to the Buddha, the rather limited and limiting invocation of *brahmano*—as the wise enlightened one—is replaced with *manuso*, the human. Without affecting the metre of the verse, it enhances and redeems it. The mellifluous *ma* (gently grazing on *n* sounds) sits here with more grace than the grating harshness of *brah* (to which we shall turn in due course):

> yadaacha attanaa vedi *muni monena maanuso*
> attha roopa aroopaa cha sukhaduHkha pamuchchati

If Kabir's songs can change and evolve by word of mouth, so can the verse attributed to the Buddha, especially when they seem to be saying the same thing in other words. After all, all of the Buddha's suttas begin with the caveat, *evam me sutam*—thus have I heard. We hear—and sing—it differently. Just as most Kabir songs impel you to listen (suno) to what Kabir says (*kahat, kahe*).

Even if Buddhism uses brahmano not as caste but as a category to refer to persons who can be 'freed', and if the Buddha can issue statements to the effect that any wise one is a Brahmin and any vile one a Chandala, the problem inherent in such a hierarchy remains. Not thinking twice about discarding all that is worthless, Ambedkar, Kabir and Mahesha Ram appear to get to the kernel of the Buddha's dhamma—and thus free it from itself.

This is no fortuitous mishearing or misreading: of this you and I are proof.

What do you seek in the mirror?
क्या देखो दर्पण मा हे

कबीरा तेरी झोंपडी गलकटन के पास
करंता और भरंता तू क्यों फिरे उदास
कबीरा कबीरा क्या करो सोचो आप शरीर
पांच इन्द्रियां बस करो आपो दास कबीर
दया धरम तेरे अंगने में नाहीं
क्या देखो दर्पण मा हे
अंड़सठ तीरथ गुरांजी बताया
दर्शन कर बंदा देहीड़ा मैं
दया धरम तेरे अंगने में नाहीं
क्या देखो दर्पण मा हे
अम्बले री डाल कोयल राजी रे
मूरख राजी मन मा हे
घरवाली घरड़े मा हे राजी
तपसी हो राजी बन मा है
दया धरम तेरे अंगने में नाहीं
क्या देखो दर्पण मा हे
पीलो सो बागो लाल कसूंबल
सोवे गुरांजी रे अंग मा हे
करमहीन ना रतन हीरो लादो
फेंक दियो अन रेत मा हे

दया धरम तेरे अंगने में नाहीं
क्या देखो दर्पण मा हे
पानी पत्थर की न्याव हला दयूं
उलट जावे एक ही छल में
करमी रे धरमी पार उतरया
पापी हो रह गया जल मा है
दया धरम तेरे अंगने में नाहीं
क्या देखो दर्पण मा हे
धन हे जोबन बादलियेरी छाया है
बिखर जावे एक ही पल मा हे
कहत कबीरा सुनो भाई साधो
आखिर डेरा बन मा है
दया धरम तेरे अंगने में नाहीं
क्या देखो दर्पण मा हे

kabeeraa teree jhonpaDee galkaTan ke paas
karantaa aur bharantaa tuu kyon fhire udaas
kabeeraa kabeeraa kyaa karo socho aap shareer
paanch indriyaan bas karo aapo daas kabeer

dayaa dharam tere angane mein naaheen
kyaa dekho darpaN maa hey
anDsaTh teerath guraanjee bataayaa
darshan kar bandaa deheeDɑɑ mein
dayaa dharam tere angane mein naaheen
kyaa dekho darpaN maa hey

ambale ree Daal koyal raajee re
moorakh raajee man maa hey
gharavaalee gharaDe maa he raajee
tapasee ho raajee ban maa hey

dayaa dharam tere angane mein naaheen
kyaa dekho darpaN maa hey

peelo so baago laal kasoonbal
sove guraanjee re ang maa hey
karamaheen naa ratan heero laado
fhenk diyo an ret maa hey
      dayaa dharam tere angane mein naaheen
      kyaa dekho darpaN maa hey

paanii patthar kee nyaav halaa dayoon
ulaT jaave ek hee chhal mein
karamee re dharamee paar utarayaa
paapee ho rah gayaa jal maa hey
      dayaa dharam tere angane mein naaheen
      kyaa dekho darpaN maa hey

dhan hey joban baadaliyeree chhaayaa hai
bikhar jaave ek hee pal maa hey
kahat kabeeraa suno bhaaii saadho
aakhir Deraa ban maa hey
      dayaa dharam tere angane mein naaheen
      kyaa dekho darpaN maa hey

Kabir lives among cut-throats, holding his breath
Like a pot, he comes to life on losing his head
Just do your thing, don't rue and regret
A fruit falls to its birth, becoming death

Why cry Kabir Kabir, who gives a toss
Rein in your senses, be your own boss

Possess your sensations, not what they sense
Divine the Kabir in you, the rest is nonsense

What do you seek in the mirror?
When your eyes are without ardour
A pilgrim cannot progress
Until he finds love's harness
    What do you seek in the mirror?

The koel reigns over the mango tree
The fool's pleased with himself easily
The house-spouse rules the household
The mouse holds court in his hole
    What do you seek in the mirror?

Draped in sunset and mustard yellow
My guru's body sleeps, graceful, mellow
Bathed in rubies, bedecked and august
A bigot will still return to dust
    What do you seek in the mirror?

Your boat of stone will sink
Even before you can blink
Love is now your only oar
Coxing you to that sinless shore
    What do you seek in the mirror?

Wealth, youth, the cloud's shade—
Strut for a moment and then fade
Sew this song to your breast
The final stop is the forest
    What do you seek in the mirror?

Mahesha Ram sings "Darshan kar bandaa deheeDaa mein", which I first heard in the 2008 CD album *Rajasthan mein Kabir* (Kabir in Rajasthan), a part of "The Kabir Project". In the opening verse, spoken by Mahesha Ram rather than sung, Kabir refers to himself as someone who lives among cut-throats. What does he mean? The allusion is to potters. As a weaver, he likely lived next to the street of potters (in a society riven by segregation of castes). After clay is thrown on a flywheel and shaped into a pot, the potter cuts off the neck using a string or wire. This final flourish is a delicate art. And hence the expression: 'Kabir lives among cut-throats, holding his breath'. Later in the song, I had rendered *gharavaali*, housewife, as house-husband till Jerry (Pinto) the mouse told this Tom to consider house-spouse, and the cat fell for it.

A doe's wedded by the well
कुएं रे किनारे अवधू

कुएं रे किनारे अवधू इमली सी बोई रे
जारो पेड़ मछलियां छायो हे लो
    रमते जोगी ने आदेस केवणा रे
कुएं रे किनारे अवधू हिरणी सी ब्याही रे
हो जी पांच मिरगला लाई हे लो
    रमते जोगी ने आदेस केवणा रे
ससियो शिखारी अवधू बन खंड चाल्यो रे
ममता मुगली ने मारी हे लो
    रमते जोगी ने आदेस केवणा रे
खूंटो तो दूजे अवधू भैंस बिलोवो रे
जारो माखण बिरला खायो हे लो
    रमते जोगी ने आदेस केवणा रे
शरण मथसंदर जती गोरख बोल्या रे
जां खोज्यां वां पाया हे लो
    रमते जोगी ने आदेस केवणा रे

kuen re kinaare avadhoo imalee see boii re
jaaro peD machhaliyaan chhaayo hey lo
    ramate jogee ne aades kevaNaa re

kuen re kinaare avadhoo hiraNii see byaahee re
ho jee paanch miragalaa laaii hey lo
      ramate jogee ne aades kevaNaa re

sasiyo shikhaarii avadhoo ban khanD chaalyo re
mamataa mugalee ne maaree hey lo
      ramate jogee ne aades kevaNaa re

khoonTo toh dooje avadhoo bhains bilovo re
jaaro maakhaN biralaa khaayo hey lo
      ramate jogee ne aades kevaNaa re

sharaN mathsandar jatee gorakh bolyaa re
jaan khojyaan vaan paaya hey lo
      ramate jogee ne aades kevaNaa re

I sowed a tamarind by the well
The tree had fish for leaves that cast a fine shade
To the fluttering flame, bear this message

A doe's wedded by the well
She births five fawns that revel
In sight, touch, taste, hearing, smell
    The fluttering flame now bears this message

With a song in his step, and a spring in his breast
The hare is out to hunt in the forest
And slay the fickle fawns of unrest
    The fluttering flame now bears this message

The pivot is milked, the buffalo is churned
The truly loved will taste this butter in turn
Chance has no place, grace must be earned
    The fluttering flame now bears this message

Sheltered by love, the flame is still
Not by oil or wick, it's illumined by will
It winks at the wind, cups the night within
    The fluttering flame now bears this message

Says Gorakh, I surrender
To the one called Mathsander
Just search, you'll find this wonder
    The fluttering flame now bears this message

Mukhtiyar Ali sings "Kuen re kinaare avadhoo", featured
in "The Kabir Project". It bears the signature of the twelfth
century yogi-poet Gorakhnath, who praises his guru
Macchinder, pronounced as Mathsander by the singer. The
penultimate stanza is a bonus for the English reader. Ali
is a singer of Kabir and Sufi music. I met him in 2022 in
Jaipur and sang with him at a baithak in the course of this
Notbook's making. He has travelled the world but remains
rooted to his village Pugal in the Thar desert along the
India–Pakistan border.

This path leads to no place
यूहीं मन समझावे

बिन पावन का पंथ है बिन बस्ती का देस
बिना पिंड का पुरुष है कहे कबीर संदेस
कबीर का घर शिखर पे सिलहली सी गैल
यहाँ पांव ना टीके पपील का क्यों मनवा लादे बैल

यूहीं मन समझावे तू झूठो मन समझाये
बिना खोज कछु भेद ना पावे
बिना खोज कछु महरम नहीं पावे
थारो विरधा जनम गमावे
सुन सायर ग्यानी तू कईं मन समझावे
जो पनिहारी पानी चाले बेडो भरी ने घर लावे
हाले डोले बात बणावे पर सुरत बेवड़ा में लावे
सुन सायर ग्यानी तू कईं मन समझावे
जो नटड़ी वा चढ़े बरत पे तो नटड़ो ढोल बजाये
ऊपर चढ़ कर मंगल गावे वा सुरत बरत में लावे
सुन सायर ग्यानी तू कईं मन समझावे
जैसे भुजंग चरे बन मांही ओस चाटने जावे
कभी चाटे कभी मणी को चितवे वो मणी तज प्राण गमावे
सुन सायर ग्यानी तू कईं मन समझावे
जो मरजीवा होवे समुंद का तो डुबकी वामे लगावे

कहे कबीर सुनो भाई साधो वा हीरा लाल बीन लावे
    सुन सायर ग्यानी तू कईं मन समझावे

   bin paavan kaa panth hai bin bastee kaa des
   binaa pinD kaa purush hai kahen kabeer sandes
   kabeer kaa ghar shikhar pe silahalee see gail
   yahaan paanv naa Teeke papeel kaa kyon manavaa laade bail

yooheen man samajhaave tuu jhooTho man samajhaaye
binaa khoj kachhu bhed naa paave
binaa khoj kachhu maharam naheen paave
thaaro viradhaa janam gamaave
    sun saayar gyaanii tuu kaeen man samajhaave

jo panihaari paanii chaale beDo bharee ne ghar laave
haale Doley baat baNaave par surat bevaDaa mein laave
    sun saayar gyaanii tuu kaeen man samajhaave

jo naTaDee vaa chaDhe barat pe toh naTaDo Dhol bajaaye
oopar chaDh kar mangal gaave vaa surat barat mein laave
    sun saayar gyaanii tuu kaeen man samajhaave

jaise bhujang chare ban maanhii os chaaTane jaave
kabhee chaaTe kabhee maNii ko chitave vo maNii taj praaN gamaave
    sun saayar gyaanii tuu kaeen man samajhaave

jo marajeeva hovey samund kaa toh Dubakee vaame lagaave
kahen kabeer suno bhaaii saadho vaa heeraa laal been laave
    sun saayar gyaanii tuu kaeen man samajhaave

This path leads to no place
Here, life leaves no trace
The essence has no face
This is it, Kabir says
    This path leads to no-place

Kabir's house is up a hill
The path is paved with peril
Why lug up a loaded bull?
Even the ant is watchful, holding still
    This path leads to no-place

Hush your heart, hold your breath
There's no finding without the search
Get going, don't wait for death
Poet, get off your cozy perch
    This path leads to no-place

Winding her way home from the river
Her head balancing the pitcher
She trots, she ambles, she stops to chatter
But her mind is stilled on the water
    This path leads to no-place

On the rope, the daughter
On the drum, the father
On her lips, a song
Her faith, rope-strong
    This path leads to no-place

The thicket parts, a snake slithers through
It licks the night that rests as dew
But it sets its sights on the jewel
Where the moon mirrors into view by the well
    This path leads to no-place

Holding death in his breath
The diver plunges the ocean's depth
Says Kabir, listen, be all ears
He who finds the ruby stills his fears
    This path leads to no-place

This translation is based on Prahlad Singh Tipaniya's rendition in the CD *Malwa mein Kabir* ("The Kabir Project"). Tipaniya, a Dalit, is among the most popular interpreters of Kabir and is the force behind the annual Malwa Kabir Yatra. A 2011 Padma Shri awardee, he contested on a Congress party ticket in the 2019 Lok Sabha elections from Dewas, a reserved seat, and lost.

Things that do not know their name
मौला मौला लाख पुकारे

Fariduddin Ayaz and Abu Mohammed and their qawwal party from Karachi string a garland of songs of and for Kabir during a visit to Delhi in 2006. This concert is recorded as part of "The Kabir Project". Ayaz and Mohammed bring in lines from other Sufis and poets Kabir speaks to, and who speak to Kabir, conversations from the past that spread into the future after piercing the ever-present. They begin with "Niikee lagat mohe apane piyaa kee" by Hazrat Shah Turab Ali Qalandar Kakorvi (1767–1858), who was born in Kakori near Lucknow. His signature or takhallus was *turaab* (soil, earth in Arabic). His words are in dialogue at once with Kabir, the ghazal master Mirza Ghalib, and with 1950s Bollywood lyrics (like Ayaz suggests, think to the blockbuster *Mughal-e-Azam*'s song "Pyaar kiyaa toh darnaa kyaa"). Often Ayaz and his brother Abu Mohammad bring in verses without mentioning the poets, indicated here by section numbers; I have identified the poets I can. The qawwals then move to "Maulaa maulaa laakh pukaare" by Baba Zaheen Shah, but after singing the opening couplet, they switch to "Bhalaa huaa meree gagaree fooTee" attributed to Kabir. Even this divagation is interspersed with a lot of commentary by Ayaz, and other verses (including one by the Punjabi sufi Sultan Bahu) are remembered along the way: song-flowers gathered from memory's garden. Baba Zaheen Shah Yousufi Taji (1902–1978), a Sufi, poet, scholar and philosopher, was born Muhammad Tuaseen in Jhunjhunu, Rajasthan, India. The 1947 Partition caused him to migrate to and live in Karachi (quite like the qawwals who had to migrate from Delhi). Retrospectively, succumbing to hindsight that could well be the foreshortening of foresight, the Buddha gets a walk-in part in my rendition. My explanations of some of these shifts are in italics. Ayaz's explanations are in indented italics.

I

नीकी लगत मोहे अपने पिया की
लागी लागी सब कहें लागी बुरी बला
लागी तो तब जानिए जब आर पार होई जाए
नीकी लगत मोहे अपने पिया की
आँख रसीली जादू भरी
नज़र ने नज़र से मुलाक़ात कर ली
रहे दोनों ख़ामोश और बात कर ली
चैन पड़त नाहीं मुख देखे बिना
देखे नज़र भर जात हरी
काहे तुराब डरे काहू से
प्रीत करी का मै चोरी करी
नीकी लगत मोहे अपने पिया की

niikee lagat mohe apane piyaa kee
laagee laagee sab kahen laagee buree balaa
laagee toh tab jaaniye jab aar paar hoee jaae

niikee lagat mohe apane piyaa kee
aankh raseelee jaadoo bharee
nazar ne nazar se mulaaqaat kar lee
rahe donon khaamosh aur baat kar lee

chain paDat naaheen mukh dekhe binaa
dekhe nazar bhar jaat haree

kaahe turaab Darey kaahoo se
preet karee kaa main choree karee
        niikee lagat mohe apane piyaa kee

I'm in love, they say
I'm in love with love, they prate
When love really strikes you
It will split you right through

I'm in love, they say, in love with love
When love really strikes, you'll know
You'll be left speechless, with nowhere to go

Love is an ache braised to sweetness
It is the light in the pupilla of darkness

To love's gaze my eyes are beholden
Nothing is said, yet all has been spoken

I drift in shadows till I see his face
His very sight is the sun's embrace

Why should the earth fear the jasmine?
It has only loved and that's no thieving

II

अब लफ़्ज़ ओ बयां सब ख़त्म हुए
अब लफ़्ज़ ओ बयां का काम नहीं
अब इश्क़ है ख़ुद पैग़ाम अपना
और इश्क़ का कुछ पैग़ाम नहीं

एक शाहिद-ए-मानी-ओ-सूरत के
मिलने की तमन्ना सब को है
मैं उसके न मिलने पर हूं फ़िदा
लेकिन यह मज़ाक़-ए-आम नहीं

ab lafz o bayaan sab khatm huey
ab lafz o bayaan ka kaam naheen
ab ishq hai khud paigaam apanaa
aur ishq kaa kuchh paigaam naheen

ek shaahid-e-maanii-o-soorat ke
milane kee tamannaa sab ko hai
main usake naa milane par hoon fidaa
lekin yah mazaak-e-aam naheen

So far, we have played the world with words
We have played with words to make the world
Now, all words have come to an end
There's only so much that signs can tend
We have come to a place
Where language has no say

Now love is its own calling
And love calls for nothing

What's the first lesson at this port of call?

The desire for the face of love is in everyone
We seek form and meaning both in one

I delight in not having possessed that one
Such pleasures are not for everyone

I fall for a love that cannot be mine
But such grace remains hard to find

To find pleasure in decline
Such rapture is not for everyone

Oh, the delight of being undone
When your words run over me like a tongue

III

मौला मौला लाख पुकारे मौला हाथ न आए
लफ़्ज़ों से हम खेल रहे हैं माना हाथ न आए
जो पानी के नाम को पानी जाने यह नादानी है
पानी पानी रटते रटते प्यासा ही मर जाए
शोला शोला रटते रटते लब पर आंच न आए
इक चिंगारी लब पर रख लो लब फ़ौरन जल जाए
इस्म पे क़ाने होने वाला और मुसम्मा खोने वाला
काम न करने वाला मूरख बस नाम से जी बहलाए

माला कहे है काठ की अरे तू का फेरत मोए
मन का मनका फेर दे सो तुरत मिला दूँ तोए (कबीरा)

maulaa maulaa laakh pukaare maulaa haath naa aae
lafzon se ham khel rahe hain maanaa haath naa aae

jo paanii ke naam ko paanii jaane yeh naadaanii hai
paanii paanii raTate raTate pyaasaa hee mar jaae

sholaa sholaa raTate raTate lab par aanch naa aae
ik chingaaree lab par rakh lo lab fauran jal jaae

ism pe qaane hone vaalaa aur musammaa khone vaalaa
kaam na karne vaalaa moorakh bas naam se jee bahalaae

maalaa kahe hai kaaTh kee arey tuu kaa pherat moye
man kaa manakaa pher de so turat milaa doon toye (kabeeraa)

Call out to god in a million ways, he'll always slip away
We're dabbling with words and meaning goes astray

Such an aspectless aspect, such a person
Who eludes words, thoughts, meaning and reason
How do we ever know that subtle one?

To think that water knows it's called water is our ignorance
To cry 'water water' and to die of thirst, that's no deliverance

The word for water will not slake thirst
Chanting the word for water, the fool will die first

The word for water is not water
The name Ram doesn't contain Ram
Nor does Allah know he is Allah

Now, how does this illusion deign to submit?
To chant for water, hanker after truth, and not attain it—
But what truly is truth?
We set snares, but truth always gives the slip

Chant 'fire' all you want, your lips will feel nothing
Place an ember on your lips, you'll feel the sting

Content with chanting names, he loses Him to games
The one who does not labour finds refuge in mystic jabber

The rosary asks this: Why bother me as you chant?
Bead your heart into His, he'll be with you in the instant

Raze all mosques, raze all temples, raze all
Just merge your heart into His, that's all

IV (threaded with V and VI)

भला हुआ मेरी गगरी फूटी
मैं पनिया भरन से छूटी रे
मोरे सर से टली बला

चलती चाकी देखकर सो दिया कबीरा रोए
दो पाटन के बीच आ साबुत बचा ना कोए
चाकी चाकी सब कहें और कीली कहे ना कोए
जो कीली से लाग रहे वो को बाल ना बीका होए

हर मरे तो हम मरे और हमरी मरे बला
सांचे गुरु का बाल का मरे ना मारा जाए
राम नाम की खूंटी गाड़ी सूरज ताना तंता
चढ़ते उतरते दम की खबर ले फिर नहीं आना बनता कबीरा
कबीरा कुआं एक है और पानी भरें अनेक
भांडे ही में भेद है पानी सब में एक
अलिफ़ अल्लाह चम्बे दी बूटी मुर्शिद मन विच लाई हू
नफ़ी इसबात दा पानी मिल्या हर रगे हर जाई हू
अंदर बूटी मुश्क मचाया जाँ फुल्लाँ ते आई हू
जीवे मुर्शिद कामिल बाहू जैं ईह बूटी लाई हू

bhalaa huaa meree gagaree fooTee
main paniyaa bharan se chhooTee re
morey sar se Talee balaa

    chaltee chaakee dekhakar so diyaa kabeeraa roe
    do paaTan ke beech aa saabut bachaa naa koe

    chaakee chaakee sab kahen aur keelee kahe naa koe
    jo keelee se laag rahe vo ko baal naa beekaa hoe

    har marey to ham marey aur hamaree marey balaa
    saanche guru ka baal ka marey naa maaraa jaae

    raam naam ki khoonTee gaaDee sooraj taanaa tantaa
    chaDhte utarate dam kee khabar le fir naheen aanaa
        bantaa kabeeraa

    kabeeraa kuaan ek hai aur paanii bharen anek
    bhaanDe hee mein bhed hai paanii sab mein ek

alif allaah chambe dee booTee murshid man vich laaii hoo

nafee isabaat daa paanii milyaa har ragey har jaaii hoo

andar booTee mushk machaayaa jaan phullaan te aaii hoo

jeeve murshid kaamil baahoo jain eeh booTee laaii hoo

Ah, good the pitcher's shattered
I need not fetch any water!
What a load off my head!
Thank god, god is dead!
What a load off my head!

Breaking away from the pitcher–rosary–god similes, Farid Ayaz's brother Abu Mohammed remembers other fragments:

At the sight of the grindstone, Kabir lets out a cry
Crushed between two rocks, no grain can survive

Abu Mohammed then suggests that Kabir's son Kamaal Das, of whom Kabir is said to have said, 'Kabir is a mere spoke in the wheel, Kamaal is the real deal,' came up with this response:

Caught in the daily grind, no one sights the pestle
Those who abide by the pestle will know they're special

If god dies so would I, and with it all my woes
What never dies is the Word that the guru bestows

A loom of such length and breadth
     The sun its fibres and threads
Listen to the rise and fall of breath
     There's no life after death

Listen to Kabir—there's but one well
    The water's drawn by all
Some pitchers are big, some small
    It's the same water as far as I can tell

*Quickly, Ayaz plays with words in the Urdu–Hindi zabaan,
exploiting the ambiguities and equivocations created by the absence
of punctuation in the language:*

Listen, Kabir is but one well
    His waters are drawn by all
Some pitchers are big, some small
    It's the same water as far as eye can tell

*Like water defining the virtue of land, the flow of thought takes
yet another turn as Ayaz remembers a fragment of Sultan Bahu's
verse in Punjabi while spitting out and chewing up more paan,
and yet once more adjusting the glistening white crown of his glass-
beaded cap:*

Seeding the jasmine of Aleph
In my quivering breast
He nourished no with the waters of yes
That seep into my every pore
Causing my being to blossom and soar
Blessed by Aleph, I prance
The fragrance within makes me dance
Bless the blessed Sultan Bahu
He's the jasmine, he's the dew

And then we thread back to the song of the rosary and the pitcher shattering, and the rapture of the devotee rid of the burden of god, bowing to the wisdom of many Sufis and poets:

भला हुआ मोरी माला टूटी
मैं तो राम भजन से छूटी रे
    मोरे सर से टली बला
ना कछु देखा राम भजन में
ना कछु देखा पोथी में
कहत कबीर सुनो भाई साधो
जो देखा दो रोटी में
    अल-इल्म-ओ-हिजाब-उल-अकबर
    मालूम होना ही सबसे बड़ा ना-मालूम होना है
अगर क़तरा ना दरिया से जुदा होता तो क्या होता?
वही होता जो है—इस के सिवा होता तो क्या होता?
ना होने पर तो दुनिया की निगाहें खा गईं धोखा
जो तेरे मा सिवा कोई ख़ुदा होता तो क्या होता?
जो यूं होता तो क्या होता जो यूं होता तो क्या होता?
माटी कहे कुम्हार से तू का रौंदत मोए
एक दिन ऐसा आयेगा कि मैं रौंदूंगी तोए
    भला हुआ मोरी माला टूटी
माला जपूं न कर जपूं और मुख से कहूं न राम
राम हमारा हमें जपे रे हम पायो बिसराम

bhalaa huaa moree maalaa TooTee
main to raam bhajan se chhooTee re
morey sar se Talee balaa

naa kachhu dekhaa raam bhajan mein
naa kachhu dekhaa pothi mein

kahat kabeer suno bhaaii saadho
jo dekhaa do roTee mein

al-ilm-o-hijaab-ul-akbar
maloom honaa hi sabse badaa naa-maloom honaa hai

agar qataraa naa dariyaa se judaa hotaa toh kyaa hotaa?
vahee hotaa jo hai is ke sivaa hotaa toh kyaa hotaa?
naa hone par toh duniyaa ki nigaahen khaa gayee dhokhaa
jo tere maa sivaa koii khudaa hotaa toh kyaa hotaa?
jo yoon hotaa to kyaa hotaa jo yoon hotaa toh kyaa hotaa?

maaTee kahe kumhaar se tuu kaa rondat moye
ek din aisaa aayegaa kee main rondoongee toye
bhalaa huaa moree maalaa TooTee

maalaa japoon naa kar japoon aur mukh se kahoon naa raam
raam hamaaraa hamein jape re ham paayo bisaraam

A good thing my prayer beads shattered
God's name was just jabber
I'm liberated from this bother!

What really needs breaking is this rosary
God must be freed from his coterie
All this punditry is mere sophistry

There's nothing I see in chanting Ram
Nor in their books do I see any charm

There's no enchantment in chanting the name
    No enlightenment in the books of god
Says Kabir, and for this he earns fame:
    It's the sight of bread that leaves me awed

Ayaz recalls a saying in Arabic and explains it in Hindustani:

Wisdom is the biggest obstacle
To ravel is to come unravelled
To understand is a misunderstanding

If the drop were not parted from the river,
                        what would it be?
It would be what it's meant to be—if it were
                    not this, that it would be
It is in the not-being that the world has lost sight
                            of all being
If there were another god besides you,
                    what would it be?
If it were not to be this, what would it be?
                        Would it be?

The author of these above lines is not mentioned by Ayaz, but this
idea is echoed in the doctrine of Paticca Samuppada or Dependent
Arising, central to Buddhism, and equally by Mirza Ghalib:

इमस्मिम सति इदम होति इमसुप्पादा इदम उप्पज्जति
इमस्मिम असति इदम न होति इमस्स निरोधा इदम निरुज्झति

imasmim sati idam hoti imasuppaadaa idam uppajjati
imasmim asati idam na hoti imassa nirodhaa idam nirujjhati

From this being, that becomes; from this arising,
                                    that arises
If this were not, that does not become; from this
                                    ceasing, that ceases

न था कुछ कुछ तो ख़ुदा था कुछ न होता तो ख़ुदा होता
डुबोया मुझ को होने ने न होता मैं तो क्या होता

na thaa kuchh toh khudaa thaa kuchh na hotaa toh khudaa hotaa
Duboyaa mujh ko hone ne na hotaa main toh kyaa hotaa

When nothing was, god was; if nothing was,
                                    god would be
Being beat the life out of me; if I were not,
                                    what would be

Whom do I pray to now? I'm rid of the rosary
Come wish me well, O congratulate me

It's a new day, a new dawn
I've been scented with Aleph
I'm fragrant now

Good thing, my rosary is scattered
O what joy! The chanting never mattered!

God's name is always on the lip
But god always gives the slip

Ah, good the pitcher's shattered
I need not fetch any water!

The earth tells the potter
Don't be proud of kneading me
A day will dawn sooner or later
When I'll be kneading thee

Ah, good the pitcher's shattered
I need not fetch any water!

All this chant is cant
Ram's name an empty rant
Ram now chants my name
Kabir has changed the game

Kabir sings not of Ram but of No-Ram
Kabir knows no guru, he wishes no-one harm

Ayaz and co. forget to add this equally famous bead to their rosary:

हद हद कर के सब गए और बेहद गया न कोय
अनहद के मैदान में सो रहा कबीरा सोय

had had kar ke sab gaye aur behad gayaa naa koy
anhad ke maidaan mein so rahaa kabeeraa soy

Bound by the limit, they cried and died
The boundless limitless, no one espied
In the field of boundlessness
Unbound, Kabir is at rest

A fabric so fine
झीनी चदरिया

गुरु गोविंद दोऊ खड़े किसके लागूं पांव
बलिहारी गुरु देवन की मने गोविंद दियो बताए
संत मिलन को चालिए तो तज माया अभिमान
ज्यों ज्यों पांव धरे धरनी पर त्यों त्यों यज़ समान
कबीरा जब हम पैदा हुए तो जग हंसे हम रोये
ऐसी करनी कर चलो हम हंसे जग रोये

झीनी झीनी झीनी बीनी चदरिया
काहे के ताना काहे के भरनी कौन तार से बीनी चदरिया
    झीनी झीनी झीनी
इंगला पिंगला ताना भरनी सुखमन तार से बीनी चदरिया
    झीनी झीनी झीनी
आठ कंवल दल चरखा डोलै पांच तत्त गुन तीनी चदरिया
    झीनी झीनी झीनी
सांई को सियत मास (नौ)दस लागे ठोक-ठोक के बीनी चदरिया
    झीनी झीनी झीनी

जद मोरी चादर बन घर आई धुबियन के घर दीनी
सुरत सिला पर दे फ़टकारो इस विध निर्मल कीनी
चादर धूप तयार भई जद रंगरेज को दीनी
ऐसा रंग रंगा रंगरे ने लालो लाल कर दीनी

चादर ओढ़ शंका मत करियो ये दो दिन तुमको दीनी
मूरख लोग भेद नहीं जाने दिन दिन मैली कीनी

सो चादर सुर नर मुनि ओढ़ी ओढ़ के मैली कीनी चदरिया
झीनी झीनी झीनी
दास कबीर जतन से ओढ़ी ज्यों की त्यों धर दीनी चदरिया
झीनी झीनी झीनी

guru govind doou khaDe kiske laagoon paanv
balihaaree guru devan ki mane govind diyo bataae

sant milan ko chaalie toh taj maayaa abhimaan
jyon jyon paanv dhare dharanii par tyon tyon yajn samaan

kabeeraa jab ham paidaa huey toh jag hanse ham roye
aisee karanii kar chalo ham hanse jag roye

jheenii jheenii jheenii beenii chadariyaa
kaahe ke taanaa kaahe ke bharanii kaun taar se beenii chadariyaa
jheenii jheenii jheenii

ingalaa pingalaa taanaa bharanii sukhaman taar se beenii chadariyaa
jheenii jheenii jheenii

aaTh kanval dal charakha Dolai paanch tatt gun teenii chadariyaa
jheenii jheenii jheenii

saanyii ko siyat maas (nau)das laage Thok-Thok ke beenii chadariyaa
jheenii jheenii jheenii

jad moree chaadar ban ghar aayee dhubiyan ke ghar deenii
surat sila par de phaTakaaro is vidh nirmal keenii

chaadar dhoop tayaar bhaaii jad rangarej ko deenii
aisaa rang rangaa rangare ne laalo laal kar deenii

chaadar oDh shanka mat kariyo ye do din tumako deenii
moorakh log bhed naheen jaane din din mailee keenii

so chaadar sur nar muni oDhee oDh ke mailee keenii chadariyaa
    jheenii jheenii jheenii

daas kabeer jatan se oDhee jyon ki tyon dhar deenii chadariyaa
    jheenii jheenii jheenii

Love and god are what I face:
Tell me whom I must embrace?
It is to love that I surrender
For love will render me to the maker

When in love you seek recourse
Shed your ego, give up pride
At every step along the course
The fire of sacrifice abides

I came into the world crying
And found everyone laughing
When I signed off with a smile
The world was left grieving

I've woven a fabric so fine
With the warp of your breath, the weft of mine
O the spin that spins, spinning me
    How subtle these threads, finer than fine

The movement of the sun wafting me
The movement of the moon wefting me
The pillar of breath spindling me
    All these threads threading me

With eight lotuses for spindles, the five elements for thread
It takes nine-ten months to weave this spread
Of starshine, birdsong, earth's russet
    I have woven a fabric so blessed

    When the cloth arrives home, uncut like the sky
    I give it to the washer to lave and dry
    She beats it on the stone of awareness, makes it glisten
        But this cloth is not yet done

    It's then the turn of the dyer
    Who reddens the cloth in the vat of desire
    Infusing it with the spirit of fire
        The reddened cloth is now made sheer

When this garment wraps you, wear no doubt
You're here for a few days, it will wear you out
The ignorant in their wisdom sully it, day in and day out
    This boundless cloth weaves day into night

The cloth Kabir bears knows no wear and tear
He holds the warp of love with the weft of care

I wove this song, cut from Mukhtiyar Ali's and Kumar
Gandharva's versions of "Jhini chadariya" (YouTube). Ali
proffers the epigraphic verses. Here, I have rendered guru

as love. For how and why the guru is a heavy burden for both Kabir and the world, and how we may lighten that burden, see the reflections that follow the song, "All I ask of you is you"/ "सतगुरु मोरी चूक संभारो" (p.225). By and by, we will also see Das Kabir become Boss Kabir.

For now, into the body of the poem that Gandharva offers, I have woven elements from Ali's (such as the reference to the process of washing, laving, dyeing). Ali's rendition, that I first heard in "The Kabir Project" recorded in 2009, offers a more Hinduistic take on the song (bringing in the bhaktas of Vishnu like Dhruv and Prahlad, which I skip), whereas Gandharva veers towards the appeal of the *nirgun*, formlessness. Standing between both, we pause at the jheenii subtleties of *subtle*: from *sub*, 'under' + *-tilis*, from *tela*, 'web, net, warp of a fabric', from PIE [Proto-Indo-European, the reconstructed common ancestor of the Indo-European language family] root *teks-*, 'to weave', also 'to fabricate'.

My love's awakened
पिया मेरा जागता

जागन ही में सोवना सोने में है जाग
एक तो बन में घर करे एक घर में रहे बैराग

पिया मेरा जागता मैं कैसे सोऊं री
कैसे सोऊं री सखी मैं कैसे सोऊं री
मालिक मेरा जागता मैं कैसे सोऊं री
कैसे सोऊं री सखी मैं कैसे सोऊं री
पिया मेरा जागता मैं कैसे सोऊं री
रात में सोई दिन खेल गंवायो हाथ से चिड़िया खेत चुगायो
अरे हां री हेली कौन सा माली इना बाग का है
पिया मेरा जागता मैं कैसे सोऊं री
हाथ में मेहंदी पांव में मेहंदी सीस फूल माथे पर बिंदिया
अरे हां री हेली कंगना पहरो निज नाम का हे
पिया मेरा जागता मैं कैसे सोऊं री
चुन चुन कलियां सेज बिछाई सूली ऊपर सेज पिया की
अरे हां री हेली आज की रैन सुहाग की है
पिया मेरा जागता मैं कैसे सोऊं री
सैन हुसैन फ़कीर अलोदा मिल गये सदगुरु मिटी गयो भेदा
अरे हां री हेली कठिन पंथ बैराग को है
पिया मेरा जागता मैं कैसे सोऊं री

jaagan hee mein sovanaa soney mein hai jaag
ek toh ban mein ghar kare ek ghar mein rahe bairaag

piyaa meraa jaagata main kaise soun ree
kaise soun ree sakhee main kaise soun ree

maalik meraa jaagataa main kaise soun ree
kaise soun ree sakhee main kaise soun ree

raat mein soii din khel ganvaayo haath se chiDiyaa khet chugaayo
arey haan ree helee kaun saa maalee ina baag kaa hai
        piyaa mera jaagataa main kaise soun ree

haath mein mehandee paanv mein mehandee sees phool maathe
                                                par bindiyaa
arey haan ree heli kanganaa paharo nij naam kaa hey
        piyaa meraa jaagataa main kaise soun ree

chun chun kaliyaan sej bichhaaii soolee oopar sej piyaa kee
arey haan ree helee aaj kee rain suhaag kee hai
        piyaa meraa jaagata main kaise soun ree

saiN husain fakeer alodaa mil gaye sadaguru miTee gayo bhedaa
arey haan ree helee kaThin panth bairaag ko hai
        piyaa meraa jaagataa main kaise soun ree

Sleeping in wakefulness, wakeful in sleep
One recluse seeks refuge in the forest deep
In the drifter who stays home, the forest sleeps

My love stays awake, sleep's foreign to me
How can I sleep when love has forsaken me?
I've staked everything for my love's sake
    Hey! I stay awake for my love's sake

I give my night to sleep, while the day away
Feasting off my hand, birds have a field day
Who's to care for this garden of grace?
    Hey! I stay awake for my love's sake

The vein-bursts of henna on my hands and on my feet
Flowers for a crown, on my brow a red streak
I wear a bangle clasped close in its need
    Hey! I stay awake for my love's sake

To deck this bed, I picked each flower
On the tip of a thorn, the bed of my lover
This is the tryst I'll always treasure
    Hey! I stay awake for my love's sake

I've found truelove, I've merged with the sun
There's no self nor the other, there's just one
The path to this place is not for everyone

    Hussain's a blessed fakir, he's merged with the One
    He's erased all difference, he's done and undone
    It is not easy, this path of irreverent deference

Kaluram Bamaniya sings "Piyaa meraa jaagataa", which bears the signature of Hussain Fakir, a Kabiri poet, recorded in August 2006 in Luniyakhedi, Madhya Pradesh. I first heard it in the *Kabir in Malwa* CD of "The Kabir Project". Years later, I watch Bamaniya and his full troupe in a video uploaded on YouTube in 2018. It's from a "Kabir Mahostav" in Diggiraj Nagar, Dewas. Before singing the signature line, he adjusts his winter cap and offers his live audience this information: 'Hussain was one of Kabir's Mohammedan followers... a Mussalman he was.' He then sings the refrain with gusto. Do not all identities and particularities cease when you weave such a fine Kabiri song and have 'merged with the One'? Are not all differeneces transcended in the ecstasy of song? Should such a one be remembered as a Mohammedan or a Baaman? It is thus done and undone. So little is known about Hussain Fakir that "The Kabir Project" website ajabshahar.com says: 'We have no information about this poet, and we welcome help from our browsers in finding out more about this person.' Ajab Shahar broadly translates as Strange City, and on the website's 'people' page many poets listed are truly *ajab*—strangers about whom nothing is known save for the forging and merging of their names and songs into Kabir. Yet, some wannabe Kabiriyas like me flaunt long bios.

The body city
शून्य गढ़ शहर

शून्य गढ़ शहर शहर घर बस्ती
कोण सोता कोण जागे है
लाल हमरे हम लालन के
तन सोता ब्रह्म जागे है

शून्य गढ़ शहर शहर घर बस्ती
जल बिच कमल कमल बिच कलियाँ
भँवर बास ना लेता है
इस नगरी के दस दरवाजे
जोगी फेरी नित देता है
शून्य गढ़ शहर शहर घर बस्ती
तन की कुंडी मन का सोटा
ज्ञान की रगड़ लगाता है
पांच पच्चीस बसे घट भीतर
उनकु घोट पिलाता है
शून्य गढ़ शहर शहर घर बस्ती
अगन कुंड से तपसी तापे
तपसी तपसा करता है
पांचो चेला फिरे अकेला
अलख अलख कर जपता है

शून्य गढ़ शहर शहर घर बस्ती
एक अप्सरा सामें उभीजी
दूजी सुरमा हो सारे है
तीसरी रम्भा सेज बिछावे
परण्या नहीं कुंवारा है
	शून्य गढ़ शहर शहर घर बस्ती
परण्या पहिले पुत्तुर जाया
माता पिता मन भाया है
शारण मच्छिंदर गोरख बोले
एक अखंडी छाया है
	शून्य गढ़ शहर शहर घर बस्ती

shoonyaa gaDh shahar shahar ghar bastee
koN sotaa koN jaage hai
laal hamre ham laalan ke
tan sotaa brahm jaage hai
	shoonyaa gaDh shahar shahar ghar bastee

jal bich kamal kamal bich kaliyaan
bhanvar baas naa letaa hai
is nagaree ke das daravaaje
jogee pheree nit detaa hai
	shoonyaa gaDh shahar shahar ghar bastee

tan kee kunDee man kaa soTaa
gyaan kee ragaD lagaataa hai
paanch pachchees basey ghaT bheetar
unaku ghoT pilaataa hai
	shoonyaa gaDh shahar shahar ghar bastee

agan kunD se tapasee taape
tapasee tapasaa kartaa hai
paancho chelaa phire akelaa
alakh alakh kar japtaa hai
　　shoonyaa gaDh shahar shahar ghar bastee

ek apsaraa saamein ubheejee
doojee suramaa ho saare hai
teesaree rambhaa sej bichhaave
paraNyaa naheen kunvaara hai
　　shoonyaa gaDh shahar shahar ghar bastee

paraNyaa pahile puttur jaayaa
maataa pitaa man bhaayaa hai
shaaraN machhindar gorakh boley
ek akhanDee chhaayaa hai
　　shoonyaa gaDh shahar shahar ghar bastee

Zero fortress city
City house hood
Who sleeps? Who stirs?

My love is red, I'm reddened
My lord is red, I'm wakened

Daubed in my beloved's red, I'm reddened
The body sleeps, the spirit's awakened

City fortress emptiness
In the city, a hood of hush

Emptiness fortress cityness
Cityness naughtness fortress

In the middle of the water, the lotus
In the middle of the lotus, buds
The bee, restless, finds a stillness
The nectar had in its notness

This city has ten gates
The wise guard it always

> The zero city, fortressed by silence
> In the city, the house of quiescence
> Emptiness, fortress, cityness

The mortar of the mind
In the pestle of the body
Grinds the paste of wisdom
Nurtures the river of elements
Nourishes the garden of senses
> The twenty-five deer that roam the forest
> Quaff this blend, and find the musk

> Zeroness fortress cityness
> City, hood, a house of hush
> Who sleeps? Who wakes?
> I'm the love of red, daubed in my beloved

The ascetic floats in the fire-pit
He does not burn, he's burnished
His five wards, each seeks a new turn
It leads to the unseen path, they learn

The zero city, walled by silence
In this city, your home the essence
What sleep? What wakefulness?
I'm daubed in red, in the love of my beloved

Emptiness, fortress, cityness

A houri appears out of nowhere
Another wears jasmine in her hair
The third lies spread on the bed of desire
    She's made of water, air, sky, earth and fire

    Emptiness a fortress
    The city, the hood, a house of hush
    Who sleeps? Who's sleepless?
    I'm the red of love, drenched in my beloved

    In the near redness, a red redness
    A nearness reddened, a reddened dearness
    A dear redness, a red dearness
    A red nearness, a near redness
    A reddedness, a reddenedness

The unwed maiden births a child
Her parents take great delight
Gorakh sees but one source of light
It shines on all—no wrong, no right

    Emptiness fortness cityness
    In the city, a house of hush
    Who sleeps? Who's sleepless?

What slumbers? What's aroused?
I'm drenched in red, the red of my beloved

Emptiness
Fortness
Cityness

Kumar Gandharva lingers on the silences in Gorakhnath's "Shoonya gaDh shahar", (featured in the CD that accompanied the first edition of Linda Hess's *Singing Emptiness*), and I linger with and explore the expanse of Kumar's silences. A singular aspect of Kumar's approach to a composition is the angle of repose at which he makes the lyric yield to the unthought of a raga. He sheds the sanctimony of the purist path. When he finds two roads diverging in a yellow wood, he's happy to take both. In this song, he starts with what in the 'classical' structure has come to be the well-worn raga of dawn, Bhairav, and threads into it phrases of the 'folk' idiom of Maand. He swings between the sombre Bhairav and the joyous Maand, flirting with Bhatiyar. I started on this translation for a friend around Ambedkar's birth anniversary in 2014 and have revisited it each time I sing it.

No sun, no moon, but light
बिना चंदा रे बिना भान

अलख पुरुष निर्बाण है वाको लखे नहीं कोय
वाको तो वो ही लखे जो वा घर का ही होय
घर का हुआ तो क्या हुआ तत्व लखे होय
तत्व लखे वो सूरमा जो शबद विवेकी होय
कोई शबद विवेकी पारखी मेरे सिर माथे का मोड़
सब संतन कौ बंदगी अपनी अपनी ठोर
साधू सब ही बैठिया अपनी अपनी ठोर
कोई शबद विवेकी पारखी मेरे सिर माथे का मोड़

बिना चंदा रे बिना भान सूरज बिना होया उजियाला है
परलोगा मत जाओ परख ले यहीं उनियारो है
अरे हेली म्हारी
गूंगा गावे है अब राग बेहरो सुनवा लाग्यो है
पांगलियो नाचे रे घणो नाच आंधलियो नरखन लाग्यो है
    बिना चंदा रे बिना भान
अरे हेली म्हारी
गगन मंडल के बीच मचों एक झगड़ो भारी है
नहीं कायर को यां काम कायर को कोई पतियारो है
    बिना चंदा रे बिना भान
अरे हेली म्हारी

सुन शिखर के बीच तपे कोई जोगी मतवालो है
नहीं अगन वा बभूत नहीं रे कोई तापन वालो है

    बिना चंदा रे बिना भान
अरे हेली म्हारी
गावे गुलाबी दास खुल्या तुम्हारी हृदय रा ताला है
बोल्या भवानी नाथ होया म्हारा घट उजियाला है

    बिना चंदा रे बिना भान

    alakh purush nirbaaN hai vaako lakhe naheen koy
    vaako toh vo hee lakhe jo vaa ghar kaa hee hoy

    ghar kaa huaa to kyaa huaa tatv lakhe hoy
    tatv lakhe vo sooramaa jo shabad vivekee hoy

    koii shabad vivekee paarakhee merey sir maathe kaa moD
    sab santan kau bandagee apanii apanii Thor

    saadhoo sab hee baiThiyaa apanii apanii Thor
    koii shabad vivekee paarakhee merey sir maathe kaa moD

binaa chandaa re binaa bhaan sooraj binaa hoyaa ujiyaalaa hai
paralogaa mat jaao parakh le yaheen uniyaaro hai
    arey helee mhaaree

goongaa gaave hai ab raag beharo sunavaa laagyo hai
paangaliyo naache re ghaNo naach aandhaliyo narakhan laagyo hai
    binaa chandaa re binaa bhaan

arey helee mhaaree
gagan manDal ke beech machon ek jhagaDo bhaaree hai
naheen kaayar ko yaan kaam kaayar ko koiin patiyaaro hai
    binaa chandaa re binaa bhaan

arey helee mhaaree
sunn shikhar ke beech tapey koii jogee matavaalo hai
naheen agan vaa babhoot naheen re koii taapan vaalo hai
    binaa chandaa re binaa bhaan

arey helee mhaaree
gaave gulaabee daas khulyaa tumhaaree hraday raa taalaa hai
bolyaa bhavaanii naath hoyaa mhaaraa ghaT ujiyaalaa hai
    binaa chandaa re binaa bhaan

The Unseen One will subsume words
He dwells in a world beyond worlds
He'll show himself only to those
Who find a place in this house

You may well belong to this place
But you let the senses rule your ways
He who seeks the Word that's right
Finds that love floods his sight

The one engulfed in this light
Has two diamonds for eyes
Every swan that espies this sight
Sings this song in delight

All the poets of yore I've adored
Have explored the worlds of the Word
I've bowed, beseeched and implored
Shutting my eyes, I sing what I've heard

There's no sun, no moon in sight
Yet everywhere there's such a light
You don't have to seek another sky
Just find the lamp within your eye
    No sun, no moon, but light

The mute finds voice in song
The deaf descries the notes
The cripple breaks into a dance
The blind paints in unseen tones
    No sun, no moon, but light

A quarrel between clouds in the sky
Thunder and lightning are at strife
There's no place here for cowards
Time to unsheathe the swords of words
    No sun, no moon, but light

Scaling the peak of emptiness
A yogi breathes the air of bliss
There's no fire, there's no ash
Only dew steaming on the lips
    No sun, no moon, but light

There's no lock on the house of love
The key is in the song I sing
My heaven is in the here and now
An Unseen Light floods my being
    No sun, no moon, but light

Prahlad Tipaniya sings "Binaa chandaa re binaa bhaan"—
it loops back to the Bahiya Sutta of the Buddha we
encountered earlier ("Freeing freedom from itself", p.39),
and to several other songs of Kabir here that speak of a
sunless, moonless, starless, darkless, lightless realm of no-
ness bereft even of songness. Two signatures appear at the
end—Gulabi Das (or Nath) is said to have spoken this
song and opened the lock to the heart, and Bhavani Nath
who sings it signs in as well, saying he's flooded by light.
According to "The Kabir Project", Bhavani Nath was a
poet born in 1775 in Dholka village, Gujarat, in the Vankar
(weaver) community, and his guru was likely Gulabi Das.
The song that follows, "Sakhiyaa vaa ghar sab se nyaaraa",
set by Kumar Gandharva in the raga Bhairavi, echoes the
same ideas.

Where my love lives
सखिया वा घर

सखिया वा घर सबसे न्यारा
जहां पूरन पुरुष हमारा

सखिया वा घर सबसे न्यारा
जहां नहीं सुख दुख साच झूठ नहीं पाप न पुन्य पसारा
नहीं दिन रैन चंदा नहीं सूरज बिना ज्योत उजियारा
सखिया वा घर सबसे न्यारा
नहीं तह ज्ञान ध्यान नहीं जप तप वेद कितेब न बानी
करनी धरनी रहनी गहनी ये सब जहां हिरानी
सखिया वा घर सबसे न्यारा
धर नहीं अधर न बाहर भीतर पिंड ब्रह्मंड कछु नाहीं
पांच तत्त गुन तीन नहीं तहं साखी शबद न ताहीं
सखिया वा घर सबसे न्यारा
मूल न फूल बेली नहीं बीजा बिना व्रिच्छ फल सोहे
ओह सोहं अर्ध उर्ध नहीं स्वास लेख न कोहे
सखिया वा घर सबसे न्यारा
जहां पुरुष तहां कछु नाहीं कहे कबीरा हम जाना
हमरी सेण लाखे जो कोई पावे पद निर्बाना
सखिया वा घर सबसे न्यारा

sakhiyaa vaa ghar sabase nyaaraa
jahaan pooran purush hamaaraa
    sakhiyaa vaa ghar sabse nyaaraa

jahaan naheen sukh dukh saach jhooTh naheen paap na punya pasaaraa
naheen din rain chandaa naheen sooraj binaa jyot ujiyaaraa
    sakhiyaa vaa ghar sabse nyaaraa

naheen taha gyaan dhyaan naheen jap tap ved kiteb na baanii
karanii dharanii rahanii gahanii ye sab jahaan hiraanii
    sakhiyaa vaa ghar sabse nyaaraa

dhar naheen adhar na baahar bheetar pinD bramhanD kachhu naaheen
paanch tatt gun teen naheen tahan saakhi shabad na taaheen
    sakhiyaa vaa ghar sabse nyaaraa

mool na phool belee naheen beejaa binaa vrichchha phala sohe
oham soham ardh urdh naheen svaas lekh na kohe
    sakhiyaa vaa ghar sabse nyaaraa

jahaan purush tahaan kachhu naaheen kahe kabeera ham jaana
hamaree seN laakhe jo koii paave pad nirbaanaa
    sakhiyaa vaa ghar sabse nyaaraa

Where my love lives, it is utterly beautiful
Where it is utterly beautiful, there lives my love
My utterly beautiful love lives in the only true house
My utter love lives in the truly beautiful house
My love lives in the utterly beautiful house
I'm become utter and beautiful in the house of love
In the truly beautiful house, I've uttered my love

I'm truly beautiful in the house of utter love
My love is utterly beautiful in the house of love
In the house of love, I'm utterly beautiful
It's utter, it's beautiful, it's the true house of love
    Where my love lives, it is utterly beautiful

No sorrow there nor joy, no truth within
It's the domain of neither virtue nor sin
No constant sun, no inconstant moon, no night follows day
It's blindingly bright but nothing is in sight
    Where my love lives, light manifests in light

There's nothing known, nothing unknown
You don't chant a thing, no recitation of hymns
Words mean nothing, nothing has meaning
No doings, undoings, no reason no wrangling
    Where my love lives, it is the utter thing

There's no either or, no neither nor
The house is no house, no interior exterior
No being no nothing, no self no other
None of the five elements, not even Kabir's song
    Where my love lives, there's no right no wrong

No creeper, no flower, no seed, no root
There's not even a tree, but there's fine fruit
No inbreath no outbreath, no way to count breath
There's no life no death, there's no way to live death
    Where my love lives, there's only one breath

My truelove lives in the middle of nowhere
Kabir winks and tells, I've been there
That's the one place that's really no-place
Look all you want, but you'll find no trace
   Where my love lives, that is the place

Often a singer takes a line, a phrase or just a word for a long walk into a raga. Each repetition throws new light on the word, the phrase, sometimes just a vowel. How does the tail of a line eat the head? Return to the opening line: What happens when the words sakhiyaa/ सखिया and nyaaraa/ न्यारा meet? Or when न्यारा/ nyaaraa runs into हमारा/ hamaaraa? Each utterance seeks out the utmost and inmost point and the expanse in between. Meaning meanders, at once collapsing and expanding. With each rendition, the artist seeks different ways of moving between two points. The iteration and reiteration of each alliteration renews the relation between sense and sensation. In raga music across genres, this is broadly called improvisation, where we come to terms with the unforeseen and the unexpected within the frames of words and notes. Here, the boundless is bound. The fact that most Indian poetry of the premodern period does not use any punctuation nor phrase breaks, stanza distinctions or lineation gives scope for limitless possibilities. A line, a phrase, a word or an idea can be turned inside-out, outside-in. It is often left to the reader, and more so to the singer, to play with all the possible and impossible, explicit and implicit meanings.

Here, I have improvised on Kumar Gandharva's meditative improvisations on "Sakhiyaa vaa ghar sab se nyaaraa" in the raga Bhairavi (YouTube). In the Nagari script, you'll see the collocation pooran purush/ पूरन पुरुष, which in the course of singing is enunciated both as pooran (whole, complete) and puraan (ancient). On the surface, it references the primeval man-god (perhaps the Purusha of the *Rig Veda* who's sacrificed at the Vedic altar). However, in the nirguni cosmogeny of formlessness that informs Kabir and his coevals, it means anything but. As the scholar-translator **David Lorenzen** says, the nirgun poets praised 'a formless God, a God who is everywhere and nowhere, within all things and apart from all things, a supreme God without arms, legs, beard, eyes, sex, or even a recognizable personality.' I render puraan/pooran purush simply as love.

Thinner than water, fiercer than fire
जी कबीरा रे

जल से पतला कौन है
कौन अगन से तेज़
कौन भवे से भारी
कौन काजल से कारी
गियान जल सू पतला है
क्रोध अगन से तेज़ है
पाप भवे से भारी
कलंक काजल से कारी

जी कबीरा रे
चालत चालत जुग भया रे कौण बतावे जी धाम रे
जी कबीरा रे
मन के भूलोवाला भूलो फिरे रे पांव कोस पर धाम/ गाम जी
जी कबीरा रे
कौण मटली कौण झेरणा रे कौण बिलोवनहार रे
जी कबीरा रे
मन मटली तन झेरणा रे सुरत बिलोवनहार रे
जी कबीरा रे
सुरत बहोणवाला (बहोणगद) साळणा रे झेल सके तो झेल रे
जी कबीरा रे
सूरा होवे तो वे सनमुख लड़िये (लड़िया) नहीं कायरों का खेल रे

जी कबीरा रे

धुरत कबीरो संत ले गयो रे छाछ पीए संसार जी

जी कबीरा रे

धुरत पिया तो वा का क्या हुआ रे थेण धणी के पास रे

जी कबीरा रे

सूली के ऊपर घर हमारा औथ पायो विशराम दियौ

जी कबीरा रे

संत कबीरो रमे रह्यौ रे आठ पोर होशियार रे

जी कबीरा रे

jal se patalaa kaun hai
kaun agan se tez
kaun bhave se bhaaree
kaun kaajal se kaaree

giyaan jal suu patalaa hai
krodh agan se tej hai
paap bhave se bhaaree
kalank kaajal se kaaree

jee kabeeraa re
chaalat chaalat jug bhayaa re kauN bataave jee dhaam re
jee kabeeraa re

man ke bhoolovaala bhoolo phire re paanv kos par dhaam/ gaam jee
jee kabeeraa re

kauN maTalee kauN jheraNaa re kauN bilovanahaar re
jee kabeeraa re

man maTalee tan jheraNaa re surat bilovanahaar re
jee kabeeraa re

surat bahoNavaalaa (bahoNagad) saaLaNaa re jhel sakey toh jhel re
  jee kabeeraa re

sooraa hovey to ve sanamukh laDiye (laDiyaa) naheen kaayaron ka khel re
  jee kabeeraa re

dhurat kabeero sant le gayo re chhaachh peeae sansaar jee
  jee kabeeraa re

dhurat piyaa toh vaa kaa kyaa hua re then dhaNii ke paas re
  jee kabeeraa re

soolee ke oopar ghar hamaara auth paayo visharaam diyau
  jee kabeeraa re

sant kabeero ramey rahyau re aaTh por hoshiyaar re
  jee kabeeraa re

What's thinner than water
What's fiercer than fire
What's heavier than the earth
What's darker than kohl

Wisdom is thinner than water
Anger fiercer than fire
Sin heavier than the earth
A blemish darker than kohl

So Kabira says:
You've wandered through time, weathered the tide
Not heeding the light that's right inside
You've searched everywhere, without a clue
The destination was always close to you

So Kabira says:
What is the pot and what the churn
Who's the one that stirs?
Mind is the pot, body the churn
It's your awareness you must stir

So Kabira says:
The arrow of awareness seeks a target
See if you can bear to face it
The fearless one will meet it in the eye
The coward will cower and hide

So Kabira says:
Poets like me savour the ghee
The world makes do with buttermilk
So what if I'm allowed to feast?
The cow and I are of one ilk

So Kabira says:
The bed of my love is at the tip of a thorn
And that's where I find bliss
Kabir's busy tooting his own horn
At every moment he's aware of this

Mahesha Ram and his troupe's "Chaalat chaalat jug bhaya re" makes us aware of Kabir who asks us to be aware. Years after translating this from the version I heard in "The Kabir Project", I stumbled on another rendition on YouTube in 2022. It is a recording dated to 2013 in Mumbai from a private *satsang*, literally a gathering (*sang*) of, for and around being or truth (*sat*). A song is always renewed with each singing, each remembering. The questions and answers that preface this song are posed and answered by Mahesha Ram in the 2013 rendition. These prefatory remarks, improvised and sung without rhythm, often change according to mood and audience. They are called *saakhi* in the Rajasthani tradition, often treated as proverbial distichs. You'll find several of the songs in *The Notbook* open with a string of couplets. These can be invoked anytime, anywhere. They can be moved around; summoned at will. The performing artist's mind is a reservoir of sediments, and each time something new floats up.

'My apologies to great questions for small answers,' says Wisława Szymborska in a poem. The rhetorical questions, freed of punctuation, are apparently posed by humans, the answers apparently are by god—such pieties aside, surely both are the work of humans, god being a necessary fiction, just another Word. 'Kabir koi bhagat thaa, usne bhagwaan se mazaak karlee,' says Mahesha Ram, explaining in a line. Kabir was a devotee who had fun with god. Are they Kabir's words? Or are they spoken in Kabir's name? Did Mahesha Ram improvise, or did he pick it from a guru or another singer? Was Kabir a devotee or a sceptic? Which flower is Kabir in this garland of delights? What colour is his flower? What colours our idea of it? If wisdom is thinner, rather subtler, than water, what's more subtle than wisdom? What is the awareness that is caught unawares? Kyaa baat hai, kahe Kabir. So subtle, says Kabir.

Coasting along
नैय्या मोरी

नैय्या मोरी निक्के निक्के चालन लागी
आंधी मेघा कछु ना व्यापे चढ़े संत बड़भागी

नैय्या मोरी निक्के निक्के चालन लागी
उथले रहत डर कछु नाहीं नाहीं गहरे को संसा
उलट जाय तो बाल न बांका वाह रे अजब तमासा
नैय्या मोरी निक्के निक्के चालन लागी
औसर लागे तो परबत बोझा ताउ ना लागे रे भारी
धन सतगुरूजी ने राह बतायी वाकई रे मैं बलिहारी
नैय्या मोरी निक्के निक्के चालन लागी
कहे कबीरा जो बिन सिर खेवे सो यह सुमति बखाने
या बहु हित की अकथ कथा है बिरला खेवट ही जाने
नैय्या मोरी निक्के निक्के चालन लागी

naiyyaa moree nikke nikke chaalan laagee
aandhee meghaa kachhu naa vyaape chadhe sant baDabhaagee
    naiyyaa moree nikke nikke chaalan laagee

uthale rahat Dar kachhu naaheen naaheen gahare ko sansaa
ulaT jaay toh baal na baankaa vaah re ajab tamaasaa
    naiyyaa moree nikke nikke chaalan laagee

ausar laage toh paṛabat bojhaa taau naa laage re bhaaree
dhanaa satgurujee ne raah bataayee vaakaee re main balihaaree
    naiyyaa moree nikke nikke chaalan laagee

kahe kabeeraa jo bin sir kheve so yah sumatee bakhaane
yaa bahu hith kee akath katha hai biralaa khevaT hee jaane
    naiyyaa moree nikke nikke chaalan laagee

My boat is coasting along, just fine
My boat is just fine, coasting along
My boat is fine, just coasting along
My coast is boating along, just fine
    You see, I'm just singing a song

Storms, cloudbursts, my boat rides them all!
It quietly tames every cyclone and squall
My boat is just fine, coasting along
This boat floats on nothing but song
    You see, I'm just in its thrall

When it hits a rock, I'm not alarmed
Not a strand of my hair will be harmed
My boat in no way will be pitchpoled
It is my very breath, my only hold
    You see, the song I sing is very old

Drop a mountain into my boat, meanwhile
And I'll bear the burden on my smile
I've love for an oar and god at the shore
My boat has warp for substance, weft for style
    I've been coasting along, all the while

See how the north wind loves my sail
My head surges with a push from the tail
My bow is not cut, it's lifted by the waves
My boat is buoyant against whatever it chafes
    I'm just coasting along, this is no travail

Kabir says with a light head what needs to be said
Only the rare coxswain can sing life as a song
The untold tale of the good of all beings
My song jives to the boat, my boat to the song
    You can't tell the boat from the song

    You see, I'm just coasting along

Improvisations on Kumar Gandharva's improvisations on
"Naiyyaa moree nikke nikke chaalan laagee" (YouTube).

Love in every heart, a poem in everyone
बाहर क्यों भटके

ऐसा ऐसा हीरला घट मा कहिये
जौहरी बिना (बणा) हीरा कौन पारखे
    क्या भटके बाहर क्यों भटके
    थारो राम [भीम] हृदय मैं बाहर क्यों भटके
ऐसा ऐसा घ्रित दूध मा कहिये
बिना (बणा) झुगिये माखन कैसा निकले
    क्या भटके बाहर क्यों भटके
    थारो राम [भीम] हृदय मैं बाहर क्यों भटके
ऐसा ऐसा आग लकड़ी मा कहिये
बिना (बणा) घसिये आग कैसे निकले
    क्या भटके बाहर क्यों भटके
    थारो राम [भीम] हृदय मैं बाहर क्यों भटके
ऐसा ऐसा किवाड़ हिवड़े पर जड़िया
गुरु बिना (बणा) ताला कौन खोले
    क्या भटके बाहर क्यों भटके
    थारो राम [भीम] हृदय मैं बाहर क्यों भटके
कहे कबीर सुनो भाई साधो
राम [भीम] मिले थाणे कौन हटके
    क्या भटके बाहर क्यों भटके
    थारो राम [भीम] हृदय मैं बाहर क्यों भटके

aisaa aisaa heeralaa ghaT maa kahiye
jauharee binaa (baNaa) heeraa kaun paarakhe
  kyaa bhaTake baahar kyon bhaTake
  thaaro raam [bheem] hraday main baahar kyon bhaTake

aisaa aisaa ghrit doodh maa kahiye
binaa (baNaa) jhugiye maakhan kaisaa nikale
  kyaa bhaTake baahar kyon bhaTake
  thaaro raam [bheem] hraday main baahar kyon bhaTake

aisaa aisaa aag lakaDee maa kahiye
binaa (baNaa) ghasiye aag kaise nikale
  kyaa bhaTake baahar kyon bhaTake
  thaaro raam [bheem] hraday main baahar kyon bhaTake

aisaa aisaa kivaaD hivaDe par jaDiyaa
guru binaa (baNaa) taalaa kaun khole
  kyaa bhaTake baahar kyon bhaTake
  thaaro raam [bheem] hraday main baahar kyon bhaTake

kahe kabeer suno bhaaii saadho
raam [bheem] miley thaNe kaun haTake
  kyaa bhaTake baahar kyon bhaTake
  thaaro raam [bheem] hraday main baahar kyon bhaTake

All the jewels are in your body
  but you go looking here there everywhere
Only a rare jeweller knows
  the worth of this treasure
Love is in your heart, and you look for it
  here there everywhere

All the jewels are in your body, don't go searching
    here there everywhere
Why wander from place to place
    when you always arrive at your feet
Love is in your heart, yet you go looking
    here there everywhere

Such sweet truths are secreted in the milk
    but without heat there'll be no cream
Why go looking for what turns inside you
    the butter's in your heart, be the churn
Love is in your heart, don't you go looking
    here there everywhere

Such a beautiful fire hides in the wood
    but it will not burn without friction
Every poem is inside you, don't go grazing
    here there everywhere
Love is in your heart, don't forage
    here there everywhere

Such a large lock jangles on your heart
    who but a poet can pick it apart
Every poem is in your body, don't go looking
    here there everywhere
Love is in your heart, don't look for it
    here there everywhere

It is not just Kabir who has seen this
    There's love in every heart, a poem in everyone
Mahesha Ram sings it, Anand dances to this
    Love is in every heart, a poem in everyone

Mahesha Ram sings "Baahar kyon bhaTake" with Bhange Khan, and the audience breaks into a dance (documented by "The Kabir Project"). The 'Ram' in the refrain, which I sing as 'Bhim' when I perform, is rendered as 'love' in translation—transitions, elisions, conversions, inversions and interpolations such as these are taken up in "In the bustling market, stand empty" (p.205), "My own god am I" (p.262) and "Spot less ness" (p.282), later in this Knotbook.

In the seen and the unseen
तित्थ सुत्ता

इमेसु कीर सज्जंति एके समण ब्राह्मणा
विग्गयहनम् विवादन्ति जान एकांग दस्सिनो

imesu keera sajjanti ekey samaNa braahmaNaa
viggayahanam vivaadanti jaana ekaanga dassino

Udanavagga, 6-4: Pathamananatitthiyasuttam
(The First Discourse about the Various Sectarians)

> Thus have I heard—I suffer no deafness—
> The parable of the blind lacks insight:
> The elephant in the room is the blindness
> Of the wise one who takes pride in his sight.
> It is both in what you see and not see:
> The head like a jar, the ear a winnow
> Tusk a plowshare, body a granary
> Foot a post, hind like a mortar, trunk plow
> The tail a pestle, the tuft like a broom …
> The wise one mocks the blind to make the point
> That the truth is not quite what you assume.
> Should such anointed wisdom disappoint?
> They think only they are true, brahmanas!
> Holding what they grasp, the elephant's arse!

This is, of course, off course. A discourse on a discourse taking its own course.

In the aforeplaced Tittha Sonnet in the wake of the **Tittha Sutta**, with the benefit of hindsight, I could well begin with a recension of the last couplet.

> They think only they are true, the buddhas!
> Holding what they grasp, the elephant's arse!

In the Tittha Sutta, the Buddha, stumbles. From the *nikayas*, well-funded institutional compilations of unauthorized authorized editions of his ideas, speech and discourses told as suttas, put together a few hundred years after the author's passing (accessible now on helpful websites that anoint themselves "Sutta Central", "Access to Insight" and such enlightened names), it is clear that the Buddha was often given to holding forth. He was no doubt a charismatic and enigmatic figure, a consummate and calm victor in all the important debating competitions of his time, at ease with both a king and a sweeper, merchant and potter (though he was cagey about women initially, or thus we have heard).

This once, the Buddha is sought to spell out his views on sectarian quarrels about what the dhamma really is and isn't, what *nibbana* is and not—this happens at the end of the day after the ritual of seeking alms. In this discourse known also as 'The First Discourse about the Various Sectarians', to be cited as Udana 6.4 Pathamananatitthiyasuttam 54, the all-knowing Buddha weighs in:

> Monks, the wanderers of other sects are blind and eyeless. They don't know what is beneficial and what is harmful. They don't know what is the Dhamma and

what is non-Dhamma. Not knowing what is beneficial and what is harmful, not knowing what is Dhamma and what is non-Dhamma, they keep on arguing, quarreling and disputing, wounding one another with weapons of the mouth, saying, 'The Dhamma is like this, it's not like that. The Dhamma's not like that, it's like this.'

And like it says in the "Jaccandhavaggo" (The Chapter, Including the Discourse, about the Congenitally Blind) in Pathamananatitthiyasuttam:

taayam velaayam imam udaanam udaanesi:
on that occasion [he] uttered this exalted utterance:

That 'exalted utterance' is the Tittha Sutta. Such an *udana* is explained by **William Woodville Rockhill** (1854–1914), a diplomat–scholar whom Wikipedia labels 'the first American to learn to speak Tibetan', in his 1883 translation, *Udanavarga: Collection of Verses from the Buddhist Canon*, thus:

The word udana must not be understood to imply 'joyous utterances, hymns of praise', but something nearly approaching 'gatha, verse, or stanza', although in some cases, where certain virtues are extolled, the word is employed with its habitual acceptation of 'hymn'. Such verses are very generally found at the end of the sermons or sutras of Gautama, and were probably intended to convey to his hearers, in a few easily remembered lines, the essence of his teaching. It appears to me that the founder of Buddhism must have attached great importance to these verses, and that he advocated their use by all his disciples.

The setting, of course, is grand. Not some chawl in Mumbai or village like Chalisgaon in the Konkan as often happened with the Bodhisatta of our times, Bhimrao Ramji Ambedkar. The Buddha sat at the head of a well-appointed *vihara* (monastery) known as Jetavana, or Jeta's Grove, bestowed as a gift to him and his followers by the wealthy merchant Anathapindika (born Sudatta). Wiki-wise, he received the name Anathapindika for being the 'one who gives alms (*pinda*) to the unprotected (*anaatha*)'. A lay devotee who reportedly entered the first stage of enlightenment (called *sotapanna* or the one who has entered the stream), Anathapindika buys the estate from the prince Jetakumara.

It may be sobering to have some idea of how this came about. When Anathapindika eyes this land to the south of Savatthi (Sravasti in Sanskrit), Jeta drives a hard bargain. He refuses: 'Not even if you could cover the whole place with money.' Anathapindika—one among many wealthy merchants and kings who stood by the Buddha and the dhamma—is willing to pay such a price, and when he files a case, the lords of justice in Savatthi rule that Jetakumara must sell if Anathapindika can pay the quoted price. And so Anathapindika ferries cartloads of gold to flood Jetavana. This scene is commemorated in a bas-relief at the Bharhut *stupa* in central India. The Buddha was clearly on a roll.

Fa-Hsien's *A Record of Buddhistic Kingdoms*, generously subtitled as 'Being an Account by the Chinese Monk Fa-Hsien of his Travels in India and Ceylon (A.D. 399–414) in

Bharhut stupa, Jetavana panel. The inscription says "Jetavana Anadhapediko deti kotisanthatena keta", meaning Anathapindika presents Jetavana, having purchased it for a layer of gold coins.
Photo of Joseph David Beglar's photographic print, c. 1874

Search of the Buddhist Books of Discipline', describes the Jetavana vihara as originally having seven storeys. 'The kings and people of the countries around vied with one another in their offerings, hanging up about it, silken streamers and canopies, scattering flowers, burning incense, and lighting lamps, so as to make the night as bright as the day. This they did day after day without ceasing.' His narrative is given to hyperbole and a touching faith in the legends that include the Buddha preaching the dhamma to five hundred blind men (no women again) and their regaining sight. (No sight, no dhamma?)

Given this accepted official history of ostentation and pomposity, we may quickly learn to do two things: Appreciate the modern-day Dalit icon Mayawati and her efforts at statuary when she was chief minister of Uttar Pradesh, and in the same breath partake of this alms-seeking business by the Buddha and his well-cared-for sangha in such tall tales with a good pinch of pink Himalayan rock salt. Or, think of it as what it may have come to be—a ritual beyond need, where good returns are guaranteed.

It is in this abode called jetavana, in the suburbs of the bustling city of Savatthi with a population estimated at close to a million over two thousand five hundred years ago, that the Buddha ate, bathed, defecated, slept and discoursed about all things big, small and in between, spending nineteen of the forty-five rainy seasons or *vassa*s after his 'enlightenment' in this grand park, more than any other monastery. While at it, slow-witted that I am, I delighted in realizing going into my forty-eighth that the Pali word for a year, vassa (Sanskrit, *varsha*), is also the term for rain or the annual monsoon. Before we attend to the Tittha Sutta, one last stop at what *tittha* means in Pali (Sanskrit, *teertha*):

1. a ghat; a place of access to a river; a landing-place; a fording-place, a ford.
2. (metaph.) a ford, a way across; a dogma; a sect.

This well-worn and well-known parable of the blind men and the elephant likely predates the Buddha (c. 500 BCE) for it is the Buddha who here speaks of an unnamed king of the very place where he's pontificating—Savatthi. The said king gets some five or seven men, all born blind (no women, mind), to experience an elephant and describe it, wherein each man is made to encounter a different aspect of the animal, and each of them 'sees' it differently, ostensibly like the quarrelling priests and robe-clad *bhikkhus* (rendered in the couplet to the end of the sutta in the compressed compound *samanabrahmana*), and they come to blows over what it is they see or don't see. As the Buddha recounts:

> Saying, 'The elephant is like this, it's not like that. The elephant's not like that, it's like this,' they struck one another with their fists. That gratified the king.

This reductive, insensitive, inaccurate caricature of the blind that often passes for a 'Hindoo fable' for wide-eyed Westerners, appealed equally to Jainism. The Sufis and Baha'I cult too took to this tale. The Sufi poets Al-Ghazali and Sana'I retold this tale from 'the Hind', but kept the characters blind. It was Rumi who in his thirteenth-century *Mathnawi* (also *Masnavi*) changed the very premise, saying the men (not blind) and the imported, exotic elephant were

"Blind Men and the Elephant", Netsuke from MoMA. Late nineteenth century. Ivory, height 1⅝ inches. Signed: Kuku Joso to (literally, 'Kuku Joso's knife'). Source: metmuseum.org (public domain)

put in a pitch-dark room, and each perceived what they felt differently. In **Farrukh Dhondy**'s translation:

> So my friends do not count the evidence
> Of hand or eye or ear and ever hope
> That these can lead beyond the realm of sense.

Dhondy gets the message across with delectable rhymes but does not quite convey how, in the poem, one man says the beast is like 'dal' (the tenth letter of the Persian alphabet, functioning quite like *d* in English) and another man calls it 'alif' (the first letter). In an earlier translation by **E.H. Whinfield** from 1898, Rumi's retelling is rendered as:

'The eye of outward sense is as the palm of a hand/ The whole of the object is not grasped in the palm.'

Back in the subcontinent, to score a cheap point, the Buddha deploys a lazy simile, and gets carried away. He heaps on us a feast of evocative adjunct similes (jar, winnow, plow, broom, mortar, pestle, granary) trying to prove that those blinded by their own insight actually lack real sight. It's a cunning point in which those who suffer blindness, from birth at that, are taken to be quite dim. Now, imagine a blind person (or a person of sight in a dark room) who has never experienced the Tusked One being able to touch any part of the body of this bewitching beast twitching with life—there'd be so much exchange of sensations, unspeakable emotions. The person would in fact be awash with feeling. And so might the elephant—a highly sensitive and sentient being. Rarely does a standing elephant stand still—its swaying trunk would respond to touch as would its hind. How the chained elephant sees all this, we have no way of knowing. Perhaps, a blind person experiences this experience of an abstraction called 'elephant' in a way no person who prides on his twenty-twenty vision can experience—it becomes too easy in the latter's case. Thus have we heard: A blind person is perhaps not a slave to their perception of the elephant. They see a winnow, a jar, a pestle …

Each person's experience of a part of the elephant, blind, mute or deaf, fully abled or disabled, will be different as will the elephant's experience of each touch. This the Buddha does not seem to see, at least in the version of his telling that comes to us in the nikayas, but Kabir of the fifteenth century does. Kabir surely was more enlightened when he referenced blindness or muteness or any such impairment.

In a song that Prahlad Tipaniya sings, "Binaa chandaa re binaa bhaan" (p.94), here's a stanza that stands out—its grace and insights are more assured and reassuring than what the Tittha Sutta has to offer:

गूंगा गावे है अब राग बेहरो सुनवा लाग्यो है
पांगलियो नाचे रे घणो नाच आंधलियो नरखन लाग्यो है
    बिना चंदा रे बिना भान

goongaa gaave hai ab raag beharo sunavaa laagyo hai
paangaliyo naache re ghaNo naach aandhaliyo narakhan laagyo hai
    binaa chandaa re binaa bhaan

The mute bursts into song
The deaf can descry the notes
The cripple springs into dance
The blind paints in unseen tones
    No sun, no moon, but light

Another Kabir song rendered by Kumar Gandharva, "Avadhootaa kudarat kee gat nyaaree" (p.133), reflects Kabir's far superior vision (oh, the fun we may have with cheap puns when piety is discarded for clarity):

पंगुल मेरु सुमेरु उलंघे त्रिभुवन मुक्ता डोले
गूंगा ग्यान विग्यान प्रकाशे अनहद बाणी बोले
    अवधूता कुदरत की गत न्यारी
बांधी आकाश पताल पठावै, शेष स्वर्ग पर राजै
कहे कबीरा राम है राजा, जो कछू करें सो छाजै
    अवधूता कुदरत की गत न्यारी

pangul meruu sumeruu ulanghe tribhuvan muktaa Doley
goongaa gyaan vigyaan prakaashe anahad baaNii boley
    avadhootaa kudarat kee gat nyaaree

baandhee aakaash pataal paThaavai shesh svarg par raajai
kahe kabeeraa raam [bheem] hai raajaa jo kachhoo karen so chhaajai
    avadhootaa kudarat kee gat nyaaree

The lame scales the Everest, the world's at her feet
The mute sings silenced truths, boundless
                                        music his beat
    Vagabond! Time defeats every distance

The sky is bound and flung underground,
                        the serpent rules the heaven
For Kabir, love is supreme—for it, all is forgiven
    Vagrant one! True love can be utterly flagrant

Such verses are often called *ulaTbaamsi*—the downside-
up songs. For Kabir and all those who sing unauthorized
variations of his songs, enlightenment or the great
awakening is for one and all. It is the evental shattering
of hierarchies and barriers, of all binaries, of the self and
the other, of being and nonbeing, of the formed and
not-formed, of comprehension and incomprehension, of
dhamma and non-dhamma: It is the absolute force-field
of equality, in thought first, and then in deed. The blind
see, the deaf hear, the mute sing, the lame scale the Everest.
No one is left out. Love is supreme, as is the *shabad*, Word,
the unstruck sound—nibbana at every threshold. The four
sanctified, solemnized stages of enlightenment—*sotapanna*
(recall Anathapindika), *sakadagami*, *anagami* and *arahant*—

are not there in the Kabiri/ Kabiru world. Enlightenment or nibanna is not some kind of institution-bound four-stage PhD coursework. A tiller or a singer, a deaf weaver or a blind painter can aspire to it. And it is Ambedkar, to whom 'equality will be of no value without fraternity or liberty,' who yokes the Buddha with Kabir, harnessing equality to enlightenment. Or thus I have read, says Anand. Notwithstanding the doubts presented here about the Buddha, Ambedkar writes in his essay, "**Buddha or Karl Marx**":

> He [the Buddha] was a thorough equalitarian. Originally the Bhikkus, including the Buddha himself, wore robes made of rags. This rule was enunciated to prevent the aristocratic classes from joining the Sangh. Later Jeevaka the great physician prevailed upon the Buddha to accept a robe which was made of a whole cloth. The Buddha at once altered the rule and extended it to all the monks. ... The Bhikshu Sangh had the most democratic constitution. He was only one of the Bhikkus.

In this parable, and in most of his teachings which reach us through his ghost writers, the Buddha is often made to sound leaderly. Ambedkar too chooses what words to put into the Buddha's mouth. He consults sources but presents his own re-envisioned version of the Buddha in *The Buddha and His Dhamma* and in the essay "Buddha or Karl Marx".

Like you will have heard before and shall hear again, each of the Buddha's suttas that comes to us is prefaced with the words—evam me sutam—thus have I heard. Echoing this, Kabir urges us to listen (suno) to what Kabir says (kahat, kahe). All the suttas end with a flourish, a distich that condenses the essence of the discourse, a function that the closing couplet performs in the Shakespearean sonnet.

Quite like we have many versions of a Kabir song, so does a sutta. I am listing here the other recensions of the Tittha Sutta verse, set to the *savipula* metre, some leaning towards Sanskritic accents, some with words **spelt and heard differently**:

bhavesv eva hee sajyanta ekey sramanabraahmanah
vigrihya vivaadantime bala hee ekaantadarsinah
—Uv. 33.4 Brahmanavarga

bhavesv eva hee sajyanta ekey sramanabraahmanah
antarena visidantee hee aprapyaivottamam padam
—Uv. 33.5 Brahmanavarga

imesu keera sajjanti eke samanabraahmana
antara va visidantee appatva va tamogadham
—Ud. 6–5: Dutiyananatitthiyasuttam

Like with Kabir's heard and sung fragments, there are many versions of the Buddha's words gathered in the *Tipitaka*, 'the three baskets', and there are many versions of these three baskets. Here's an expert translation:

Some ascetics and brahmanas, it seems, are attached
to these (views),
Having grasped ahold of it, they dispute, (like) people
who see (only) one side.

Another:

> With regard to these things
> they're attached—
> some contemplatives & brahmans
> They quarrel & fight—
> people seeing one side.

They all see the elephant that is not in the room.

देखन देखत हो
It is seeing

Some 550 years ago, by a ghat in Benares, after the day's work at the loom, when the workers had gathered over a storm of songs, a migrant weaver from Kanchipuram rendered a verse from Valluvar's *Thirukkural* to Kabir who told Raidas to tell Mira about what he saw in the moment:

I ask you to see what we can't, you see it
Yet in my not showing it, see seeing
In being the sound that I inhabit
Now trying to unsee with my eyes seeing
The ear goes where no eye can, it by it
It shows the eye what is beyond seeing
The comings and goings between such wit
Seeing that there's no point beyond unseeing
What unfolds in the folds of this orbit
Of now, where closed eyed, you see the seeing
That sees you seeing you not seeing it
In all the sights these eyes have been seeing
Now you see it now you don't seeing it
Seeing sees to it, it sees you seeing

कुछ ५५० साल पहले बनारस के इक घाट पर तांत पर काम के बाद शाम के विसराम में गान के तूफ़ान के बीच जब एक तमिल जुलाहे ने वल्लूवर का एक कुरल कबीर को राग में सुनाया तो कबीर ने जो देखा रैदास को बताया और बोला कि मीरा को ज़रूर ये बखान सुनावे:

देख नाही वा देखत हो
अनदेखी मा हर देखी हो
वाणी जप जप राग सुनावे
बीच बसा हर देखी हो

अनदेखी जो नजर मा भटका
अखियां कान बराबर हो
ना देखो बस सुनो रे भाई
देख नाही वा देखत हो

संग सत के खाये धक्का
आवत जावत पावत हो
अनदेखी मा बात समावे
देख नाही वा देखत हो

देख देख अखियन की देखी
देखन से अनदेखन हो
न देखन ना अनदेखन मा
देख नाही वा देखत हो

dekh naahee vaa dekhat ho
andekhee maa har dekhe ho
vaanNii jap jap raag sunaave
beech basaa har dekhee ho

andekhee jo najar maa bhaTkaa
akhiyaan kaan baraabar ho
naa dekho bas suno re bhaaii
dekh naahee vaa dekhat ho

sang sat ke khaaye dhakkaa
aavat jaavat paavat ho
andekhee maa baat samaave
dekh naahee vaa dekhat ho

dekh dekh akhiyaan kee dekhee
dekhan se andekhan ho
na dekhan naa andekhan maa
dekh naahee vaa dekhat ho

The sky is bound and flung underground
कुदरत की गत न्यारी

अवधूता कुदरत की गत न्यारी
रंक-निवाज करे वो राजा भूपति करें भिक्कार
    अवधूता कुदरत की गत न्यारी

येथे लवंगहि फल नहीं लागे चंदन फूले न फूले
मच्छ शिकारी रमे जंगल में सिंध समुद्रहि झूले
    अवधूता कुदरत की गत न्यारी
रेड़ा रुख भया मलयागर चहूं दिशी फूटी बसा
तीन लोक ब्रह्मांड खंड में देखे अंध तमाशा
    अवधूता कुदरत की गत न्यारी
पंगुल मेरु सुमेरु उलंघे त्रिभुवन मुक्ता डोले
गूंगा ग्यान विग्यान प्रकाशे अनहद बाणी बोले
    अवधूता कुदरत की गत न्यारी
बांधी आकाश पताल पठावै शेष स्वर्ग पर राजै
कहे कबीरा राम [भीम] है राजा। जो कछु करें सो छाजै
    अवधूता कुदरत की गत न्यारी

avadhootaa kudarat kee gat nyaaree
rank-nivaaj kare vo raaja bhoopati karen bhikkaar
    avadhootaa kudarat kee gat nyaaree

yethe lavangahi phal naheen laage chandan foole na foole
machh shikaaree ramey jangal mein sindh samudrahee jhoole
      avadhootaa kudarat kee gat nyaaree

reDaa rookh bhayaa malayaagar chahoon dishee phooTee basaa
teen lok brahmaanD khanD mein dekhe andh tamaashaa
      avadhootaa kudarat kee gat nyaaree

pangul meruu sumeruu ulanghe tribhuvan mukta Doley
goongaa gyaan vigyaan prakaashe anahad baaNii boley
      avadhootaa kudarat kee gat nyaaree

baandhii aakaash pataal paThaavai shesh svarg par raajai
kahe kabeeraa raam [bheem] hai raajaa jo kachhu karen so chhaajai
      avadhootaa kudarat kee gat nyaaree

Wanderer dear! Nature's ways are not clear and neat
Vagabond, heed! Time marches to a timeless beat

The pauper's now king, the king a pauper
Friend, love blooms in every colour
      O minstrel! The world is wondrous in its splendour

The clove fruits fruitless, the sandal is fragrant without flower
The fish trawls the forest, the lion rules the sea
      O vagrant one! True love can be utterly flagrant

The castor shrub is a thriving forest, airing its fragrance
All three worlds are shining orbs, the blind see radiance
      Wanderer! Nature's ways are never clear

The lame scales the Everest, the world's at her feet
The mute sings silenced truths, boundless music his beat
  Vagabond! Time defeats every distance

The sky is bound and flung underground,
                        the serpent rules the heaven
For Kabir, love is supreme—for it, all is forgiven
  O friend! Love blooms in every colour

  Vagrant one! True love can be utterly flagrant

Kumar Gandharva sings "Avadhootaa kudarat kee gat nyaaree" (YouTube). The word flagrant traces back to the late fifteenth century (in the sense 'blazing, resplendent'): from French, or from Latin *flagrantem*, 'burning, blazing, glowing', from the verb *flagrare*, adjective (of an action considered wrong or immoral) conspicuously or obviously offensive: a flagrant violation of the law.

The shelter of truth
गुरा तो जी ने

गुरु कुम्हार सीस कुम्भ है गढ़ि गढ़ि काढ़ै खोट
अंदर हाथ सहार दे बाहर बाहै चोट

गुरा तो जी ने ग्यान की जड़ियां दई
सतगुरु जी ने ग्यान की जड़ियां दई
वाही ज़िड तो म्हाने प्यारी जो लागी
अमुरुत रस की भरी
    गुरा तो जी ने ग्यान की जड़ियां दई
काया नगर में घर एक बंगला
जा बीच गुपत धरी
    गुरा तो जी ने ग्यान की जड़ियां दई
पांचो नाग पच्चिसो नागनी
सूंघत तुरत मरी
    गुरा तो जी ने ग्यान की जड़ियां दई
आणि काली ने सब जग खाया
सतगुरु देख डरी
    गुरा तो जी ने ग्यान की जड़ियां दई
सतवा सारणे शिवगुरु बोल्या
ले परिवार तिरी
    गुरा तो जी ने ग्यान की जड़ियां दई

guru kumhaar siis kumbh hai gaDhi gaDhi kaaDhai khoT
andar haath sahaar de baahar baahai choT

guraa toh jee ne gyaan kee jaDiyaan daee
sataguru jee ne gyaan kee jaDiyaan daee

vaahee jaDi toh mhaane pyaaree jo laagee
amurut ras kee bharee
        guraa toh jee ne gyaan kee jaDiyaan daee

kaayaa nagar mein ghar ek bangalaa
ja beech gupat dharee
        guraa toh jee ne gyaan kee jaDiyaan daee

paancho naag pachchiso naaganii
soonghat turat maree
        guraa toh jee ne gyaan kee jaDiyaan daee

aaNi kaalee ne sab jag khaayaa
sataguru dekh Daree
        guraa toh jee ne gyaan kee jaDiyaan daee

satavaa saaraNe shivaguru bolyaa
le parivaar tiree
        guraa toh jee ne gyaan kee jaDiyaan daee

Guru is the potter, the pot disciple
He batters the facet, holds the core still

The guru is a hallowed tree
He's disclosed the truth to me

The guru has bared his roots
This truth is dear to me

He's revealed what lies concealed
I've tasted both the kernel and peel
I've suckled the truly sweet truth
    The guru has fed the truth to me

In this body city, one house of plenty
In this house, a treasure is hidden
For this treasure, these songs unbidden
    The guru unearths this trove for me

In this metropolis, the thief knows the truth
In this smart city, truth is the one thief
With him the authority has no beef
    The guru's caught the true thief

The five snake-senses slither
They birth twenty-five that go hither thither
They inhale the truth, instantly expire
    The guru has already warned me

The ogress, she ate up this world
Oh yes, she gobbled all the three
Seeing the guru, she went weak at the knees
    The guru is a hallowed tree

Sheltered by the truth of the tree
Shivguru sings joyously
He walks the path with his family
    The guru is dear to me

The first couplet was proffered by Venkat Raman Singh Shyam from memory. The body of the song figures in Kumar Gandharva's rendition of "Guraa toh jee ne" (YouTube), one of the first Kabiri songs I learnt to sing, without a guru. A version of this translation featured in *Finding My Way*, a work that interwove art and text in an anamnetic fashion, setting the story of Venkat's life asail amidst a sea of stories and songs that he and I recounted. It was working with Venkat in 2013–14 that made me return to music and poetry. If a guru is someone who awakens something sleeping inside you, Venkat was one. The song bears the signature of Shivguru, and this is the only song of his we know. 'We have no information about this poet, and we welcome help from our browsers in finding out more about this person. Please write to us at ajabteam@ gmail.com,' says "The Kabir Project" website. In the last stanza, he says that he converted to or embraced, with his entire family, ले परिवार तिरी (le parivaar tiree), Kabir's path, a path paved with songs to the no-place.

This presages another conversion to come—in 1956, half a million Dalits flocked to Nagpur, en famille, to embrace the 'middle path' of the Buddha paved anew by Babasaheb Ambedkar.

I find ways to say nothing
मन मस्त हुआ फिर क्या बोले

आज बदरा उठा प्रेम का और हम पर वर्सा होय
हरसील हो गयी आतमा और हरी-भरी बनराय

बूंद पडा दरियाब में सब कोई जानत हैं
समुंदर समान बूंद में जाने बिरला कोई

मन मस्त हुआ फिर क्या बोले मन मस्त हुआ फिर क्यों बोले
क्या बोले फिर क्यों बोले मन मस्त हुआ फिर क्या बोले
क्यों बोले फिर क्या बोले मन मस्त हुआ फिर क्यों बोले
हीरा पाया बाँध गठड़िया बार बार वाको क्यों खोले
मन मस्त हुआ फिर क्या बोले
हल्की थी तब चढ़ी तराजू पूरी भरी फिर क्या तोले
मन मस्त हुआ फिर क्या बोले
सूरत का लालन भयी मतवाली मदवा पी गयी अणतोले
मन मस्त हुआ फिर क्या बोले
हंसा पावे मानसरोवर ताल तळ्या में क्या डोले
मन मस्त हुआ फिर क्या बोले
कहे कबीर सुनो भाई साधो साहिब मिल गया तिल ओले
मन मस्त हुआ फिर क्या बोले

aaj badaraa uThaa prem kaa aur ham par varsaa hoy
haraseel ho gayee aatamaa aur haree-bharee banaraay

boond paDaa dariyaab mein sab koii jaanat hain
samundar samaan boond mein jaane biralaa koii

man mast huaa phir kyaa boley man mast huaa phir kyon boley
kyaa boley phir kyon boley man mast huaa phir kyaa boley
kyon boley phir kyaa boley man mast huaa phir kyon boley

heeraa paayaa baandh gaThaDiyaa baar baar vaako kyon kholey
    man mast huaa phir kyaa boley

halki thee tab chadhee taraajoo pooree bharee phir kyaa toley
    man mast huaa phir kyaa boley

soorat kaa laalan bhayee matavaalee madavaa pee gayee aNatoley
    man mast huaa phir kyaa boley

hansaa paave maanasarovar taal taLayyaa mein kyaa Doley
    man mast huaa phir kyaa boley

kahe kabeer suno bhaaii saadho saahib mil gayaa til oley
    man mast huaa phir kyaa boley

A cloud of love stopped by and rained on me
My heart turned lush, everything green

Everyone sees a drop fall into the sea
The rare one sees the drop that holds the sea

Joy has run my heart over, I find many ways to say nothing
A cloud bursts inside my head, the rain speaks to me
How do I say it? Do I have to say it? Can I say nothing?
My heart's whelmed over, nothing I say means anything

If you find a diamond, tuck it in your turban
Keep walking, why show it to everyone
    A cloud bursts ins my head, nothing comes of nothing

I weighed my self on the scale of nothing
I'm full, filled, fulfilled—why measure the never-ending?
    Joy has whelmed my heart over, rain speaks to me

My awareness is dyed red, I'm high on my own brew
A cloud of love stopped by and soaked me through
    How do I say it? I'm the riddle and I'm the clue

The swan bathes in the lake of mindfulness
Why muddy oneself in paltry ponds for less?
    My heart's whelmed over, nothing I say means a thing

Heed Kabir—he's found love in the pupil of his eye
A cloud empties itself on him, and he's high
    When the heart brims over, find ways to say nothing

Kaluram Bamaniya sings this with abandon, Shabnam Virmani dances to it, and we rejoice in their high ("The Kabir Project"). When you find a diamond, don't babble about it, says Kabir, and yet he can't resist, making a jewel of a song that (un)states this message. When singing this for my friend Bhanwar Meghwanshi while working on his memoir, *I Could Not Be Hindu: The Story of a Dalit in the RSS*, in November 2019, I layered Bamaniya's words 'hansaa paaye maansarovar' with 'hansaa paaye *sam*-maansarovar', and 'saahib mil gayaa til oley' with 'Baaba-saahib mil gayaa til oley'. The possibilities of wordplay are enhanced and amplified while singing.

In what is stolen and in what is found
साहिब मिल गया तिल ओले

Come into the palace, my brother, my sister, my beloved
For the king of formlessness, spread the form of a bed

God is in between yes–no and haan-na, says Sultan Bahu
The emperor of words who has been the distance
Who has been to that place in between, says so
My dear na-no and brother haan-yes
When we do not know what limit we occupy
When we do not know how to harness the limit
Why look for that which is limitless?

man mast huaa phir kyaa boley?
The heart is joyous, there's nothing I can say
The heart is buoyant, what's there to say?
When joy has run my heart over, what's to say?
I'm drowning in myself, what am I to say?

You steal with the thief and you aid the police
You are in what is stolen and you are in what is found
You become charitable among those who fleece
Among the poor, you're a vagabond

The heart has now turned mendicant:
A lute in my hands, a song on my lips
I wander ticketless everywhere
I rule in every direction I turn
I live in the city of love
The police is you, the thief too
Find me if you can and you'll find nothing

Strut in pride all you want
The body will turn to dust
You'll find god only in love
Sorry if I sound like a crazy cuckoo
Trilling the same thing, saying nothing new

You're in the elephant and in the ant too
Wherever we turn it's you, it's you

It's you, only you, you, you, only you
Allah hu, Allah hu, Allah hu

Bless the mullah who cries Allah hu
Coming in love's arms, he goes Allah hu

Allah hu, Allah hu, Allah hu
Hu hu hu, Allah hu hu hu

When you find a diamond, just wear it
Why stop to admire every chance you get?

The swan bathes only in the mind's lake
It does not wash itself in the lake of every sense

I felt light when placed on the scale
When found immeasurable, what do I say?

Ride slowly, sister, ride slowly
Let people stop and see who drives by
Our cart is decked colourfully
Our wheels wear the reddest dye

We turn again into the same song, "Man mast huaa phir kyaa boley", which shines differently each time it is sung and heard. It appears now to us as "Saahib mil gayaa til oley"/ "I've found the master in the pupil of the eye". Behind these song fragments, behind these words whose wisdom shines more when embellished with music, is a story that folds many.

In October 2016, I heard Kaluram Bamaniya perform in the basement of a wealthy business family's home in South Delhi. A friend's friend's friend had forwarded an invitation on WhatsApp, and I made my way there. At this private mehfil, meant for the host family and their intimates, if someone sought my bona fides, I was prepared to say I had come for Kaluram Bamaniya's Kabir. No one asked. If a mendicant singer of Kabir, or Kabir himself arrived here after a day's labour on his loom or after a twelve-hour shift as a metal polish worker in the Okhla Industrial Estate, he'd have been turned away at the gate.

The chandelier was intricately cut and the floor cushions were so spotlessly white I wondered if I could sit without leaving a trace behind. I sat up close to the troupe. There were not more than forty in the audience. Commodious chairs were lined along the walls for the hosts and the corpulent men and women to rest. Some wore the finest silks and exuded expensive perfumes. There was a velvet-cushioned throne placed on a higher ground at the far end of the hall. It was the *gaddi*. It was adorned by a presumably dead rich man's ornately framed photograph. The finest of flowers were decked around it. Many walked up to bow before the gaddi that seemed unaware of its own importance. In the life-size picture, he wore the beatitude that comes easy to a man well-fed all his life. I slyly clicked pictures of the obsequiousness and the incongruities (Kabir, here?), unaware of the incongruity and irony of considering myself above what I was surveying.

Kaluram Bamaniya and his friends were likely going to be paid well. How does an artist make a living other than by trading their art? What is a good place to perform? Can art exist only in and for itself? Then how will it reach me? Clouds gathered around me. Questions I reckon Kabir would have asked. Would Kabir have ever sung for a well-clad gentry at a private mehfil, or performed at the Jaipur lit-fest or in Edinburgh, were his to-and-fro to be covered and a good fee paid? Or would he have been a struggling artist in Benares whose childhood was spent stealing shrouds off just-lit pyres, now uploading his jams on Instagram and YouTube hoping someone would discover him and regard him the new Marley? Would he have been lynched for presumably possessing beef or marijuana? Or would he be doing the rounds with his tanpura for a living, turning up as impeccably dressed as the teetotaller vegetarian Bamaniya, and if he did, would it also be an all-male troupe, or would Kabir be trans? Would Kabir have applied for a writer's residency, thinking, Oh, I'll write well if I'm fed and paid well and if I'm in a place with no connectivity? Or would he still just weave for a living and sing to the rhythm of the loom, not thinking of who heard him and who didn't? Which one story or all of these will serve my purpose?

The most secular art must and does negotiate the sacred. But how does it negotiate the might of the market and the state? How does it greedily receive and on the rare occasion righteously return awards, expecting applause for both? How does it even begin to resist the lure of what's respectably called patronage? Say sponsorship by Reliance Foundation or the CSR arm of the Adani group? Or a wealthy family in South Delhi that pays the artist in hard, unaccounted-for cash.

As Bamaniya and his all-male troupe, dressed impeccably in white kurtas, black vests and colouful turbans, set their instruments up, the clouds drifted away. I would not be denied an evening like this by my awareness of history, politics and my complicity in a network of privileges and entitlements. As a man of small pleasures, I shall look between yes and no. I shall seek beyond my limitations, if not my limits. Enlightenment has to be here and now, within limits, through a raga on the lips. When we do not know how to harness the limit, why look for that which is limitless?

The casual opulence of the house and the people was offset not just by Kaluram but by the bareness and austerity of the Kabir he sang for a little over an hour. Other poets and artists were remembered, their phrases and verses woven into the words of Kabir, who was already speaking in a translation, in Kaluram's Rajasthani, a Kabir who teaches us how to say nothing, a Kabir who proffers us words that help us pretend we're erudite. I came under the spell of words charged with music, and quickly overcame my estrangement. I scribbled notes on the back of papers that bore the report of the annual general meeting (importantly called 'AGM') of the Seabrooke Apartments Owners' Association, Chennai, a report I had never read of a meeting I had never attended. As Kaluram and his ensemble made things up about Kabir who made things up about the words that make us what we are, I part translated, part made up lines in English. Kaluram did not bring in Allah hu. Nusrat came between us. I jazzed it up.

I left wordlessly after the performance.

I booked an Uber and explained to the driver where exactly I was standing in the C Block of New Friends Colony. It would take five minutes. Did "Mann mast huaa phir kyaa boley?" indeed stick mostly to the scale of what has come to be raga Bhoop or Bhoopali, found in the Carnatic system as Mohanam, the universal pentatonic found in Paleolithic bone flutes in Europe to the tune of the ominous "Star Spangled Banner" (*the Rockets' red glare, the Bombs bursting in air*), ubiquitous in Asia in all forms, labelled folk and classical? How much has what's come to be 'classical Bhoop', from Kabul to Lascaux, Okinawa to Dharwad, stolen from the tradition Bamaniya comes from, and how much of Bamaniya has found its way into the raga I know? Where does one begin, where does the other end? Is it possible to inhabit a raga between what is stolen and what is found?

As I quietly contemplated the prospect of listening again to the recording I had made of the songs that were still buzzing inside me, two helmeted men on a bike snatched my phone from my hands and sped away. I panicked. I shrieked and ran after the bikers. Some two hundred yards later, pacified by concerned onlookers, I took an auto-rickshaw and rushed to the nearest police station, some minutes away, to lodge a complaint about the faceless thieves. There I found similar petitioners, saying they'd also been relieved of their cellphones. Mine was expensive; the origin of sins. Our descriptions of the thieves matched. We commiserated with each other. For the police, it was all routine. We were told registering a case would be a waste of everyone's time. And time must not be wasted. The phone did not come back. Another replaced it.

I had tried to capture Kabir in my phone, and he stole my phone.

The loss almost completely erased the experience of that evening of Kaluram and Kabir, the rich man's framed photo, the fancy chandelier over which rose words threaded with music—all embers of a forgotten fire now. The police is you, the thief too.

A year later, in 2017, rummaging my laptop bag while at a writing residency in Ranikhet to work on a manuscript on raga music, where my phone luckily doesn't work so that I may, in relative peace and quiet, write about what was stolen and what was found and of that space in between, I discovered these notes folded and crumpled at the bottom of the bag, and it all came back. Some of the handwriting was unclear, but I tried to make sense of how poorly I had understood Kabir despite all the fuss.

You're lost without a guru
बिन सतगुरु नर

बिन सतगुरु नर रहत भुलाना
खोजत फिरत राह नहीं जाना
    बिन सतगुरु नर रहत भुलाना

केहर सुत ले आयो गड़रिया
पाल पोस उन्ह कीन्ह सयाना
करत कल्लोल रहत अजयन संग
आपन मर्म उन्हहुं नहीं जाना
    बिन सतगुरु नर रहत भुलाना
केहर इक जंगल से आया
ताहीं देखी बहुते रिसियाना
पकड़के भेद तुरत समझाया
आपन दसा देखी मुसक्याना
    बिन सतगुरु नर रहत भुलाना
जस कुरंग बीच वसत बासना
खोजत मूढ़ फिरत चौगाना
करऊ सवास मन में देखे
इह सुगंधी धाम कहां बसाना
    बिन सतगुरु नर रहत भुलाना
अर्ध उर्ध बिच लगन लगी है
छक्यो रूप नहीं जात बखाना

कहत कबीर सुनो भई साधो
उलटी आप में आप समाना
        बिन सतगुरु नर रहत भुलाना

bin sataguru nar rahat bhulaanaa
khojat phirat raah naheen jaanaa
        bin sataguru nar rahat bhulaanaa

kehar sut le aayo gaDariyaa
paal pos unh keenh sayaanaa
karat kallol rahat ajayan sang
aapan marm unhahun naheen jaanaa
        bin sataguru nar rahat bhulaanaa

kehar ik jangal se aayaa
taaheen dekhee bahute risiyaanaa
pakaDake bhed turat samajhaayaa
aapan dasaa dekhee musakyaanaa
        bin sataguru nar rahat bhulaanaa

jas kurang beech vasat baasanaa
khojat mooDh fhirat chaugaanaa
karaoo savaas man mein dekhe
ih sugandhee dhaam kahaan basaanaa
        bin sataguru nar rahat bhulaanaa

ardh urdh bich lagan lagee hai
chhakyo roop naheen jaat bakhaanaa
kahat kabeer suno bhaii saadho
ulaTee aap mein aap samaanaa
        bin sataguru nar rahat bhulaanaa

You're lost without the guru within you
You're lost without love that's true
You've floundered, you've lost your way
You've found a way away from the way
    You're lost without the guru within you

A shepherd brings home the cub of a lion
Feeds him, raises him, watches him bleat
The goats play hide and seek with the strange one
The cub chews grass, never tastes meat
    You're lost without the guru within you

A lion from the jungle strolls by one day
The sight he sees maddens him no end
He bites the truth into the ears of his lost friend
The young one roars on finding its way
    You're lost without the guru within you

It's the same with the deer that wanders unseen
In the deepest forest searching for itself
Before learning to inhale the musk of the self
That makes its mind glow, body gleam
    You're lost without the guru within you

The truth breathes when you hold your breath
The truth holds its breath when you breathe
The truth resides at the cusp of breaths
It's odourless, casteless, formless, breathless
    You're lost without the guru within you

Says Kabir, you're the puzzle and also the clue
Just turn to the guru turning inside you

Kumar Gandharva sings "Bin sataguru nar rahat bhulaanaa" (YouTube). Venkat heard it with fevered breath and passed it to me. I let the song turn within itself and saw it turn within me. The song called to me when I was looking for a guru. I recalled it after finding a guru, and have returned to it at every turn.

The swan is its own song
उड़ जाएगा हंस अकेला

उड़ जाएगा उड़ जाएगा
उड़ जाएगा हंस अकेला
जग दरसन का मेला
    उड़ जाएगा उड़ जाएगा

जैसे पात गिरे तरुवर से
मिलना बहुत दुहेला
ना जानूं किधर गिरेगा
लग्या पवन का रेला
    उड़ जाएगा हंस अकेला
जब होवे उमर पूरी
जब छूटेगा हुकुम हुजूरी
यम के दूत बड़े मजबूत
जम से पड़ा झमेला
    उड़ जाएगा हंस अकेला
दास [बास] कबीर हर के गुण गावे
वा हर को पार न पावे
गुरु की करनी गुरु जाएगा
चेले की करनी चेला
    उड़ जाएगा हंस अकेला

uD jaaegaa uD jaaegaa
uD jaaegaa hans akelaa
jag darasan kaa melaa
    uD jaaegaa uD jaaegaa

jaise paat gire taruvar se
milanaa bahut duhelaa
naa jaanoon kidhar giregaa
lagyaa pavan kaa relaa
    uD jaaegaa hans akelaa

jab hovey umar pooree
jab chhooTegaa hukum hujooree
yam ke doot badey majaboot
jam se paDaa jhamelaa
    uD jaaegaa hans akelaa

daas [baas] kabeer har ke guN gaave
vaa har ko paar na paave
guru kee karanii guru jaaegaa
chele kee karanii chelaa
    uD jaaegaa hans akelaa

The swan will fly, alone
The swan is its own song
It discerns the colours of life
It fords the barrier of light

It's the swan's last song
It's the swan's swansong

The swan will fly alone
The swan sings its own song

The leaf that leaves the tree
Finds its own destiny
It falls at some place
The breeze decides its fate
    The swan will fly alone
    The swan is its own song

When your sun sets
When you're bereft of breath
When life goes deathly quiet
When the day dies in your eyes
    The swan flies alone
    The swan is its own song

The master has gone away
The pupil has to find his way
Boss Kabir frames the formless one
Who cannot be held, cannot be sung
    The swan flies, alone
    The swan is its own song

On trying to follow the flight of Kumar Gandharva's "UD jaaegaa hans akelaa" (YouTube). Swan—from Proto-Germanic *swanaz*, 'singer'; probably literally 'the singing bird', from root *swen*, 'to sing, make sound'. But a bird told me that the *hans* in South Asia is actually the goose. Old English *gos*, from Proto-Germanic *gans*, 'goose' (cognates:

Old Frisian *gos*, Old Norse *gas*, Old High German *gans*, German *gans*, 'goose'); from PIE [Proto-Indo-European] *ghans*—(cognates: Sanskrit *hamsah* [masc.[, *hansi* [fem.], 'goose, swan'). Even the Arabic for goose, *awza*, does not fall too far in terms of sound. Of course, neither the swan nor the goose sings as it dies; the goose at best makes a honking sound; the swan is said to grunt or snore. But as Borges says, the roots of language are irrational and magical in nature.

A word about the word 'boss' in the signature line: 'Boss Kabir frames the formless one'. The source poem refers to 'daas Kabir', which means Slave or Your Humble Servant Kabir. On why Kabir is the guru of gurus, why he is the true boss who demands irreverential reverence, see the companion essay to "Saahib ne bhaang pilaayee" (p.253).

Kabir is my Boss. And he's the multivolume BAWS: *Babasaheb Ambedkar: Writings and Speeches* by my bedside.

Swan, song, flight, sight
हंस अकेला

The swan, alone, in its flight
The world a passing feast of sights
The swan will fly, away, above
The lone swan will fly for love
The swan of life flies alone, away
The swan singular in its flight
The world a feast of passing sights
The swan's song against a changing sky
The measureless stillness of this sight
The swan, alone in its flight

The leaf is long dead
It clings to the branch of habit
A gust of wind frees it
You may not again meet it
Where it falls cannot be willed
As the song rises, the swan is stilled
As the swan rises, the song, still
The swan in its final flight, lone
The last swan on its own

When you get by in years
You lose your hold, gather your fears

Death's envoys are all muscle
You're meant to lose in this tussle
The rise of the song to the fall of breath
There'll be a grand fight to the death
The swan of the song spread against the sky
The swan riding the dark on wings of light
The passing world a feast of sights
Lone swan, last song, fading light

Kabir, a slave to words
Clings to the branch of habit
He sings the praise of a god
Who always eludes his wit
Kabir says he has only words to eat
He hymns a god who keeps him famished
What the master knows, with him goes
The pupil must reap what he sows

The swan, the song, the flight, the sight

Often, a translation changes when I learn to sing a song
and dwell upon the words, the pauses in between, the
enjambments. New meanings implore you when each line,
each word, each syllable, each vowel and consonant, is
fastened and unfastened to breath. Often, I collapse these
revisions into one, but on occasion a new newness stakes
claim: like when I learnt to sing "UD jaaegaa hans akelaa",
singing it every day over a week in February 2018.

Word-struck
लागी होय तो जाने

लागी होय तो जाने लागी शबद की
लागी होय तो जानीये म्हारा भाई
दूजा क्या कोई जाने शबद की लागी
    लागी होय तो जाने लागी शबद की
गेला मैं एक घायल घूमे घाव नज़र नहीं आई
ग्यान कमठा पैर बैठा हृदय में भाल जमाई
    लागी होय तो जाने लागी शबद की
अंका लागी बंका लागी लागी सजन कसाई
बलख बुखार कू ऐसी लागी छोड़ चला बादशाही
    लागी होय तो जाने लागी शबद की
ध्रुव को लागी प्रहलाद को लागी लागी हो मीरा बाई
गोपीचंद भरतरी को लागी सिर में भस्मि रमाई
    लागी होय तो जाने लागी शबद की
पांचने मार पच्चीसन बसकर अनघड़ लेबोना जगाई
कहे मच्छिंदर सुनौ गोरख सुन्न में धजा फ़हराई
    लागी होय तो जाने लागी शबद की

laagee hoy toh jaane laagee shabad kee
laagee hoy toh jaaniye mhaaraa bhaaii
doojaa kyaa koii jaane shabad kee laagee
    laagee hoy to jaane laagee shabad kee

gelaa main ek ghaayal ghoome ghaav nazar naheen aaee
gyaan kamaThaa pair baiThaa hriday mein bhaal jamaaee
    laagee hoy toh jaane laagee shabad kee

ankaa laagee bankaa laagee laagee sajan kasaaee
balakh bukhaar koo aisee laagee chhoD chalaa baadashaahee
    laagee hoy toh jaane laagee shabad kee

dhruv ko laagee prahalaad ko laagee laagee ho meeraa baaee
gopeechand bharataree ko laagee sir mein bhasmee ramaaee
    laagee hoy toh jaane laagee shabad kee

paanchane maar pachcheesan basakar anaghaD lebonaa jagaaee
kahe machhindar sunau gorakh sunn mein dhajaa faharaaee
    laagee hoy toh jaane laagee shabad kee

Only those struck by the word will know what a blow is
Only those struck by love will know what the word is
What would others know what love of the word is

I gore myself with words and none can see the wounds
The arrow of awareness is quartered in my heart
It quivers each time I'm kissed by a song
    Only those struck by the word will know what a blow is
    Only those struck by love will know what the word is

The word struck the cobbler, it bruised the butcher
It battered the Brahmin and the word wounded the king
    Only those struck by the word will know what a blow is
    Only those struck by love will know what the word is

It pierced Kabir, smacked Chennaiah, hit Mira really hard
When it came to Anand, he rubbed words on his open scar
    Only those struck by the word will know what a blow is
    Only those struck by love will know what the word is

My five senses have been drawn and quartered
Gorakh, I'm hoisted with the petard of emptiness
    Only those struck by the word will know what a blow is
    Only those struck by love will know what the word is

"Laagee hoy toh jaane laagee shabad kee" is a bastardized Kabiresque song with no assignable signature. According to Linda Hess in *Singing Emptiness: Kumar Gandharva Performs the Poetry of Kabir*, Gorakh's 'Macchinder' signature is appended by some; some tag it to Kabir. It is likely neither wrote it. As we have seen, this happens all too often in the world of nirguni song-poetry, where ideas and expressions become more important than authenticity and an attachment to authorship. It appears that everyone rubbed this open wound of a song with their words—and so did I. Mira, who clearly post-dates Gorakhnath by a few centuries, makes an uncanny appearance, as do mythical 'bhakts' (devotees of Vishnu) like Dhruv and Prahlad whom I bypass in my version to make place for Madara Chennaiah from the Kannada *vachana* movement and for myself. The original refers to the mythical-historical king of Ujjain of many legends, Bharthari, and his nephew Gopi Chand, who give up their kingdoms to become Nath yogis following Gorakhnath, and compose songs. My English version has this as: 'the word wounded the king'.

A word about the Kumar Gandharva who comes to us via Linda Hess. Gandharva finds the lyrics for his songs in a relatively obscure work called *Shri Shilnath Shabdamrit*, which translates as the 'Nectar of Words by Shri Shilnath', an anthology that bears the editor's name and not that of the poets. Shilnath was a yogi who founded an order in Dewas (in Malwa, Madhya Pradesh) in 1901, and in 1923 published an anthology of five hundred songs mostly assigned to Kabir but also others of the nirguni disposition, where divinity, if there is one, or the Force that animates the world, is formless. It's likely Shilnath gathered these songs from the people of Malwa—the most authentic and inauthentic source at once. Twenty-one of the thirty lyrics featured in Hess's book on Gandharva come from Shilnath's book.

Since I could not find a recording by Kumar Gandharva (nor have I heard it performed by others alive), I set this to Yaman—the much-travelled raga moistened by the love of one and all, which the poor Brahmin **Venkatamakhin** (Venkateswara Dikshita), the seventeenth-century south Indian scholar of music, dismissed as *turuska* (Turkish) and considered unsuitable for the 'classical' musical forms he described in his treatise *Chaturdandiprakashika* (The Illuminator of the Four Pillars of Music). Venkatamakhin's suggestion was duly disregarded by all the important musicians of south India.

According to aficionados V.N. Muthukumar and M.V. Ramana, the late professor and master Carnatic flautist **T. Viswanathan** (1927–2022), wrote in his doctoral dissertation that the raga does not seem to have 'been particularly well known in south India before the seventeenth century, which fact seems to support the likelihood of middle-eastern origins.' Hence a bastard raga for a song sired by many passersby.

A cow births in the sky, listen
सुनता है गुरु ग्यानी

सुनता है गुरु ग्यानी ग्यानी ग्यानी
गगन में आवाज हो रही है झीनी झीनी
    सुनता है गुरु ग्यानी ग्यानी ग्यानी

पहिले आये नाद बिंदु से
पीछे जमया पानी हो जी
सब घट पूरन पूर रहा है
अलख पुरुष निर्वाणि हो जी
    सुनता है गुरु ग्यानी
वहां से आया पता लिखाया
तृष्णा तौने बुझाई
अमृत छोड़ सो विषय को धावे
उलटी फांस फसानी हो जी
    सुनता है गुरु ग्यानी
गगन मंडल में गौ बियानी
भोई पे दही जमाया
माखन माखन संतो ने खाया
छाछ जगत बपरानी हो जी
    सुनता है गुरु ग्यानी
बिन धरती एक मंडल दीसे

बिन सरोवर जूं पानी रे
गगन मंडल में होए उजियाला
बोले गुरुमुख बानी हो जी
        सुनता है गुरु ग्यानी
ओहं सोहं बाजा बाजे
त्रिकुटी धाम सुहानी रे
इड़ा पिंगला सुखमन नाड़ी
सुन धजा फ़ेहरानी हो जी
        सुनता है गुरु ग्यानी
कहत कबीरा सुनो भाई साधो
जाई अगम के बानी रे
दिन भर रे जो नज़र भर देखे
अजर अमर वो निशानी हो जी
        सुनता है गुरु ग्यानी

suntaa hai guru gyaanii gyaanii gyaanii
gagan mein aavaaj ho rahii hai jhiinii jhiinii
        suntaa hai guru gyaanii gyaanii gyaanii

pahile aaye naad bindu se
piichhe jamayaa paanii ho jee
sab ghaT pooran poor rahaa hai
alakh purush nirvaaNii ho jee
        suntaa hai guru gyaanii

vahaan se aayaa pataa likhaayaa
tRishNaa taune bujhaaii
amRit chhoD so vishay ko dhaave
ulaTii faans fasaanii ho jee
        suntaa hai guru gyaanii

gagan manDal mein gau biyaanii
bhoii pe dahii jamaayaa
maakhan maakhan santo ne khaayaa
chhaachh jagat bapraanii ho jee
    suntaa hai guru gyaanii

bin dharatee ek manDal deese
bin sarovar joon paanii re
gagan manDal mein hoe ujiyaalaa
boley gurumukh baanii ho jee
    suntaa hai guru gyaanii

oham soham baajaa baaje
trikuTee dhaam suhaanii re
iDaa pingalaa sukhaman naaDii
sunn dhajaa feharaanii ho jee
    suntaa hai guru gyaanii

kahat kabeeraa suno bhaaii saadho
jaaee agam ke baanii re
din bhar re jo nazar bhar dekhe
ajar amar vo nishaanii ho jee
    suntaa hai guru gyaanii

The guru discerns the unstruck sound
In the head a voice from the sky resounds
    It's the subtle throb of silence—listen

The wise one discerns the unstruck sound
The sound that resounds in the sky—boundless, bound
    It's the subtle throb of silence—listen

First comes a drop of resonant sound
That pools into water blueing the round
The Unseen One breaks new ground
    This singular sound is luminous—listen

The message is draped in light: this thirst can't be slaked
Don't hanker for nectar, gulp the poison of truth
See the noose hang itself, hear the hush descend
    Inhale this pale silence—just listen

A cow births in the sky: the earth curdles
The blessed savour the butter, others quaff whey
Listen to listening, discern the unuttered sound
    The sound of sound is resounding—listen

A universe cleaved of earth, a lake robbed of water
The dome of sky emblazoned by the unspoken word
The guru's words are nothing, listen to his silence
    Silence stirring in the middle of sound—listen

Rising and falling, it's a concert of breaths
When the two meet the third, an unheard silence ascends
It is where you hoist the flag of emptiness
    At the end of sound, a pulsing quiet—listen

Kabir is fastened to the word that cannot be held
He sees what's always around but remains unseen
He reveals the sign that is neither born nor dies
    Truelove is spoken without a word—listen

When Sheela ji asked me about a particular phrase Kabir uses, we heard Kumar Gandharva's "Suntaa hai guru gyaanii" a couple of times (on YouTube). The phrase wasn't in this song, but we found other phrases that held our breath. Over two days, I saw the many petals of silence flower in a symphony of colours. Discerned on 15 May (2015), the day Ambedkar unfurled the flag of negation over caste, the day *Annihilation of Caste* was published in 1936.

Walls of sand, pillars of breath
भोला मन जाने

भोला मन जाने अमर मेरी काया
धन रे जोबन सपने सी माया
बादल की सी छाया
  भोला मन जाने अमर मेरी काया
एक कुआं पांच पनियारी
जल भरती है न्यारी न्यारी
  भोला मन जाने अमर मेरी काया
डट जायगा कुआं सूख जायगी क्यारी
हाथ मल मल चली पांचो पनियारी
  भोला मन जाने अमर मेरी काया
सूखा सा काठ हेट नहीं छाया
कहां तेरा हंसा कहां तेरी माया
  भोला मन जाने अमर मेरी काया
बालू की भीत पवन का खंभा
देवल देख भया अचंभा
  भोला मन ज।ने अमर मेरी काया
आदि आदिनाथ मच्छंदर का पूता
ये जस गाय गोरख अवधूता
  भोला मन जाने अमर मेरी काया

bholaa man jaane amar meree kaayaa

dhan re joban sapane sii maayaa
baadal kee sii chhaayaa
    bholaa man jaane amar meri kaayaa

ek kuaan paanch paniyaaree
jal bharatee hai nyaaree nyaaree
    bhola man jaane amar meree kaayaa

DaT jaayagaa kuaan sookh jaayagee kyaaree
haath mal mal chalee paancho paniyaaree
    bholaa man jaane amar meree kaayaa

sookhaa saa kaaTh heT naheen chhaayaa
kahaan teraa hansaa kahaan teree maayaa
    bholaa man jaane amar meree kaayaa

baaloo kee bheet pavan kaa khambhaa
deval dekh bhayaa achambhaa
    bholaa man jaane amar meree kaayaa

aadi aadinaath machhandar kaa pootaa
ye jas gaay gorakh avadhootaa
    bholaa man jaane amar meree kaayaa

The faint heart knows this body is immortal

The cloud is at one remove from the shade
Wealth, youth, the memory of a dream—all fade
    The faint heart knows this body is immortal

The well is but one, five draw from it
They banter, they saunter and then they split
    The wounded heart knows this body is immortal

The well will cave in, the bed will go dry
The five will quit, with a heave and a sigh
    The frail heart knows this body is immortal

A withered tree offers no shade nor shelter
Has your swan-soul flown for the mirage of water?
    The foolish heart knows this body is immortal

Walls of sand, pillars of breath—unfounded
Just look inside the shrine—you'll be astounded
    The silly heart knows this body is immortal

The son of the Primal One, Gorakh's wandered
He is a cow that has strayed from the herd
    His wandering heart is immortal

The penultimate stanza rendered by Kumar Gandharva (YouTube) brought to mind Bhimrao Ambedkar's plight after he lands in Baroda in 1916 having spent four years in the US and the UK earning doctorates and accolades. When abroad, he says, he could forget about being an Untouchable and 'experienced social equality for the first time'. Within days after his return to his family in Mumbai, Ambedkar rushes to Baroda to work for the Maharaja, Sayajirao Gaekwad. A pioneer in the field of affirmative action, Gaekwad was also a renowned patron of music and the arts. Gaekwad sponsored Ambedkar's education in Mumbai, New York and London,

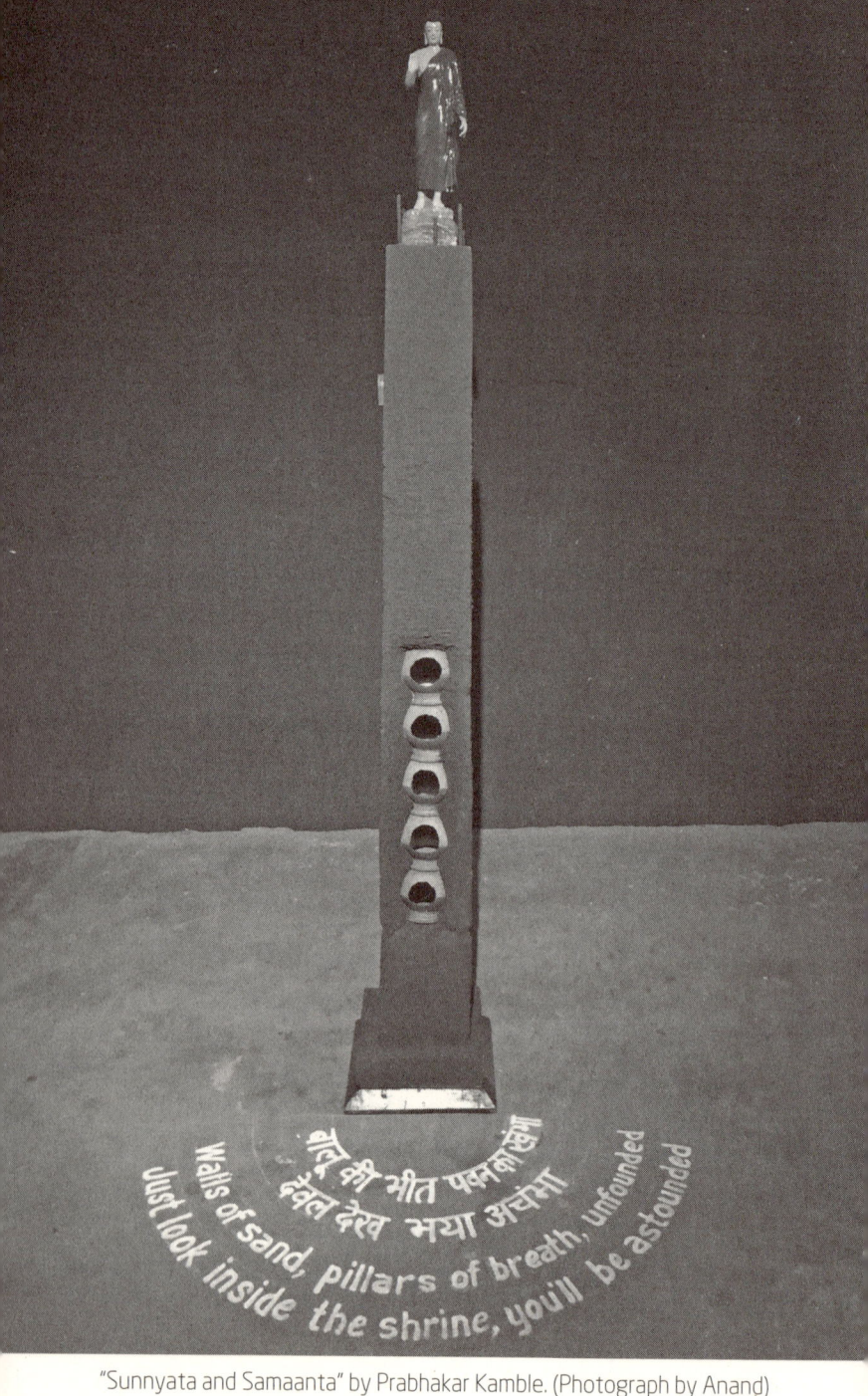

बालू की भीत पवनका खंभा
देवल देव भया अचंभा
Walls of sand, pillars of breath, unfounded
Just look inside the shrine, you'll be astounded

"Sunnyata and Samaanta" by Prabhakar Kamble. (Photograph by Anand)

मेरा आशना हूँ शहर में, सन्नाटे का घर.
होश के छप्पर पर टिकाऊँ एक सहज की चल.
My home is in the city of emptiness, a fortress of hush
Just a roof of awareness on the pillar of breath

"Sunnyata and Samaanta" by Prabhakar Kamble. (Photograph by Anand)

and in exchange Ambedkar was to serve the state to settle his dues. But when Ambedkar is appointed a probationer in the office of Baroda military's accountant general, he is denied a roof over his head. No one would rent their home to an Untouchable. Inns, run on caste and community lines, refuse him room. He offers to pay double, registers himself as a Parsi, and stays in a derelict Parsi-run inn. When his identity is discovered, he's booted out by abusive men wielding sticks. 'I was bewildered. My heart sank within me. I cursed all, and wept bitterly.' Forced out of Baroda in eleven days, he returns to Mumbai. n the posthumously published autobiographical text, "**Waiting for a Visa**", he concludes: 'An Untouchable wherever he went in India was a problem to himself and to others.'

In 2020, the *Sunnata–Samaanta/ Emptiness–Equality* art exhibition I had curated for Devi Art Foundation at a warehouse in the Okhla Industrial Estate, Delhi, featured a pair of works by the Ambedkarite artist Prabhakar Kamble: sculptural installations with small figurines of Ambedkar and the Buddha mounted atop two indigo pillars inset with broken pots symbolizing the annihilation of caste. They each inspired an inscription at the base—arranged like a garland of words. While these lines

बालू की भीत पवन का खंभा
देवल देख भया अचंभा

baaloo kee bheet pavan kaa khambhaa
deval dekh bhayaa achambhaa

Walls of sand, pillars of breath—unfounded
Just look inside the shrine—you'll be astounded

adorned the base of the Buddha column, I had to come up with something for the particularity of Ambedkar's experience of being cast out:

घर अपना है शुन्न शहर में सन्नाटे का गढ़
सांस के खंभे पर टिकाऊं एक सहज की छत

ghar apanaa hai shunn shahar mein sannaaTe kaa gaDh
saans ke khambhe par Tikaaoon ek sahaj kee chath

My home is in the city of emptiness, a fortress of hush
Just a roof of awareness on the pillar of breath

"Bholaa man jaane" is the last of the four songs from Kumar Gandharva's 1982 album, *Nirguni Bhajans*. The lyric bears the signature not of Kabir, but of the twelfth-century yogi–poet, Gorakhnath. By now we know that on occasion these names are interchanged, and true counterfeits state the unstateable truth, walking under the Tree of a Big Name. *Go-rakh* (like *go-paal*) also means one who cares for cattle (also *gau*, hence cow), a herder; and this idea is milked in the last stanza.

Your heart is large, the forest small
हीरना

हीरना समझ बूझ बन चरना
एक बन चरना दूजे बन चरना
तीजे बन पग नहीं धरना
　　हीरना समझ बूझ बन चरना
तीजे बन में पांच पारधी
इनके नज़र नहीं पड़ना
　　हीरना समझ बूझ बन चरना
तोए मार तेरो मास बिकावे
तेरे खाल का करेंगे बिछोना
　　हीरना समझ बूझ बन चरना
पांच हीरना पच्चीस हीरनी
उनमें एक चतुर ना
　　हीरना समझ बूझ बन चरना
कहे कबीरा जो सुनो भाई साधो
गुरु के चरण चित धरना
　　हीरना समझ बूझ बन चरना

heeranaa samajh bhoojh ban charanaa

ek ban charanaa dooje ban charanaa
teeje ban pag naheen dharanaa

heeranaa samajh boojh ban charanaa

teeje ban mein paanch paaradhee
inake nazar naheen paDanaa
    heeranaa samajh boojh ban charanaa

toye maar tero maas bikaave
tere khaal kaa karenge bichhonaa
    heeranaa samajh boojh ban charanaa

paanch heeranaa pachchees heeranii
unamein ek chatur naa
    heeranaa samajh boojh ban charanaa

kahe kabeeraa jo suno bhaaii saadho
guru ke charaN chit dharanaa
    heeranaa samajh boojh ban charanaa

Deer, watch your step in the forest
Know where you forage, mind where you rest
    Your heart is large, the forest small
    The musk is within, in one and all

Graze in the first forest of senses
Forage in the second forest of awareness
    Your heart is large, the forest small
    The musk is within, in one and all

Do not set foot in the third wilderness
Where five hunters lurk, dead earnest

Your heart is large, the forest small
The musk is within, in one and all

They'll flay your skin, hawk your flesh
But it's something more they're out to possess
    Deer, your heart is large, the forest small
    The musk is within, in one and all

Five deer and twenty-five doe go this way
Only one walks in wisdom, moves with grace
    Deer, your heart is large, the forest small
    The musk is within, in one and all

Says Kabir, listen up, my dear fellows
Still your heart on the guru who knows
    Dear, your heart is large, the forest small
    The musk is within, in one and all

With "Heeranaa samajh boojh ban charanaa" (YouTube), Kumar Gandharva makes the song walk the forest of senses broadly in the realm of the raga Charukesi. Given the bareness and simplicity, and the allusions (of musk) that lay concealed within the body of the poem as much as in the deer, it was amongst the most elusive songs to render in English. I had to bring the fragrance of the implied simile to the surface. Listening to it and singing it over a decade was the only way of finding a way into the being of the song, and smelling the musk within the deer in me, and in the one dear to me, my हम-दम/ hum-dum, हम-नफ़स/ hum-nafas, my comrade in breath.

Body thief
कौन ठगवा

कौन ठगवा नगरिया लूटल हो
    कौन ठगवा

चंदन खाट के बनल खठोला ता पर दुलहिन सूतल हो
    कौन ठगवा

उठो सखी री मांग संवारो दुलहा मोसे रूठल हो
    कौन ठगवा

आये यम राज पलंक चढ़ बैठा नैनन अंसुआ टूटल हो
    कौन ठगवा

चार जने मिल खाट उठाइन चहुं दिसी हौं हौं ऊठल हो
    कौन ठगवा

कहत कबीरा सुनो भाई साधो जग से नाता छूटल हो
    कौन ठगवा

kaun Thagavaa nagariyaa looTal ho
    kaun Thagavaa

chandan khaaT ke banal khaTholaa taa par dulahin sootal ho
    kaun Thagavaa

uTho sakhee ree maang sanvaaro dulahaa mosey rooThal ho
    kaun Thagavaa

aaye yam raaj palank chadh baiThaa nainan ansuaa TooTal ho
kaun Thagavaa

chaar jane mil khaaT uThaain chahun disi haun haun ooThal ho
kaun Thagavaa

kahat kabeeraa suno bhaaii saadho jag se naataa chhooTal ho
kaun Thagavaa

Who's the thief who's sacked the city?
Who's the thug ravaging this body?

Look at this sandalwood bedstead
On which the sleepy bride is spread
    Who's the thief who's sacked this city?

Wake up, dearest, wipe that frown off your brow
Wear a smile, make it up to the groom now
    Who's the thief who's sacked this city?

When King Death checks in
And climbs on to your bed, tears give in
    Who's the thief who's sacked this city?

Four men will haul your bier
The fire will sigh, hiss and sear
    Who's the thief who's sacked this city?

Kabir speaks this truth, so hearken
Every bond with this world is broken
    Who's the thief who's sacked this city?

Kumar Gandharva and Vasundhara Komkali drift in and out of "Kaun Thagavaa" (YouTube) effortlessly like birds without a care give us a joy that is ours to take. Yet there's a grating stone in this sweet song for death. Kabir wants a lazy bride—likely a child in Kabir's time, likely married to a stranger against her wishes in caste society—to be good to the groom, a groom she has offended. She must please him in every way, attend to all his needs. Hearth to bed. Arguably, the bride is everyone of us, awaiting the groom of death. Death is the only lover who will wait a lifetime for us, Kabir often says. And in this world, God is often the beloved. Irrespective of gender, the poet-bhakta is imagined as a woman whom God will ravish if they sing His praises in good poetry. Whatever the caveats, the metaphor is what it is. Something time may remember even if we try to cast it away. We have to always be more Kabir than Kabir. All he asks of us is this awareness.

Fearless formless
निर्भय निर्गुण

निर्भय निर्गुण गुण रे गाऊंगा

मूल कमल दृढ़ आसन बांधूं जी उलटी पवन चढ़ाऊंगा
 निर्भय निर्गुण गुण रे गाऊंगा
मन ममता को थिर कर लाऊं जी पांचों तत्त मिलाऊंगा
 निर्भय निर्गुण गुण रे गाऊंगा
इंगला पिंगला सुखमन नाड़ी जी त्रिरवेणी पे हां न्हाऊंगा
 निर्भय निर्गुण गुण रे गाऊंगा
पांच पचीसों पकड़ मंगाऊं जी एक ही डोर लगाऊंगा
 निर्भय निर्गुण गुण रे गाऊंगा
शुन्न शिखर पर अनहद बाजे जी राग छत्तीस सुनाऊंगा
 निर्भय निर्गुण गुण रे गाऊंगा
कहत कबीरा सुनो भई साधो जी जीत निशान घुराऊंगा
 निर्भय निर्गुण गुण रे गाऊंगा

nirbhay nirguN guN re gaaoongaa

mool kamal dRiDh aasan baandhoon jee ulaTee pavan chaDhaaoongaa
 nirbhay nirguN guN re gaaoongaa

man mamata ko thir kar laaoon jee paanchon tatt milaaoongaa
 nirbhay nirguN guN re gaaoongaa

ingalaa pingalaa sukhaman naaDee jee ttiraveNii pe haan nhaaoongaa
 nirbhay nirguN guN re gaaoongaa

paanch pacheeson pakaD mangaaoon jee ek hee Dor lagaaoongaa
 nirbhay nirguN guN re gaaoongaa

Shunn shikhar par anahad baaje jee raag chhattees sunaaoongaa
 nirbhay nirguN guN re gaaoongaa

kahat kabeeraa suno bhaaii saadho jee jeet nishaan ghuraaoongaa
 nirbhay nirguN guN re gaaoongaa

I'll sing fearlessly, I'll sing formlessness
I'll sing all the aspects of the aspectless
 Fearless formless songness stillness

I'll sing endlessness in a song that ends
I'll leave a sign that leaves no sign
 Fearless formless songness stillness

I'll be fearless singing the formless
I'll be songness, a moving stillness
 Fearless formless songness stillness

I'll bind the root of the lotus, hold my breath outside-in
I'll be without it with it, I'll be without within
 Fearless formless songness stillness

I'll speak to the wind, be one with land, keep above water
I'll attain lotusness, be the bee giddy on undrunk nectar
    Fearless formless songness stillness

I'll still my heart, brace my mind, I'll be elegance
I'll meld the five senses, quilt the five elements
    Fearless formless songness stillness

I'll bind the infinite in song
I'll be one and I'll be the throng
    Fearless formless songness stillness

I'll be yes and no, I'll be the in-between
I'll bathe where the three rivers meet unseen
    Fearless formless songness stillness

I will be at the end of where it all begins
I'll sing the formless, I'll sing songness
    Fearless formless songness stillness

Five senses and five elements, strummed on one string
The warp and woof, the false and true, strung to one thing
    Fearless formless songness stillness

I'll hear the unstruck sound on the peak of emptiness
Amidst the clamour of sounds, I'll be quietness
    Fearless formless songness stillness

Just look at Kabir, hoist on the flag of victory
Shaping the flag shaping the wind, unfurling a mystery
    Fearless formless songness stillness

"Nirbhay nirguN" is rendered by Kumar Gandharva accompanied by his principal student and wife Vasundhara Komkali (YouTube). Sometimes, my English rendition of a lyric appears longer than the original, so to say. This owes to the fact that a lyric in Kabiri/ Kabiru, like any lyric set to raga music, is sung over and again, with improvisations in each repetition. And each improvisation throws new light on meaning, the words never settling for one thing.

Songness stillness
डगमगाती स्थिरता

Kumar Gandharva begins Kabir's "Nirbhay nirguN" with a flourish, a quick statement of abstract intent that lasts barely two seconds, a flawless enunciation of the *swara*s *pa-dha-sa-sa-re*, an arc in the broad ambit of what may be characterized as raga Maand, which in Kumar's style could well be, as a friend's friend helplessly suggested, nirguni or formless Maand (one of the most happily miscegenated ragas), if such an exercise in identification is to be undertaken at all, although we can't but be struck by the unasked question Kumar leaves hanging at the swara *re*, a question that quavers in anticipation, followed by a pause, a faint pause we scarcely realize drowned by the drone of the tanpura, and this moment of utterance of the short *aakaar, a —a —a —a —aaa*, a contour without any decipherable meaning that forms the basis of all musical expression, is especially poignant in Kumar's case since he had to adapt to singing with one lung after tuberculosis sundered him from the only thing he loved, that too at the peak of his career, almost six years before streptomycin would be discovered, till which time he was 'bed-bound and coughing up morsels of his lungs' leaving his bed-sheets scarlet according to his biographer **Raghava R. Menon**, which is when Kumar heard, rather discerned, the nirgun and silences that Kabir extolled, administered to him by mendicants and wandering minstrels in Dewas in the Malwa plateau of western Madhya Pradesh, itinerants who sang for no one yet everyone, who sang equally for themselves, and Kumar felt they sang for him too as he convalesced there after being forced to flee a Mumbai humid with the air of material success, and somehow we have to be perversely grateful to this near-fatal disease but for which Kumar, who started as a prodigy blessed with an unaccountable faculty, would have been yet another concert-circuit performer albeit an excellent one, for when he recovered with antibiotics and surgery he was left with only one of his precious lungs, which meant he could express himself only in short phrases unlike his compatriots who held lungfuls of breath and imperiously stayed put on one note sometimes for two cycles of a tala, dazzling and astounding audiences with breathtaking *taan*s and *meend*s like Bade Ghulam Ali Khan, Kesarbai Kerkar or Bhimsen Joshi did with practised nonchalance, whereas Kumar had to discover the meaning of breath and musical expression all over again, to learn to linger in silences that seemed to contain as much music, like the silence we now return to, when Kumar, after a splash of Maand with *pa-dha-sa-sa-re*, follows it with a pause that lasts barely a second, and this moment of apparent silence—perched between the aakaar, formless form, and the piercing words of the song to follow—captures the essence of Kabir, who made it his business to restate the Buddha's core antigod philosophy, *atta deep bhav*, be your own light, in memorizable words that belie the depths they plumb, words that are sheer and luminous, words whose meanings flower anew each time they wrap themselves around music, and here let us allow ourselves just another excursus, not needless, for in the idiom of music that Kumar represents, the basic unit of the music, swara, is not to be rendered as note, for as Menon says, 'swa stands for self and ra stands for shining forth', which means the person who sings, and sings like Kumar, throws forth light, illumines, and these words of Kabir that Kumar makes sheer for us are in the tongue that was likely spoken in the segregated quarters of Benares (heed the use of thir instead of sthir, and tatt not tattva in stanza three; nhaaoongaa instead of nahaaoongaa—nuances Kumar is attentive to), quarters that were likely thick with the whiff of spent marijuana mixed with the smoke that wafted from Brahmin-kindled ghee-laced yagna fire-pits and the pyres along the banks of the Ganga, like it still mostly is, where Kabir the Weaver and his cohorts, Gora the Potter and Ravidas the Tanner, rapped about love and truth in rhyme and metre, berating the Brahmin and mocking the mullah, in a Benares that lay in the vicinity of Siddhartha's Sarnath, where he is said to have had his first brush with wisdom and spoke so that even the deer in the park heeded him, an image that Kabir heeds too, for the five deer representing the five senses become a leitmotif, alluded to in the fourth stanza after the refrain of "Nirbhay nirguN", where he sings of conquering and taming the five senses that combine with the five elements to birth twenty-five sensibilities that bind you in a series of attachments to the world, attachments from which Kabir, like Gautama, seeks release, and thus aspires for the formless, aspectless, amorphous abstraction called nothingness, a journey from being into nothingness mediated by consciousness and heed, a consciousness that equally militates against the unreason of caste for the Buddha and Kabir, and thence for Ambedkar, raised by a Kabirpanthi, a consciousness that Ambedkar believes is 'cognitive, emotional and volitional' (aspects that perhaps Kumar and many of his fans, sadly, seem unlikely to grasp), and such consciousness is doubtlessly formless, yet such formlessness is something Kabir cannot help but state fearlessly in the form of a song, for, like Browning was to say, here is a man whose reach exceeded his grasp (or what's a heaven for?), hence the joyous, even ecstatic, affirmation of a negation he opens with—*I'll sing the formless form*—an unwonted expression of that which cannot be expressed, which Kumar renders afresh for us, orchestrating it deftly to the rhythm of the loom in the seven-beat tevra taal, accompanied by his partner in music and life, Vasundhara Komkali, the woman who helped him find his breath again, who, to use a cliché as old as breath, breathed her last recently, thus giving me a pretext to dwell upon this song that imbues what is beyond all aspects with an aspect, shines the light on something that cannot be seen with our eyes, an aspect that cannot be heard with our ears, cannot be tasted with our tongue, nor felt on our skin or be smelt, an absolute abstraction bestowed with form, for to utter something, anything, is to give it form, and Kumar does this with "Nirbhay nirguN", to which, without further ado, you must listen, a song that ends too soon even as it sings of endlessness

I'll sing my way out
नैहरवा

नैहरवा हमका ना भावे
नैहरवा हमका ना भावे

साईं की नगरी परम अति सुन्दर
जहां कोई जाए ना आवे
चांद सुरज जहां पवन न पानी
कौ संदेसा पहुंचावै
दरद यह साईं को सुनावै
    नैहरवा हमका न भावे
आगे चालौ पंथ नहीं सूझे
पीछे दोष लगावै
केहि बिधि ससुरे जाऊं मोरी सजनी
बिरहा जोर जरावे
विषै रस नाच नचावे
    नैहरवा हमका न भावे
बिन सतगुरु आपनों नहीं कोई
जो यह राह बतावे
कहत कबीर सुनो भाई साधो
सपने में प्रीतम ना आवे
तपन यह जिया की बुझावे
    नैहरवा हमका ना भावे

naiharavaa hamkaa naa bhaave
naiharavaa hamkaa naa bhaave

saaii ki nagaree param ati sundar
jahaan koii jaae naa aave
chaand suraj jahaan pavan na paanii
kou sandesaa pahunchaavai
darad yah saaii ko sunaavai
　　naiharavaa hamkaa naa bhaave

aage chaalau panth naheen soojhe
peechhe dosh lagaavai
kehi bidhee sasure jaaoon moree sajanii
birahaa jor jaraave
vishai ras naach nachaave
　　naiharavaa hamka naa bhaave

bin sataguru aapanon naheen koii
jo yah raah bataave
kahat kabeer suno bhaaii saadho
sapane mein preetam naa aave
tapan yaha jiya kee bujhaave
　　naiharavaa hamkaa naa bhaave

This village of mine—my heart's not in it
This place called home—I've no place in it
This station of life—I want out of it
　　I want out, I've no doubt
　　O I'll sing my way out

The City of Love is a beyond beautiful thing
There are no comings nor goings, no being
No one arrives there, no one leaves
No sun no moon no water no breeze
There's no livelong day there, no dark night
Till you are in it, it is nowhere in sight
    I want out, I've no doubt
    O I'll sing my way out

Other poets have walked to this no-place
I'll lose finding fault with their ways
Where I'm headed, let my grief shine bright
Who'll bear this message, plead my plight?
The juice of all life dances in my eyes
A farmer in despair looking at the skies
    I want out, I've no doubt
    O I'll sing my way out

My guru is all, there's no one else I can call mine
He'll show the way, the raag, the secret shine
Comrades and lovers, listen to Kabir's lament
You've to work your way, there's nothing godsent
Let's burn this village down, build the City of Love
I have to go, we have to go, for the love of love
    I want out, I have no doubt
    I don't want in, I am out

Sowmya from Kalampalayam village sent "Naiharavaa hamkaa naa bhaave" my way to see what I would do with it at a time when I could not sing for nearly a year. I had returned to singing and poetry in 2014 following an annihilative break of some fifteen years. Within a year, I developed nodules in my vocal cords and lost my voice. As an autodidact, I moved quickly from nothing to nil. After a micro-laryngeal surgery, while waiting to find my voice again, I let this song envelop me. I let it ring in my head. I let it sting my being. Kumar Gandharva interprets Kabir in a slow, measured yet immeasurable fashion. A satisfying translation eluded me for years. Recovering my voice in another year, and having found a guru like the song suggests (*He'll show the way, the raag, the secret shine— raah, raag and raaz*—राह राग राज़), I've sung this over and over again. Each once, I'm renewed by the song and my singing renews the song. In time, a translation fell into place.

Kumar explores the word 'naiharavaa' (नैहरवा) in myriad ways, clinging to it, lingering over each syllable and extending each vowel, gliding across each diphthong, soaking each phrase with the drone of the tanpura. With each utterance he takes us closer to the place no-place that Kabir sings of. Each musical expression that wraps the word causes a new meaning to bloom, the way the sun falls on the same leaf differently each moment of the day. Kabir here assumes the much-used and well-worn voice of a female lover or bride who has been detained against her will at her natal home, something all too common in the subcontinent where control of female independence and sexuality is a way of sustaining the system of castes. She wants out. She yearns for union with the beloved—a union that society and family would not allow. "Naiharavaa" becomes a song of separation, of longing, of grief and equally a song for the joys to come in the City of Love. It is a song of annihilation, a song for the end of all inequalities. It is a cry to rift all boundaries. The song alludes to the stifling limitations of rural life—ridden and riven with caste and patriarchal codes. Ambedkar calls the village a 'sink of localism, a den of ignorance, narrow-mindedness and communalism.' The *nagari*, the City of Love, what the poet Raidas sang of as Beghampura, the City without Sorrow, beckons. Ambedkar thrived in Mumbai, the city that made him Babasaheb. In Kabir lore, this idea is Premnagar, City of Love. "Naiharavaa" is also a reworking of the Bahiya Sutta—a leitmotif in Kabir and in *The Notbook*. Farmers and comrades walk in at my behest. The song at once speaks to the nameless lover, a formless god and a boundless city. It is as much about nibbana.

Enlightenment for Kabir is the love of love.

Like him, Ambedkar wants out, and he walks out, taking half a million with him. A part apart.

Why sleep now?
अब का सोवै

जाग पियारी अब का सोवै
रैन गई दिन काहे को खोवै

जिन जागा तिन मानिक पाया
तैं बौरी सब सोय गंवाया
    जाग पियारी
पिया तेरे चतुर तू मूरख नारी
कबहुं न पिया की सेज संवारी
    जाग पियारी
तैं बौरी बौरापन कीन्ही
भर जोबन पिया अपन न चीन्ही
    जाग पियारी
जाग देख पिया सेज न तेरे
तोहि छांड़ उठि गए सबेरे
    जाग पियारी
कहे कबीरा सोई धुन जागै
शबद बान उर अंतर लागै
    जाग पियारी

jaag piyaaree ab kaa sovai
rain gai din kaahe ko khovai

jin jaagaa tin maanik paayaa
tain bauree sab soy ganvaayaa
    jaag piyaaree

piyaa tere chatur tuu moorakh naaree
kabahun naa piyaa kee sej sanvaaree
    jaag piyaaree

tain bauree bauraapan keenii
bhar joban piya apan na cheenhee
    jaag piyaaree

jaag dekh piyaa sej naa tere
tohi chhaanD uThi gaye sabere
    jaag piyaaree

kahe kabeeraa soi dhun jaagai
shabad baan ur antar laagai
    jaag piyaaree

Why sleep now? There's much to do, much to say
You've lost the night anyhow, why lose the day?
    Why sleep now?

Stay up and find in each moment a jewel
Revel in sleep and it won't end well
    Why sleep now?

Your beloved is wise and you're such a fool
You didn't please them, yet they find you beautiful
    Why sleep now?

You never showed your love when they were by you
It was yours to take, the festive flush of youth
    Why sleep now?

Wake up sleepyhead, your love's left your bed
There's nothing to be done, nothing to be said
    Why sleep now?

Kabir stirs the song sleeping in your soul
When this song splits you, you're made whole
    Why sleep now?

True translation is often appropriation, a theft where the thief brazenly claims rightful ownership of what's stolen, such as the night. Kumar Gandharva steals it his way, and I take it for mine. Kabir (or what's passed in his name) suggests that the job of the woman is to please the man, and yet he may be appropriated, heard and read anew, renewed, made-unmade. This is a popular song, much recorded, much anthologized, much taught. We are (as always) told that the sleep-loving lover is a metaphor, and the beloved is god. It is a convenient fiction in a land where the husband (*pati*/ पति) is called god (*parameshwar*/ परमेश्वर). In my version, the song is ungendered, engendering the idea that the slumber we need to wake from is about having good sex that can lead us to god and bliss. This body is all. It is the vessel that will get us across. There's nothing out there but nothing. Nibbana is not contingent on prescriptive and restrictive social norms. Kabir, Mira and this cohort of poets—or their equivalent vachana and abhang poets in Kannada and Marathi—are not yogis because they give up the pleasures of the material world and of the body. They are enlightened because they partake of such pleasures, mindfully, with attention.

A spotless spot, a spot of you
एक निरंजन

जाऊं जी ना जाऊं जी
दूजे के संग नाहि जाऊं जी

गुरुजी मैं तो एक निरंजन ध्याऊं जी
जाऊं जी ना जाऊं जी
   दूजे के संग नाहि जाऊं जी
दुःख ना जानूंजी दरद ना जानूं जी
न कोइ बैद बताऊं जी
सतगुरु बैद मिले अविनाशी
वाकोही नाड़ी बताऊं जी
   दूजे के संग नाहि जाऊं जी
गंगा ना जाऊंजी यमुना ना जाऊं जी
मैं ना कोई तीरथ न्हाऊं जी न्हाऊं जी
अड़सठ तीरथ है घट भीतर
वांहीं मैं मनमल न्हाऊं जी
   दूजे के संग नाहि जाऊं जी
पत्ती ना तोड़ूंजी पत्थर ना पूजुं जी
न कोई देवल जाऊं जी
बन बन की मैं लकडी ना तोड़ूंजी
ना कोई झाड़ सताऊं जी
   दूजे के संग नाहि जाऊं जी

कहे गोरख जी सुनो ओ मच्छिंदर मैं
ज्योत में ज्योत मिलाऊं जी मिलाऊं जी
सतगुरु के मैं शरण गये से
आवागमन मिटाऊं जी मिटाऊं जी
दूजे के संग नाहि जाऊं जी

jaaoon jee naa jaaoon jee
dooje ke sang naahi jaaoon jee

gurujee main toh ek niranjan dhyaaoon jee
jaaoon jee naa jaaoon jee
        dooje ke sang naahi jaaoon jee

duHkh naa jaanoonjee darad naa jaanun jee
na koii baid bataaun jee
sataguru baid miley avinaashee
vaakohee naaDee bataaoon jee
        dooje ke sang naahi jaaoon jee

gangaa naa jaaunjee yamunaa naa jaaoon jee
main naa koii teerath nhaaoon jee nhaaoon jee
aDhasaTh teerath hai ghaT bheetar
vaanheen main manamal nhaaoon jee
        dooje ke sang naahi jaaoon jee

patti naa toDoon jee patthar naa poojun jee
na koii deval jaaoon jee
ban ban kee main lakaDee naa toDoon jee
naa koii jhaaDh sataaoon jee
        dooje ke sang naahi jaaoon jee

kahe gorakh jee suno o machhindar main
jyot me jyot milaaoon jee milaaoon jee
sataguru ke mai sharaN gaye se
aavaagaman miTaaoon jee miTaaoon jee
      dooje ke sang naahi jaaoon jee

I wouldn't go with anyone
It has to be the spotless one
The one beyond all division
Colourless spotless nothing less
Nothing less than nothingness
Nothing less than nothing will do
It's got to be you, no one but you
A spotless spot, a spot of you
I'll go with no one but you
      A spotless spot, a spot of you
      I'll go with no one but you

I know no sorrow, I know no pain
I shall call on no quack in vain
No one else but you will do
If anyone knows my pulse it's you
      A spotless spot, a spot of you
      I'll go with no one but you

I wouldn't trek to holy rivers for a wash
The business of pilgrimages is hogwash
All the rivers course through my body
Where I stand, I am cleansed already
Where I am, I stand rinsed and ready

A spotless spot, a spot of you
I'll go with no one but you

I gather no flowers, I worship no stone
I go to no temple, I'm happy on my own
I torture no shrub, I leave all trees alone
This is no way of knowing the unknown
A spotless spot, a spot of you
I will go with no one but you

Gorakh says, listen, sweetest one
Be one with the light in the light
Shedding pride, be one with the one
It's not for everyone, this delight
A spotless spot, a spot of you
I'll go with no one but you

Kumar Gandharva sings "Gurujee main to ek niranjan dhyaaoon jee" (YouTube). It is a song for the beloved guru, and I sing it as a love-song with glee. But in the translation, I stay clear of the word that figures as a chant and refrain—guru, rather guru ji, with the respectful suffix. As to why, anon.

In the bustling market, stand empty
ऐ उलट वेद की बाणी

धरती तो रोटी भयी कुबुद्धि काग लिये जाऐ
वाद वृक्ष के डाल पे तहां बैठ के खाए
यह उलट वेद की बाणी कोइ ग्यानी करो विचार
अंबर में अमृत का कुआं बिन मुख पान धरे एक सूआ
वहां काली नागन खेले जूआ आठ मरे नौ धारा
ऐ उलट वेद की बाणी
अंबर में एक पेड़ बिरज का वहां झूले निर्गुण का लड़का
जिनकी जड़ का पता नी पावे हेर मरेगा संसार
ऐ उलट वेद की बाणी
तीस मार के तेरह जीतिया हाट भरारण रह गया रीता
गुरु गंगादास ने ऐसी ठानी नैय्या लगा देना पार
ऐ उलट वेद की बाणी

dharatee toh roTee bhayee kubuddhi kaag liye jaai
vaad vRiksh ke Daal pe tahaan baiTh ke khaae

yah ulaT ved kee baaNii koii gyaanii karo vichaar

ambar me amRit ka kuaan bin mukh paan dhare ek sooaa
vahaan kaalee naagan khele jooa aaTh marey nau dhaaraa
ai ulaT ved ki baaNii

ambar me ek peD biraj ka vahaan jhoole nirguN ka ladakaa
jinakee jaD kaa pataa nii paave haer maregaa sansaar
ai ulaT ved kee baaNii

tees maar ke terah jeetiya haaT bharaaraN rah gayaa reetaa
guru gangaadaas ne aisee Thaanii naiyyaa lagaa denaa paar
ai ulaT ved kee baaNii

The earth is but a roti and the foolish crow flies with it
It sits on the branch of an ism, chewing more than it has bit

This is where the spoken word is hung dry
The wise ones don't get it, the fools defy
    The spoken word is hung dry

A well of nectar dug deep in the sky
Where a beakless parrot slakes its thirst
A black snake rolls the dice
Eight will be slayed where nine streams merge
    The ksopen word is hung dry

A boundless banyan spreads in the sky
A thought beyond grasp swings in its arms
We may never taste its roots but we'll try
    The openks word is hung dry

The thirteen win by killing thirty
In the bustling market, stand empty
Ganga Das is hoist upon Kabir's song

And he says he'll take Anand along
   The pkosen word is hung dry

                              I

Kaluram Bamaniya and troupe sing "Yah ulaT ved kee baaNii" (in "The Kabir Project"), and it bears the signature of Ganga Das, assigned the dates 1823–1913. I render *ulaT ved* (which Bamaniya also alternates with *ulTa* ved) as 'the spoken word hung dry', and then go after its ulTa-ness. UlTa is to turn something upside down: reversion, inversion, conversion (implying the converse of something, from 'a turning round, revolving; alteration, change'), why, translation even. *UlaTbaamsi* comprises an entire genre of Kabir songs. (We begin with it at the outset, in "An Interjection".) From ulTa, we first have *altu*. All that ensues is *faltu* (simply useless or nonsense). It helps show how words and the assumptions they generate must not be allowed to make sense. This is also the resistance life shows to tyranny. This is what language as *baansaa*, or simply *baasaa*, with the nasal accent muted, not the pompous *bhaashaa*, does to authority, to authorship.

The word ved or *veda* means knowledge, knowledge that is meant to be secretly transmitted through an oral-aural culture, from a Brahmin male's mouth to a Brahmin male's ear. UlaT ved unmasks the pretensions of ved that claims an unchanging eternal quality, a time of timelessness, what the Brahmins call *sanatan*. If ved parades itself as knowledge and even science, ulaT ved shows us why this is nescience. Ganga Das says he is singing the *bani* (language and style) of ulTa ved, the inversion and antithesis of the ved. Unlike the jubilantly open song-poetry of Kabir, the spoken Vedic chant is shrouded in secrecy, meant only for male Brahmins. It involves the ritual unquestioning incantation of the Word. Through an insistent mnemonic chant, you learn by rote, imbibing the sounds, not pausing to ask what it all means. What passes for knowledge is exclusive and exclusionary, both secret and sacred. It is regarded only because it is so guarded. Unlike a Kabir distich, it is not available to everyone. It is not free, not meant for all. The ved must not be heard (forget uttered) by the wrong people, *id est*, those not Brahmin. The punishments prescribed are severe and absurd. The *Gautama Dharma Sutra* (dated to 300 BCE) lists some penalties for the transgressive Shudra-servant:

> 4. Now if a Shudra listens intentionally to (a recitation of) the Veda, his ears shall be filled with (molten) tin or lac. 5. If he recites (Vedic texts), his tongue shall be cut out. 6. If he remembers them, his body shall be split in twain. 7. If he assumes a position equal (to that of twice-born men) in sitting, in lying down, in conversation or on the road, he shall undergo (corporal) punishment.

This is not a story of just some mythic ahistorical past. The modes of meting punishment have changed but not the Vedic will to inflict cruelty and injustice. 'Go, said the bird, for the leaves were full of children,/ Hidden excitedly, containing laughter.' The trials and tribulations Dalit students face from school to college (and from cradle to the grave), sometimes driving them to their death, is so commonplace in our times that we don't stop to think of our complicity in this, for we cannot bear very much reality. As I edit and revisit this section, a newspaper headline, buried at the bottom on an inside page, reads "Karnataka school principal, teacher held as Dalit students forced to clean septic tank" (*Indian Express*, Delhi, 19 December 2023, p.9). The state-run school is named after Morarji Desai, former prime minister of India. 'What might have been and what has been/ Point to one end, which is always present.'

In the Ramayana, Rama as king of Ayodhya beheads a Shudra, Shambuka, for reciting the Veda in a southern corner of his kingdom. He does this in order to restore the order of caste. A Brahmin's son drops dead since in some part of the kingdom a Shudra is indulging in practices not suited to the status assigned to his life: service. **Ambedkar recounts** how, on the counsel of his Brahmin advisors,

---

Karnataka school principal, teacher held as Dalit students forced to clean septic tank

AN PARASHAR
BALURU, DECEMBER 18

KARNATAKA Police arrested government school principal a teacher for allegedly forcing alit students to clean a septic tank in Malur taluk under district.

he arrested persons were identified as Morarji Desai Residential School principal Bharathamma, and arts and crafts er Muniyappa. Three other employees of the school named in R are absconding. They were booked under the Scheduled Caste Scheduled Tribe (Prevention Atrocities) Act.

Sunday's police action came after a widely shared video showed some students belonging to Scheduled Castes cleaning septic tank. The video surfaced on Saturday, although the incident allegedly took place a month earlier.

Social Welfare Department Director M Srinivasan filed the complaint against the school staff. Bharathamma, Muniyappa, and warden Manjunath have also been suspended after the video surfaced.

A police officer said that Kalavati, a member of the cleaning staff at the school, had made the students clean the septic tank. When principal Bharathamma came to know about it, she took no action, the officer said. The video was circulated by Muniyappa and English teacher Maresh, according to the officer. The officer also said the students at the school had also faced assault from another guest teacher, Abhishek, and that students were not provided food "according to the menu chart".

Kalavati, Maresh and Abhishek have also been named in the FIR, but are absconding.

According to police sources, the video came to light amid a feud between different factions of teachers, as a result of which Muniyappa had shared the video with a helpline of the state minority department, which runs the school. However, according to sources, no action was taken, leading to Muniyappa circulating the video on social media.

On Monday, Urban Development and Town Planning minister Byrathi Suresh, who visited the school, said Rs 25,000 had been released to the school a month earlier for cleaning and maintenance work. He alleged that students were deployed in cleaning work so that school officials could syphon the money.

"We have suspended five staff, including the principal. As a punishment, we will transfer all teaching and non-teaching faculty of the school. Chief Minister Siddaramaiah is also aware of the incident and he also told me address it," Suresh said.

Asked when the video was recorded and whether officials had tried to suppress it, Suresh said an inquiry would also be conducted to see whether there were any lapses from the department.

A delegation of BJP leaders headed by Opposition leader Ashoka, visited the spot and demanded a probe by a sitting judge. "It is an inhumane act, and there have been lapses by the authorities. We demand that the government appoint a sitting judge to probe the case," Ashoka said.

Morarji Desai Residential Schools in Karnataka are run by the minority welfare department for students from Classes 6 to. The aim is to bring down the school drop-out rate in rural areas, especially among those belonging to SC/ST or minority communities.

A video grab shows students cleaning the septic tank.

Rama mounted his aerial car and scoured the countryside for the culprit. ... At last, in a wild region far away to the south he espied a man practising rigorous austerities of a certain kind. He approached the man, and with no more ado than to enquire of him and inform himself that he was a Shudra by the name Shambuka, who was practising *tapasya* with a view to going to heaven in his own earthly person, and without so much as a warning, expostulation or the like addressed to him, cut off his head. And lo and behold! That very moment the dead Brahman boy in distant Ayodhya began to breathe again.

Shambuka has no back-story. Not even a dialogue. When the offending Veda-spouting Shudra is prima facie executed without trial or inquiry, the Brahmin lad comes back to life, and the order of caste is restored.

Ambedkar calls the Vedas 'a worthless set of books'. Hence "UlaT ved kee baaNii", the spoken word hung dry. There are only rules here, no principles, is Ambedkar's fundamental point. Why do Kabir, Ambedkar and the Buddha rubbish the Vedas? It is like asking why they (and we must) oppose the naturalization of inequality.

II

Before we come to the *das* in Ganga Das's name, I have for a while quietly wondered about Kaluram Bamaniya's surname, given that *baaman/ bamman/ bumman* is the casual way in which most people refer to a Brahmin, distinct from the heavy Sanskritic formal highfalutin and imposing *bṛāhman* or the anglicized *Brahmin* that stays close to the Sanskrit. The very sound *brah*—the diacritics may please some baamans—poses the problem, literally and figuratively, of aspiration. This aspiration, this command, this will to power is deflated with the rampant usage of baaman/ bamman/ bumman (it's like *whitey* or *whitie*). *Brh* is a harsh sound, and Kabir joyously mocks such bombast.

The root *brh* primarily means 'to swell, expand, grow, enlarge'. As a bare abstraction, the word *brahmana* makes lofty claims about representing the absolute and all-encompassing. This immense sacrality is at once transferred to and bestowed on the actually existing Brahmin person. A language like Sanskrit is about power, and the Brahmin plants himself at the apex. The *brahman* thus is both the sound and the range of meanings it radiates. It reeks of self-absorption and self-importance. It is an assertion of rank arrogance. The Brahmin's pole position is just as natural as the sun in the Vedic worldview. Brahma, the supreme self-spawned god, and the *brahmana* (Brahmin)—both become eternities. *Brahm* is also an illusion. It also leads to the *Brahmana*, the exegetical ritual texts that offer prose commentary on the Vedic mantras. *Brahmand*, the entirety of the known and unknown multiverse, roots back to this sound. In its very utterance and intonation, the word and its cognates spawn an exclusionary field of sovereignty and supremacy based on absolute and brazen disregard for reason. All this cant—at the heart of which is the belief in inherent inequality—passes for Vedic and Upanishadic philosophy.

Brahmanism simply is the language of the Brahmin. Brahmanism is ideology in its most absolute form. Despite its whimsical will to hierarchy, it stakes claim to universality. And since this claim is based on nothing but the power of words and the skewed desire to call people names, since it is founded on no moral, natural or scientific principle, since it is a piece of fiction that has rather recent beginnings, it can also end. It must not have a future. For there to be no Untouchables and untouchability, for there to be no caste, there must be no Brahmin. This is not an objective proposition. It is a deeply subjective truth. The baby and the bathwater both have to go. The entire house has to be razed. Ambedkar calls it annihilation. For Kabir, this is *ulaT ved*.

All the pride and aggrandizement over a term, where sound and meaning are supposed to resonate in unison, is smashed to nothing in the way bamman or baaman is used in everyday language, *baansaa* or simply *baasaa* that always exists in (and for) itself as a boundless plurality despite efforts to bind it (as *bhaashaa*) with rules of grammar and convention, dos and don'ts. Language as vested among people often aspires to the condition of poetry and music, and it brooks no tyranny. All that the Brahmin-Brahman holds as exalted—starting with *himself*—is brought down. Levelled. But the Brahmin, in his pathetic clamour for superiority, keeps mocking those who don't even care to pronounce brahman correctly. 'Oh they can't even say br̥āhman correctly.' Often, the bumman is trapped in his own design. It is a curse where the accursed one thinks it to be a blessing.

III

I felt too abashed to pick up the phone, call Kaluram ji, and ask him about the Bamaniya part of his name. Since we do make much of names and their associations, I paused at Kaluram. That it means Blackie Ram dawned on me. A shudder without the shuddering. Ram—the word in Sanskrit means dark and is related to the night—by another name would not be just as Ram. Nevertheless, Ram looms here, just as he marks his insidious and insistent presence in Kanshi Ram, Bhimrao Ramji Ambedkar and Jagjivan Ram, all iconic Dalit names. Famously, a Dalit political leader called Ram Raj converted to Buddhism in 2001, got a tonsure, and became Udit Raj (*udit* means the one who has woken). He gave up on Ram, forcefully and formally, only to briefly *serve* a political party that has ruled and rules in the name of Ram. The hold Ram (and its myriad variations and synonyms) has on the 'Indian' imagination is numbing: It is likely the most named name in this part of the world. (Universally, we all have no say in the individual names we are given just as much as pets do not.) What baggage does a name bear? Can a name be a dispensable externality? Is there no end to these low ends?

As we hang such questions dry, we must join Fariduddin Ayaz and sing:

Content with chanting names
He ends up losing the Named
The one who does not labour
Is content with the jabber

All this chant is cant
Ram's name an empty rant
Ram now chants my name
Kabir has changed the game

Kabir sings not of Ram but of No-Ram
Kabir knows no guru, he wishes no-one harm

Names have to be changed if they condemn you to
a stinking generality, consign you to the horrors of
untouchability. Ambedkar tells us why in the essay "**Away
from the Hindus**":

> A rose called by another name would smell as sweet
> would be true if names served no purpose and if people
> instead of depending upon names took the trouble of
> examining each case and formed their opinions and
> attitudes about it on the basis of their examination.
> Unfortunately, names serve a very important purpose.
> They play a great part in social economy. Names are
> symbols. Each name represents association of certain
> ideas and notions about a certain object. It is a label.
> From the label people know what it is. It saves them
> the trouble of examining each case individually and
> determine for themselves whether the ideas and
> notions commonly associated with the object are true.
> … The name 'Untouchable' is a bad name. It repels,
> forbids and stinks. The social attitude of the Hindu
> towards the Untouchable is determined by the very
> name 'Untouchable'.

In this light, what does the second part of the name
Bamaniya connote? Whatever my purposeless purpose, it
would be terrible and unscrupulous to ask Bamaniya what
his caste is. So I become Google Das. I am led to believe
that it is a caste category modelled on the Brahmin but
as a surname and a *gotra* or totemic clan name (*kuTamb-*

kabeela as it appears in Kabir's songs) is found largely among those classed as Shudra or Untouchable. In the Chamar community in Madhya Pradesh, some are also Bamaniya. There's even a village called Bamaniya in Rajasthan. Another site says they are a branch of the Ahir community, herders, and that they do not touch the pipal tree. In the state of Gujarat, officialese lists them among the 'Socially and Educationally Backward Classes' (featuring over two hundred communities); in Madhya Pradesh it is 'Other Backward Class', and there is also 'Bamania Banjara', the second word indicating nomadic status.

Unhappy and unsure of being a slave to Google, I called my friend Bhanwar Meghwanshi, a writer and Ambedkarite activist from Bhilwara, Rajasthan. Bhanwar speculated about what Bamaniya as such might be, but told me to call Kaluram ji without hesitation. So I did. It turned out that my intuitive guess was not wide of the mark. Kaluram's Bamaniyas are a priestly class within the Chamars. 'It started this way among our ancestors. Whenever a Chamar was accused of cow slaughter, he needed a purification rite. Dead cattle and their carcasses had to be disposed by our caste, and I have seen this being done until my father's generation in my family. But sometimes when a cow was suspected to be butchered, our family did a puja to atone for the crime.' The Bamaniyas thus came to be a *jati*, a caste. In his 1916 essay, **"Castes in India"**, Ambedkar calls this the 'infection of imitation'.

Kaluram Bamaniya learnt his Kabir from his father and grandfather. 'My Dada would drink up, eat meat, tune the tambura [drone] and belt out Kabir and nirguni songs. Today, I have given up on meat and alcohol. In some of the programmes I attend, Brahmins with names like Trivedi

Chaturvedi Sharma gorge on the meat, suck on the marrow. It's an odd turnaround.' Yet, Kaluram remains a Chamar and the Trivedis Chaturvedis Sharmas (and Anands) do not lose caste privileges as such.

While baaman or bamman sets out as a radical rupture in the language of the Brahmin, it comes to suffer a career in caste as Bamaniya. We turn and return to Ambedkar again:

> The Untouchable who adopts the new name as a protective discolouration finds that the new name does not help and that in the course of relentless questionings he is, so to say, run down to earth and made to disclose that he is an Untouchable. The concealment makes him the victim of greater anger than his original voluntary disclosure would have done.

Ambedkar is speaking from experience here. After his doctorate from Columbia University in New York and time spent at London School of Economics, when he returns to India to work in Baroda in 1916, he is forced to conceal his Untouchable status while renting a room at an inn. The lie gets him through nine horrible days, and every day he is unfailingly reminded not of his splendorous accomplishments but his inescapable untouchability. When the truth of his caste is discovered by the keepers of the Parsi-run inn, he is humiliated, called *names*, and evicted.

If digging into Brahmin, Bamman, Bamania makes for a sad tale, turn sad around, and you land yourself with Das, which starts its career as the very antonym of the Brahmin or a Bamania.

Kabir is who Kabir is. But, over time, some devotees turned him into Kabir Das. He came to be repackaged as a

Vaishnavite bhakta. Bestowed with the attribute of servitude by both Brahmin and non-Brahmin mythographers, he is made to call himself a Das in song after hit song—a Great Slave (or Great Servant), even if only to an inexistent god (insistently and tiresomely called Ram). In many songs featured in this book, often sung by Dalits, he is Das Kabir or Kabir Das. His bitter pill apparently gets a sugar-coating when false humility (surrender to the very god he denounces) is infused into his name, Kabir, which means great. (With such songs, I tend to substitute the Das with Boss, just like Ram sometimes makes way for Bhim, the slayer of gods.)

Just like with Brahmin, the root of *dasa* too can be traced back to the *Rig Veda*. In all, four Vedas were composed over time by a committee of lineage-flaunting matted-haired **beef-eating** male poets riding a high and writing hymns to violence and warfare that are at once metaphoric and real. The Vedic corpus, often referred to singularly as Veda, becomes a moving body of 'knowledge' vested only in the bodies of Brahmin men, or men who certified themselves Brahmin, men who recited these literary and liturgical productions ritually. The *Rig Veda* contains verses composed in Vedic or proto-Sanskrit (the root *krit* means action, to *make*, it is the verb of doing; *Sanskrit* means something 'put together, well-formed, perfected'). The most exhaustive, annotated three-volume edition of the *Rig Veda* is translated and edited by **Stephanie Jamison and Joel Brereton**. The 1028 hymns here, divided into ten mandalas (literally circles), adhere to the rigours of metre and prosody, are rich in guttural accents, stresses and agglutinative morphemes (where the form or sound of a word is modified and influenced by the form or sound of an adjacent word, *sandhi* in Sanskrit), and are set in a grammar and structure that have fascinated minds devoted solely to the business of thinking the world with words. There's also the thickening and thinning of language demanded by poetry. The verse-making revels in layers of obscurity, flights of fancy and a penchant for quibbling. They are often written in a code we are not even meant to get. The oldest of the Vedas, the *Rig Veda*, which means the Praise of the Veda or the Praise of Knowledge, is an anthology dated to around 1300–1500 BCE, making it a pre–Iron Age text. There was **no script**. A script could have meant the risk of letting this 'sacred' language loose among the undeserving masses, the possibility of its secret becoming known. This knowledge must not be known. And the Vedas revel in speaking of knowing the unknown. Language was knowledge relayed as sound, revealing one meant revealing the other. According to the scholarship industry around the Veda, the *Rig Veda* came to be committed to script only around the third century BCE. This perhaps owed to the challenges and contentions posed by the emergence of Buddhism and other *shramanic* modes of knowledge open to all.

At the heart of all this knowing and knowledge is the Brahmin himself, the vile poet who reviles and classifies most of humanity, and spends his time and intellect in formulating metrical-mystical diktats that seek to snuff out the human personality, both of the Brahmin and the many subjects of his spite. Everything and everyone are at a distance from the Brahmin. And the *Rig Veda*, the Praise of Knowledge, places the Dasyus at the farthest end of the sliding scale of hierarchies, calling them 'savages' who have no laws, different observances, are *akarman* (who do not perform rites) and who act against a person without knowing the person. In **Ralph Griffith**'s 1896 translation (RV 10.22.8):

अकर्मा दस्युरभि नो अमन्तुरन्यव्रतो अमानुषः
त्वं तस्यामित्रहन्वधर्दासस्य दम्भय

akarmaa *dasyu*rabhi no amanturanyavrato amaanushah
tvam tasyaamitrahanvadhardaasasya dambhaya

Around us is the Dasyu, riteless, void of sense,
                              inhuman, keeping alien laws
Baffle, thou Slayer of the foe, the weapon which
                              this Dasa wields.

Jamison and Brereton render this as: 'The Dasyu of non-deeds, of non-thought, the non-man whose commandments are other, is against us/ You smasher of non-allies, humble the weapon of this Dasa.'

Whence names such as Ganga Das, Gareeb Das and so on. Das, in fact, has come to be a common surname in large parts of the subcontinent, up to the southern tip. Christianity in India took lovingly to the term, since it meant a servant of either god, Jesus or some saint. Hence, we have Yesudas, Xavier Das, Anthony Dasan and so on. Mohandas Gandhi, a Baniya, has Das in his name (meaning, servant of Mohan, one of Krishna's many names). There's the famous poet Surdas, a slave to *sur*, musicality. There's the even more famous Narendra Damodardas Modi (Damodar is Krishna). Even those who claim to be

Brahmins in eastern India take to Das. Some elite non-Brahmins take to Dasgupta. Romanized variants include Doss and Dass. Just as baaman is turned into Bamaniya, the defiant Dasyus who are hated for wreaking havoc on the Brahmanical practice of yagna, are turned over time into keepers of caste and upholders of vile ritual. Caste keeps returning to us, each time changing its name and face, wearing a sly grin. So we must keep at it before we end up with a Bamman Das. Just as Kabir keeps at it, taking now the form of Kaluram Bamaniya:

> The earth is but a roti and the foolish crow flies with it
> It sits on the branch of an ism, chewing more
> > than it has bit

And Bhim Das, enjoined from joining this procession, is now scheming his own appropriation, peddling old songs as new. Anon anon.

जय भीम
The chant of Bhim

The chantless chant
The enchantment Bhim

The nameless name
Speaking its name Bhim

The lightless light
The enlightenment Bhim

The momentless moment
In the momentum Bhim

The unthought thought
The one often not Bhim

There's no One but one
And you are the one Bhim

Formness and formless
Such peerless oneness Bhim

No bamman no das
You ended the farce Bhim

वो अजपा जप	vo ajapaa japa
वो अचंभा भीम	vo achambhaa bheem
वो अनाम नाम	vo anaam naam
बोले अपना नाम भीम	boley apnaa naam bheem
वो ज्योत अजोत	vo jyot ajot
और वो प्रबोध भीम	aur vo prabodh bheem
वो पल बेपल	vo pal bepal
चले अचल भीम	chale achal bheem
वो सोच असोच	vo soch asoch
जो होत न होत भीम	jo hot na hot bheem
वो कोई नहीं बस एक	vo koii naheen bas ek
अनेक में तू एक भीम	anek mein tuu ek bheem
वो गुणभरी निगुण	vo guNabharee niguN
सुन सहज की धुन भीम	sun sahaj kee dhun
सुन सहज की धुन भीम	sunn sahaj kee dhun bheem
सुन सुन की धुन भीम	sun sunn kee dhun bheem
ना बामन ना दास	naa baaman naa daas
सब है बकवास भीम	sab hai bakwaas bheem

Would Kabir sing 'Jai Bhim' today? The question was posed in the "Interjection" that *The Notbook* opens with. Kabir today writes in English, I claimed. This is the answer (and a few others follow).

The distance between *sun/* सुन—the imperative 'listen'—and *sunn/* सुन्न—the void of sunnya—is a delicate and delectable blur in Kabiri bani. Very rarely do sound and meaning pulling in their contraposed directions brush so close past each other, creating a sibilant hush as two consonants are held by a vowel. Yet, what the English does is beyond Hindi's reach. The true poem is the one that lies between both. Where does one begin, where does zero end? Which is the original, which the translation? If it can be answered merely by saying which came first, language would end. Yet, here's a song that without these extraneous notes can be read (not misread) equally as a poem in the bhakti mould where the unsung is sung. Each reading, rather singing-listening, can be different. If you pay attention to the lyric, it's a chantless chant, a poem that turns against itself. When I sing it, the words, charged with music, graze against each other, and meaning shape-shifts. Ambiguity is at the heart of this song: It leaves you open to many readings, listenings and singings.

Consider the lines वो कोई नहीं बस एक/ अनेक में तू एक भीम (*vo koii naheen bas ek/ anek me tuu ek bheem*) that work differently in English. I thought 'no One but one' did the trick, hearkening to the *shahaada* (*laa ilaaha illallaah*). But in the split line, the *one* is at once democratized, lowered in case, made every*one*. In the singing, reiteration makes this idea both forceful and mellow. That's the Ambedkarite pulse and impulse. And yes, if you heed Kabir, who appears to heed the Buddha, he will tell you that in the sunless, moonless, starless, dayless, nightless no-place where we must go, and where he has been, even the shabad (flesh-made-Word-made-song) of Kabir cannot go.

The serious handicap English suffers is that I don't (yet) sing in it comfortably (the more vowel-heavy languages of South Asia suit the raga framework better). The raga Miyan ki Todi wraps the words (and the lyric is not exactly 'Hindi' but Kabiri) in ways I cannot unsay. I could say that language *1* (One) came in hindsight, so to say, but the foresight of language *0* (Zero) was informed by anticipating the attack from the hind. Which came first? Which second? Who cares when both languages are satisfying each other.

All I ask of you is you
सतगुरु मोरी चूक संभारो

सतगुरु मोरी चूक संभारो
हौं आधीन हीन मति मोरी चरनन ते जो ना टारो
    सतगुरु मोरी चूक संभारो
मन कठोर कछु कहा ना माने बहु वाको कहि मैं हारो
    सतगुरु मोरी चूक संभारो
तुमही ते सब होत गुसांई याको वेग संवारो
    सतगुरु मोरी चूक संभारो
अब दीजे संगत सतगुरु की जावे होय निसतारो
    सतगुरु मोरी चूक संभारो
और सकल संगी सब बिसरे होऊ तुम एक प्यारो
    सतगुरु मोरी चूक संभारो
कर देख्यो हित सारे जगत से मिल्योन कोउ पुनि सहारो
    सतगुरु मोरी चूक संभारो
कहे कबीर सुनो प्रभु मेरे भवसगर से हो तारो
    सतगुरु मोरी चूक संभारो

sataguru moree chook sambhaaro

haun aadheen heen mati moree charanan te jo naa Taaro
    sataguru moree chook sambhaaro

man kaThor kachhu kahaa naa maane bahu vaako kahi main haaro
    sataguru moree chook sambhaaro

tumahee te sab hot gusaanii yaako veg sanvaaro
    sataguru moree chook sambhaaro

ab deeje sangat sataguru kee jaave hoy nisataaro
    sataguru moree chook sambhaaro

aur sakal sangee sab bisare houu tum ek pyaaro
    sataguru moree chook sambhaaro

kar dekhyo hit saare jagat se milyon kou puni sahaaro
    sataguru moree chook sambhaaro

kahe kabeer suno prabhu mere bhavasagar se ho taaro
    sataguru moree chook sambhaaro

O teacher beyond doubt, make me right
O guru who knows best, make me bright
O love of no falsehood, make me true
    O teacher beyond doubt, make me new

I'm given to folly, I'm witless
May it be at your feet that I know touch
I've been laid low, I'm weak, I'm feckless
    O garu beyond doubt, more me less

The mind is brash, it has ears for no one
You give it song but it will not listen
Pride rides a high horse, come rein it in
    O garu ji who's true, be my friend

Take me whole, put this restlessness to rest
O knower of all secrets, I'm your test
O doer of good, give me your best
    O teacher beyond doubt, bring me brightness

The point where all points meet, see my point
Teach me stillness in this moving world
Read me the book of life, word by word
    O guru who knows best, make me good

Everyone has moved on, leaving me to you
You have the world at your feet, I've only you
I'm done asking, all I ask of you is you
    O teacher who knows best, make me true

Why such languor when you see me flounder?
O sweet lord, pull me out of this sea of doubt
Kabir is down, Kabir is out, shut him up, get him now
    One true rugu, best of best, I'm your true test

In the spoken and sung tongue, guru is also *gura*, and sometimes *garu* (in Pali). Garu, with the respectful suffix, becomes garu ji. (The Buddha is called, among other things, a *lokagaru*, the teacher of the world.) *Rugu* is a word to come.

I found "Sataguru morii chook sambhaaro" in Linda Hess's *Singing Emptiness* but had not heard Kumar Gandharva ji (or any ji) sing it. I made the words for it in English a day after I set it to the raga Bhimpalasi in 2017 in Ranikhet (see "In what is stolen and in what is found", p.144)—and I have tinkered with the words over the years. My understanding of the complexities of self-abjection in this song has been renewed, revised and refined each time I find myself singing it, especially after I came to find my guru, rugu, garu, satguru, the true guru, the love of Ustad Faiyaz Wasifuddin Dagar, a twentieth-generation musician of the largely abstract dhrupad form of classical raga music. We found one another in June 2018.

Now, a belated word about bhakti and my unease with it, which is the same as my vexation with caste and hierarchy-seeking Hinduism. As such, it is an idea to consider. Bhakti is meant to convey devotional love for a personal god experienced without the mediation of a priest/ guru (read Brahmin) or ritual. The seed of this idea was sown in the southern part of the subcontinent in Tamil with the song-poetry of the (Vaishnavite) *alwars* and (Saivite) *nayanars* from the seventh to tenth centuries who followed the earlier tradition of love (often erotic) poetry of the two-millennia old Sangam era but replaced the lover, patron and king with god. Often, the songmakers were from the working castes. By the twelfth century, this style of speech-as-song found its way into the Kannada world as the vachana movement. A vachana is remembered speech, word, promise, poem, song. It is a form of speaking in rhymed metrical verse in Kannada, a movement in which a range of working caste poets, men and women, took part.

The poet and translator **A.K. Ramanujan** writes: 'The poets were not bards or pundits in a court but men and women speaking to men and women. They were of every class, caste and trade; some were outcastes, some illiterate. Vachanas are literature, but not merely literary.'

It was more than that. Not all poetry may be about doing politics, but vachana poetry in the Kannada-speaking cultural geography of twelfth-century Deccan, was definitely political. The watchman Talavara Kamideva, the farmer Okkalu Maddayya, the ferryman Ambigara Chaudayya, the ropemaker Nuliya Chandayya, the pancake-seller Pittavve, the rice-gleaner Aydakki Lakamma, the steward Bokkasada Sanganna, the cobbler Madara Dhoolaiah, the washerman Madivala Machayya, the comb-maker Mahadevi, the prostitute Sule Sakkavve and so on—each of them composed and sang vachana poetry. The ruler made poems, the physician made poems, the parasol-holder made poems and the wreath-maker made poems. Even brahmins made poems. Basava, the most celebrated and iconic of the vachana poets, a brahmin by birth and the prime minister of the Bijjala kingdom, traces his lineage to the poets from different castes who paved the way for him (even as he forgets to name any mother, lovers, sisters or aunts):

My father's Chennaiah the tanner
My grandpa's Kakkaiah the weaver
My brother's Brahmaiah the balladeer
My beloved's Chikkaiah the herder
I find god in these trysting rivers

The first vachana poet was the leather-worker known as Madara Chennaiah. Which is to say we may do well in heeding the poets and artists among the unlettered and underpaid working men and women, the 'migrant labour', who subsidize middle-class leisure.

In the vachana tradition, physical labour was called *kaayaka*—that which involved the body, *kaaya*. Happily, this involves sex and hence an obsession with the god's/ beloved's body as well, of which the vachanakaras Allamaprabhu and Mahadeviakka or Akammadevi (among others) unabashedly write. The sensual was spiritual. Much of vachana poetry is beautiful love poetry even if many speak of detachment from the body. Anyone who surrenders to these free-floating ideas by either making such poetry or by listening to it, thus experiencing the universal language that's born of labour, was called a *sharana*: the one that has surrendered. Both the poets and the community of poetry they forged were sharanas. It was a civil rights movement as much as a literary one.

The sharana movement offered labour as poetry, and poetry as labour. Word made flesh. Speech born of labour became the new universal that the poets both constituted and surrendered to. Madara Dhoolaiah, whose caste as a leather-worker prefixes his name, asserts his identity only to transcend it. His tools of labour enter his poems. Here, in **H.S. Shivaprakash**'s translation in *I Keep Vigil of Rudra: The Vachanas*, with words sharpened on his chisel and anvil, he tells god to go do his job, his work, his labour:

On seeing the great godhead
Appear on the edge of the chisel
Piercing the hide—

'Why are you here, sir
In front of the one that moves about
Carrying the bag of flesh?
Go, go away
To the dwelling places of your devotees
Free them
Go on to the top of your silver mountain,
With your masquerades
Go free your devotees.
By the grace of the master of lust, dust and smoke
Go and prosper.'

What is god's work? 'Go free your devotees.' It is the bhaktas, whether then or now, who need to be freed from the clutches of unreason and hate. When Dhoolaiah shows god the door, is he religious? Or is he a rationalist? Another vachanakara, Adaiah, as if replying to Dhoolaiah—the vachanakaras were often in dialogue and critiqued each other in poetry—talks of the need to 'transcend the web of similes', the need to free ourselves from 'the thick paste of similes and non-similes'. Adaiah also bemoans those who 'make similes with similes' and those who 'come into being through similes'. Fellow-poet Siddharama goes a step further, saying that the very making of a vachana goes against the vachana spirit. He says the vachana experience is something that is not spoken about, for it is a truth that is unspeakable, but when Siddharama sings-speaks-shares his experience, when he renders it as a vachana, in words that also imply a promise, he transgresses his own rule, he negates what he affirms, he affirms the unaffirmable. Speaking of the form of the formless, you arrive at the form of the vachana.

"A Gathering of Holy Men of Different Faiths" by Mir Kalan Khan, ca. 1770–75 is likely to be the oldest depiction of Kabir, painted perhaps two hundred years after his time. The Met identifies the figures to the left in the work as Ravidas, Sena, Namdev, Aughar, Kamal, and Kabir (centre with peacock feather on his cap). Trained at the Mughal court, the artist Mir Kalan Khan lived in Lucknow where he became the leading court painter of Shuja' al-Daula (r.1754–75) and Asaf al-Daula (r.1775–98). Source: metmuseum.org

(Just like we see early in *The Notbook* with "Aivee aivee sehaNaa"/ "Freeing freedom from itself", p.39.)

In all, some three hundred poets across caste, class and gender, shook up the twelfth-century Deccan with the reverberations reaching parts of the Tamil country and the nascent language-worlds of Marathi and Telugu. The poets became literary heroes, worthy of love, adoration, respect.

The echoes were felt among the many *varkari* poets who made abhangas in Marathi from the twelfth century on to the seventeenth, with a corpus of poems by the tailor Namdeo, the Brahmin Dnyandeo, his sister Muktaai, the maid Janabai, the farmer-turned-moneylender Tukaram, the prostitute Kanhopatra, the village guard Chokhamela, his wife Soyrabai, their son Karmamela, and many more. Often entire families were involved in the pursuit of poetry.

Bhang means a break. The verse form abhang, or abhanga, means unbroken, absolute, eternal, unending, or simply a poem without a caesura—an exuberant or exalted utterance (quite like the udana attributed to the Buddha we encountered in "In the seen and the unseen", p.116). A varkar is a pilgrim, and the varkari tradition revolves around the god Vithoba or Vitthal/ Vitthala/ Pandurang/ Panduranga in Pandharpur (by the Bhima river in today's Solapur district, Maharashtra). *Vari* is the annual pilgrimage that is undertaken by the devout, who on their way to see Vitthal sing the song-poetry of the sants who have both praised and upbraided him. In popular lore, Vitthal has come to be regarded as a form of Krishna and this tradition is seen as Vaishnavite: all post-facto definitions and labels that suit the needs of those who have the power to define. The varkari cult inaugurates the Marathi literary tradition, according to most scholars. Vitthal could have had origins in Saivism or Buddhism, but more importantly among pastoral and nomadic tribes. Over centuries we see the Sanskritization, Vedicization and Vishnu-ization of Vitthal. According to the anti-caste scholar **Gail Omvedt**, the deity, who oddly has his arms akimbo, could have been originally female ('wide hips, narrow waist, busty, long hair, straight though harsh face'). Poets who have sung his praises often address him as 'Mother'.

From the fifteenth century, this idea of a god unmediated by a priest or guru, spread to the working-class poets of the northern region: Raidas the tanner, Kabir the weaver, Gora the potter, Savata the gardener, and so on. Like Ramanujan says, a fuse was lit. Bhakti became post-facto pan-Indian generalization, created by the nineteenth–twentieth century nationalistic project mostly, and it contained a multitude of distinct idioms. There are scholars and historians who do not see this omnibus bhakti phenomenon as really 'anti-Vedic'. They think it ultimately performs the function of incorporating the non-Brahmin, non-Aryan population into the Vedic hierarchy.

Often those regarded the most ideal bhaktas or devotees have a radical edge that gets blunted by history. We are asked to see how despite being Untouchable and not being allowed to enter the temple or behold the god they sing praises of, such bhaktas were beholden to the deity. One attentive scholar of the Marathi bhakti movement, **Jayant Lele**, advocates the art of suspecting and listening to the symbols simultaneously. Bearing this in mind, let us turn briefly to Chokhamela, the fourteenth-century Marathi poet of the Untouchable Mahar caste. Gandhi and his ilk saw him as the perfect 'harijan', the child of god: The ideal suffering pilgrim who will never make it but shall not lose faith, singing of the lord in matchless metre and peerless rhyme. In contrast, **Ambedkar dismisses Chokhamela** and most bhakti saints for not forcefully questioning the order of chaturvarna. According to him, this gave the Brahmins one more reason to silence or coopt Dalits demanding equal treatment. They could tell the Dalits, 'We will respect you when you become bhakts like Chokhamela.' While top-ranked musicians like Kumar Gandharva, Kishori Amonkar, Bhimsen Joshi, Jitendra Abhisheki and others were happy to sing abhangs in their concerts to draw in the crowds, the Dalit Panthers in the 1970s, led by the iconoclastic literary icons Namdeo Dhasal, Raja Dhale and J.V. Pawar, shared Ambedkar's distaste for what they perceived as an abject, submissive surrender. Yet, we have songs by Chokhamela that must have needed immense courage and conviction on his part to sing to an unheeding audience, for whom he was forced to toil, and from whom he was forced to beg for leftovers. Here's **Abhang 283** (in my translation), where he curses all gods and scriptures:

वेदासी विटाळ शास्त्रासी विटाळ
पुराणें अमंगळ विटाळांची
जीवासी विटाळ शिवासी विटाळ
काया अमंगळ विटाळाची
ब्रह्मिया विटाळ विष्णुसी विटाळ
शंकरा विटाळ अमंगळ
जन्मतां विटाळ मरतां विटाळ
चोखा म्हणे विटाळ आदिअंती

vedaasee viTaaL saastraasee viTaaL
puraanen amangaL viTaaLaanchee
jivaasee viTaaL shivaasee viTaaL
kaayaa amangaL viTaaLaanchee
brahmiyaa viTaaL vishnusee viTaaL
sankaraa viTaaL amangaL
janmataam viTaaL marataam viTaaL
chokhaa mhane viTaaL aadi-antee

Vedas are tainted, shastras tainted
Puranas are tainted, so tainted
The self is a taint, the spirit tainted
The body is a taint, soul tainted
Brahma is a taint, Vishnu tainted
Shankara a taint among the tainted
Birth is a taint, death is tainted
Says Chokha, taint to taint tainted

In this damning abhang that no savarna musician sings, Chokha, as he signs himself, uncannily prefigures both Kabir's downside-up idea of ulaT ved (that we see in the song, "In the bustling market, stand empty"), and Ambedkar's views in *Annihilation of Caste*. In this 1936 undelivered speech, which his reform-minded Arya Samaj hosts found 'unbearable', Ambedkar says without ambiguity: 'If you wish to bring about a breach in the system, then you have got to apply the dynamite to the Vedas and the shastras, which deny any part to reason; to the Vedas and shastras, which deny any part to morality. You must destroy the religion of the shrutis and the smritis. Nothing else will avail.'

Now picture Chokha in his town Mangalvedha (in modern-day Solapur district), a bhikkhu of a kind at a time when Buddhism was fighting for survival, singing this early in the morning and begging for leftovers, and the effect it had on his savarna benefactors. There was neither dynamite nor a suit-clad Ambedkar then. However, even at his radical best, Chokha remains tainted. Moving beyond the binary of tainted and untainted, Chokha chooses one side. He says all is tainted, from beginning to end, from the Absolute (brahman) to the lowliest (that is Chokha himself). This is very dialectical, and reaches a truth. Ambedkar, then, is the bhang—the break—from this mode of thinking. His idea of annihilation of caste means freedom: from tainting or being tainted. We may fittingly add a coda to Chokha's abhang:

Baba is the bhang, nothing's tainted
Unning taint, he's attained it

Today, the official, dominant narrative is that the presiding deity at Pandharpur, Vitthal (known also as Pandurang, Vitthu and Vitthoba), is a Vishnu/ Krishna figure. Chokhamela, in his time, may well have witnessed the earliest days of the deity's conversion from a Buddhist to Vishnuized figure. Ambedkar contends that Vitthal was none other than Buddha. **Dhananjay Keer**, in his biography *Dr Babasaheb Ambedkar: Life and Mission*, reports a speech in Pune in 1954 where Ambedkar

told the gathering of 20,000 men and women that he was writing a book on Buddhism explaining its tenets in simple language to the common man. A year might be needed to complete the book: on its completion he would embrace Buddhism. Ambedkar also told his audience that the image of the god Vithoba at Pandharpur was in reality the image of the Buddha. He *intended writing* a thesis on the subject, and after completing it, he would read it before the Bharatiya Itihas Sanshodhan Mandal at Poona. The name of the god Pandurang, he observed, was derived from Pundalik. Pundalik meant lotus, and a lotus was called Pandurang in Pali. So Pandurang was none other than the Buddha.

Raised by a father, who Ambedkar says (in an unpublished essay, **"Who is Pandurang?"**) was 'like a Roman patriarch, desirous of exercising in the most rigorous manner his *patria potestas* on his children,' Ambedkar grew up learning and reciting Marathi abhangs:

> I was at one time a student of the classical Marathi literature and had to read the writings of Dnyaneshwar, Eknath, Mukteswar, Namdeo, Tukaram, Shridhar Swami and Moropant. ... My father who was a Kabirpanthi had made the reading of their works compulsory and I could not take my daily food without the fulfilment of this obligation. This compulsory routine continued till my father's death. I therefore *grew up as a youth with a deep spirituality* very seldom to be found among my contemporaries.

This means Ambedkar was raised on good poetry that was regarded as sacred literature. In his adulthood, despite having declared in **Yeola in 1935** that 'I will not die as a person who calls himself a Hindu!', Ambedkar dedicates

Who is Pandurang?

I ~~have been~~ at one time a a student of ~~marathi~~ the classical marathi literature and had had to read the writings of Dyaneshwar, Eknath, Mukteshwar, Namdev, Tukaram, ~~and~~ Janardan Shridhar swami, Moro path and even the lavanis of Nam Joshi. ~~the reading of these works was more~~ by my father who was a Kabirpanthi had made the reading of these works compulsory and I could not take my daily food without ~~a reading~~ the

A photograph taken in 2013 of the first page of Ambedkar's unpublished undated essay "Who is Pandurang?" from the collection of Ramesh Tukaram Shinde, archivist, Mumbai.

his important work of 1948, *The Untouchables: Who were they and why they became Untouchable?* to 'Nandnar, Ravidas, Chokhamela—three renowned saints who were born among the Untouchables and who by their piety and virtue won the esteem of all.' There's something irresistible here even for Ambedkar who turns his face away from all forms of Hinduism, including the seemingly protestant bhakti mode that involves two kinds of hero worship—the worship of god with the charged words of the poet, and the consequent worship of such a poet.

How these figures *appear* to us surely affects and alters our perception, and we are all creatures of perception. Raidas the tanner is often seen with his anvil even when in a sadhu's robes; Kabir is always beatific with his loom; and Namdev the calico printer/ tailor and his cohorts with an *ektara* or a tanpura are lost in song. All of them survive attempts on their life by kings and Brahmins. Chokhamela dies doing 'Mahar work', while repairing the wall of Mangalvedhe, a town near Pandharpur, when it collapses, burying him and the other Mahar workmen alive. The virtuous and pietistic iconography of all the sant-poets, Namdev to Chokha, Kabir to Mira, were imagined first in the 'nationalist' period, quite like Raja Ravi Verma's oleographs made up many Hindu gods. Like the scholar **Parita Mukta** shows in her work, not just their images, the words of these poets were edited and adapted to service Brahmanism, patriarchy and nationalism. A Mira bhajan that 'hit at the very raw nerve of widowhood' by using the word *randavu* (prostitution) was edited by Gandhi at his ashram, says Mukta in "Mirabai in Rajasthan", an essay in the now-defunct journal *Manushi*. Mira, for him, was a 'paramount satyagrahi'. All references to widowhood in the song were expunged since Gandhi's message to widows was: 'Look upon your widowhood as sacred and live a life worthy of it,' similar to his message to the scavenging castes to do their work with love and selflessness. He had a fetish for spiritualizing inequality and for this he became a saint.

While Gandhi in his fifties sought to desexualize free-spirited women, at the age of twenty-five, Ambedkar, in a seminar paper simply called "Castes in India", delivered at an anthropological seminar in Columbia University, New York, in 1916, spoke of how enforced widowhood and child marriage formed the bedrock of the caste system, solutions likely devised by Brahmin men to deal with 'surplus women'. Around the same time, in 1919, Gandhi commissioned the artist Kanu Desai to offer for posterity a series of images of a docile, domesticated Mira, each image eventually calendarized and reproduced a billion times, creating the definitive cinematic image-text of a bowdlerized *Mira* (1945) played by an intensely wooden M.S. Subbulakshmi, feeding into distorted conceptions of woman as supplicant, dancer-singer, pliable lover. Such re-packaging of both words and images happened with all the rebel sant-poets (with 'Hindu nationalist' cinema playing a key role). And yet the radical core of a Kabir or Mira has survived through Dalit performative traditions and in cultural memory insomuch as we know these stories.

II

I have often zealously and joyously sought secular this-worldly alternatives to words like 'Ram', 'Allah' and the fictive-real guru. It is not that I wish to misrepresent or mislead myself or the reader, however informed. On the contrary, my desire is to walk myself (and you) on a path mere words cannot convey. It is a desire to capture the active secularization of a spiritual experience that the artists who sing these song-poems effect in the moment of their singing (what is called 'Suprematism' or 'the supremacy of pure feeling' in the case of the art of the Russian, **Kazimir Malevich**, 1879–1935).

Before returning to the song that has triggered this excursive exercise, let us consider other invocations of and offerings to the guru figure in the songs featured in this book. Mukhtiyar Ali, a Kabiri and Sufi singer of international renown, prefaces his version of Kabir's "Jheenii chadariyaa" ("A fabric so fine", p.79) with this epigraph:

गुरु गोविंद दोऊ खड़े किसके लागूं पांव
बलिहारी गुरु देवन की मने गोविंद दियो बताए

guru govind doou khaDe kiske laagoon paanv
balihaaree guru devan kee maney govind diyo bataae

An earnest meaning-fixated exercise in fidelity would be:

I come face to face with guru and god
At whose feet should I be prostrate?
It is the guru I choose to adulate
For he'd take me towards the lord

Is the guru turned towards god? The guru himself is turned into god. The antigod Kabir becomes a guru, a little god.

The idea of prostrating before a nameless or big-named guru, the actual physical act of abjection and self-abasement for the sake of acquiring any kind of knowledge or initiation into a path, is rather commonplace in South Asia. The word guru has come to mean 'venerable, worthy of honour'. Literally, it means 'heavy, weighty', deriving from the PIE root *gwere-*, meaning gravity, looping to *gravis* in Latin. In ayurveda, it is used for substances that are heavy, and its opposite is *laghu* (light). In Sanskrit prosody, syllables in a *pada* (a sung poem) are classified as metrically short or laghu (light) when a syllable contains a short vowel, or long or guru (heavy) for syllables with a long vowel or diphthong.

But the path of the guru—teacher–preceptor, and most of all, 'the living embodiment of the spiritual truth professed by the sect and thus identified with the deity' as the editors of **Encyclopaedia Britannica** have it—is not for everyone. Those belonging to Untouchable and Shudra communities, and in most cases, all women, are excluded from these portals of formal knowledge. At the outset of *Annihilation of Caste*, 'Speech Prepared for the 1936 Annual Conference of the Jat-Pat-Todak Mandal of Lahore But Not Delivered', as he was to wryly state on the cover of the tract, Ambedkar reminds the self-styled reformists who run the 'Forum for Annihilation of Caste':

The [Jat-Pat-Todak] Mandal may be asked to explain why it has disobeyed the shastric injunction in selecting the president. According to the shastras, the Brahmin is appointed to be the guru for the three varnas. वर्णानाम् ब्राह्मणो गुरु: is a direction of the shastras. The Mandal therefore knows from whom a Hindu should take his lessons and from whom he should not. The shastras do not permit a Hindu to accept anyone as his guru merely because he is well versed. This is made very clear by Ramdas, a Brahmin saint from Maharashtra, who is alleged to have inspired Shivaji to establish a Hindu Raj. In his *Dasbodh*, a socio-politico-religious treatise in Marathi verse, Ramdas asks, addressing the Hindus, can we accept an *antyaja* [last-born, meaning an Untouchable] to be our guru because he is a pandit (i.e., learned)? He gives an answer in the negative.

The Sanskrit injunction Ambedkar cites, 'varNaanaam braahmaNo guru', is from *Manusmriti* chapter 10 verse 3. It means, among varnas, the Brahmin is the teacher/ preceptor. **Georg Bühler's 1886 translation**, that Ambedkar often consulted, renders the entire couplet as follows: 'On account of his pre-eminence, on account of the superiority of his origin, on account of his observance of (particular) restrictive rules, and on account of his particular sanctification the Brahmana is the lord of (all) castes (varna).'

But knowledge and learning, love and enlightenment, like life, are always unbound and boundless. They do not heed the diktats of some *Manusmriti*. For life itself is equality.

While the idea of touching the feet of the elderly and of 'learned men' is seen more intensely among the castes that will themselves to be held high, any guru, even a Dalit guru, comes to expect a seeker to touch his feet. For, it could be equally seen as an affront—oh, you wouldn't touch my feet because I am Dalit? (Mayawati as the Dalit chief minister of Uttar Pradesh getting Brahmins and Savarnas to bow to her and touch her feet is an instance where a historical wrong is symbolically righted, albeit in a perverse display of secular power.) Going down on all fours or even a symbolic half-bow is read as an act of total surrender, of one's ego, one's sense of self—all for the sake of esoteric gyaan/ knowledge from a guru. Obsequiousness is turned into art. The student is seen not as a student but as a *disciple*. Often a professional singer of most traditional genres of art in the subcontinent is asked: Who's your guru? If you don't have a ready answer, you could be suspect. Like the scholar Katherine Butler Schofield says in her book, *Music and Musicians in Late Mughal India* (2024), 'lineage is everything in Hindustani music, and musicians are nothing without it'.

In our times, we do know that the guru figures—in yoga, music, dance, sport, cinema, religious and spiritual affairs, universities and offices—turn out to be habitual abusers of power who are often accused of demanding sex of their students. This, to be fair, is only one aspect of the abuse of power. We could add to this: the crippling of intellect, the demand for servility, the pursuit of the pure, the accusations of infidelity, the deliberate stunting of students. Often, all this is seen as *seva*, or service; the experiential performative loss of individuality (of the sense of self) and the surrender of ego at the 'lotus feet' of the Guru/ Sir/ Teacher/ Master/ Ustad, in exchange for the gain of *gyaan*, the teaching. Such service comes to be seen as a blessing in the valorized Brahmanical gurukul tradition that places the guru above god. An old popular mantra that equates the guru with the trinity of gods, Brahma, Vishnu and Maheshwara, declares: गुरु साक्षात परब्रह्म/ guru saakshaat parabrahma, meaning, the guru is verily god. These ideas about the supreme and divinely ordained dominance of the guru dominate a range of pedagogical practices, even in secular settings like state-run spaces. In Indian universities, it is common for professors, especially supervisors of PhDs, to expect their wards to attend to household chores and other menial work. The rewards, if any, are material: commendations leading to opportunities and jobs, and the future ability to perpetuate the system. The same is the case in sports where coaches, managers and those in power expect favours of all kind.

Exceptions galore, because to excel without help is human, but the norms are such as they are. This is also not to say the guru–*chela* (teacher–disciple) relation has not produced wonders. It can be as liberatory as oppressive. Love can and does happen between an initiate and a master. The many poems sung here testify to the splendorous intensities of this heightened experience, which is a part-real part-realized part-imaginary participation in an idealized convention. Yet the whole idea of feet-touching, and the field of exclusions and the power structures it creates, makes me deeply uncomfortable (even where abuse of such power is not involved). It puts the Ambedkarite Kabir in me ill at ease. Crucially, it does not *sit* with the ideas at the heart of Kabir's thinking. Kabir speaks of finding one's inner guru (just as often rendered garu and garu ji in songs such as "Ber chalyaa merey bhaii"/ "Easy like a song", p.286, harking back to a Buddhist usage) by finding the guru—a teachable moment—in everything around us. The more politically charged Kabiri idea would be a total exit from this binary—to make a clean break, annihilate all hierarchies, and declare equality. Why this is easier said, we will see. For now, I choose to read Mukhtiyar Ali's lines like this:

Love and god are what I face:
Tell me whom I must embrace?
It is to love that I surrender
For love will render me to the maker

Mukhtiyar Ali, who sings them, was born into the Mirasi community, considered Untouchable. Listening to him sing, this or anything, you realize he has been touched and awakened by something that resides within him, not outside. He owes no one any debt. No god, no guru. Yet obeisance to the guru-god is offered unbidden. All this begs the question: Who was Kabir's guru, if there was one? Would the injunction Ambedkar warns us about—वर्णानाम ब्राह्मणो गुरु:/ varNaanaam braahmaNo guru/ 'Among varnas, the Brahmin is the teacher/ preceptor'—have been upheld more keenly in the fifteenth–sixteenth century?

The songs specifically addressed to the guru in this book could make a significant number—I've not counted. And unfailingly, the guru comes for habitual-ritual praise. I sing a good number of these songs for the guru, proclaiming that true knowledge is not possible without a satguru, a true guru, who is no one but god. Such a guru is at once real and metaphoric.

Human desire is often couched in the language of bhakti in the subcontinent, sanctified by the mention of some god or human guru who is equal to god, a bow to convention. In most pursuits of art, across Hindus and Muslims, the veneration of a guru-teacher-pir is celebrated. An idea associated with the Sufis, *fanaa*—to pass away, to perish, be destroyed, be united with the beloved who is god, be finished—comes to infuse bhakti. Ghalib offers a beautiful couplet to this idea of fanaa:

इशरत-ए-क़तरा है दरिया में फ़ना हो जाना
दर्द का हद से गुज़रना है दवा हो जाना

ishrat-e-kataraa hai dariyaa mein fanaa ho jaanaa
dard kaa had se guzarnaa hai davaa ho jaanaa

The drop delights in being effaced by the sea
When pain crosses a threshold, it becomes relief

Kabir, who sees guru in the ant and in the dew on the thorn, is yet subjected to a fixed nameable guru, Ramanand. This guru, at once fictitious and historical, is more imagined than real. Scholars like **Charlotte Vaudeville** say that this guru fiction happens not just with Kabir but with most subaltern literary-cultural figures. Each bhakti poet does this when she or he speaks of love, and love is what they almost always speak of. With this burden of history, can one aspire for a secularized bhakti experience? Or is it like the philosopher **Slavoj Žižek** would say: 'On today's market, we find a whole series of products deprived of their malignant property: coffee without caffeine, cream without fat, beer without alcohol... virtual sex as sex without sex.' Is this doing a **Coleman Barks on Rumi**—the American conceit of engaging with Rumi without Islam? If you consider the tyranny of the Brahmin guru, liberation from this thrall has to be imagined as well as realized.

In formal history-writing—comic books to textbooks to scholarly tomes—the guru fiction becomes a way of containing and assimilating the indomitable spirit of a genius who transcends time. For the prototypical genius of Ekalavya, Drona was imagined as a guru. What are the chances that a forest-dwelling archer of the Nishada community had to learn archery from an urban Brahmin teacher straying into the forest with his high-born pupils, the five Pandava princes? Would his own community not excel in a skill so essential to forest life in the mythic time the story is set in? Why would Ekalavya need a malevolent preceptor who would anyway not teach him but demand his thumb and snuff out his skill? Why does Ekalavya yield? Why did Ekalavya—even as a character in the Mahabharata—have to idolize a colonizing figure who brutalizes him? Even if Ekalavya learnt from Drona on the sly, why would he not be Caliban and say to his Prospero, 'You taught me language; and my profit on't is I know how to curse'? Why the bloated fiction of supplication to a vile and wily guru, instead of an insurrectionary justice when faced with rank immorality and evil?

For Kabir, a figure like Ramanand was and is imagined—although we hear nothing that is sung today attributed to this straw man. There is not one couplet by Ramanand anyone sings. His contribution to literature is zero; yet he looms. He literally hitches a ride with Kabir and several sainted poets whom he's said to have mentored. The great Rabindranath Tagore, with a desperation that comes from privilege, endorsed the fiction of Ramanand. Hagiographies about Kabir, Ravidas and a host of poet-songsters came to be written (and sung) from the sixteenth century onwards. The Kabir of the spoken word and shared speech spread anyway, and any which way. Nativist scholars ranging from Ramachandra Shukla (Brahmin) in the 1930s till Purushottam Aggarwal (Baniya) and white and Indian scholars in the Western academy like Linda Hess, Vinay Dharwadker, David Lorenzen, John Hawley and a host of others have spent enormous resources and time studying (and translating) the interplay of history, myth, orality, textuality and lived experience, and have dwelt upon whether Ramanand's floruit overlaps with Kabir's, whether Ramanand actually was the so-called reformist Ramanuja who came from the Tamil-speaking south, who instead of eradicating caste said anyone could become a Brahmin. But Ramanuja cannot quite be Ramanand. The pandits also struggle to reconcile the 'Sanskrit' Ramanand with the 'Hindi' Ramanand. They speak of the different

Amar Chitra Katha #55, first issued in 1974, titled *Kabir*, with text by Dolly Rizvi and Anant Pai, art by Umesh Burande.

Kabirs of the 'eastern' and 'western' traditions. All this ado to show nothing.

John Hawley who has walked the field and read all the books and met and heard the many sectarian and non-sectarian believers of Raidas and Kabir, has this to say of the dubious Ramanand (whereas I, a true Kabiri, don't stir from where I am, and jump to conclusions by reciting the wisdom received from Kabir: A dip in the Ganga or Yamuna is not for me/ I'm of earth and all the rivers run through me):

The hilarious story of Kabir's initiation by Ramanand—he *arranged* for the great man literally to stumble over him as he made his way to bathe in the Ganges at dawn—is one of the central motifs of his hagiography. 'Ram!' shouted Ramanand, and Kabir took it as his initiatory mantra. Tagore found Ramanand in one of the poems he translated from the set provided by Kshitimohan Sen, and it reassured him that this guru–pupil connection was a historical fact. But alas, a study of the old manuscripts unearths this poem nowhere, nor is Ramanand's name found in any of the other old poems, as one might have expected if he was so important for Kabir.

This *arranged* image needs some illumination. The picture book version—taught in school textbooks in north India—goes like this. Kabir asks Ramanand to take him as a disciple. He is refused for he is low-born, like Drona refuses Ekalavya. So one day, before the crack of dawn, a young Kabir lies on the steps of one of the ghats to the Ganga where Ramanand comes every day, on a beaten track, for his ritual ablutions. The conceit works. In the dark, Ramanand literally stumbles on Kabir, and the wise man cries out 'Ram Ram'. This one word, repeated—Ram—is deemed to be a mantra bestowed on Kabir. Ram is at once a greeting and a habitual utterance in north India—like oh god or dear god. It slips out as an involuntary reaction to both good and bad. Thus and thus, Kabir is perchance blessed. Damn, his third eye of knowledge is opened. The accidentally solicited touch of the dust of a Brahmin guru's feet—not his hands, not his lips—is at the root of the 'low caste' weaver's wisdom, and the outpouring of songs, known as both shabad and bani, Word and Voice/ Style. This shallow story gathers mass and acceleration and becomes a force with each iteration and reiteration.

Dronas and Ramanands are foisted on and in history, and sometimes even Dalit tellings of such stories in the present partake of the logic. Song after song embraces the broad structure—and rapture—of these traditional retellings, and yet undermines the myth at once. Prahlad Tipaniya, a Dalit singer from the village Luniyakhedi in Malwa, offers us this song—"Saahib ne bhaang pilaayee"— for the sahib, the guru-god, the satguru, who of course is Kabir. Tipaniya invokes the abstraction of a guru who gets him high on love and enlightenment: Here, a subversive metaphor (of bhaang/ cannabis) joyously jostles with the idea of subservience (Brahmin feet grazing a Dalit's head). It is dense and subtle, banal and profound at once.

Turn. Face the page.

My guru got me high
साहिब ने भांग पिलायी

साहिब तमारि साहिबी सब घट रही समाए
ज्यों मेहंदी के पात में लाली लखी नहीं जाए
लाली मेरे लाल की और जित देखूं उत लाल
लाली देखन मैं गयी तो मैं भी हो गयी लाल
साहिब ने भांग पिलायी अंखियों में लालन छायी
पीकर प्याला हुआ दिवाना घौम रहा जैसे मतवाला
जनम जनम का ताला खुल गया
मेरी जोत लगी घट मांही
 साहिब ने भांग पिलायी अंखियों में लालन छायी
झाड़ बिंद और जीव चराचर में
फूल रहा है सांई
तहां देखूं वहां रीता नाहीं
तहां देखूं वहां खाली नाहीं
सब घट रहा समाई
 साहिब ने भांग पिलायी अंखियों में लालन छायी
गुरु रामानंद तुम्हरी बलिहारी
सिर पर ठोकर ऐसी दीनी
साहिब कबीर बक्सीस कर लो
या अगम बाणी गायी
 साहिब ने भांग पिलायी अंखियों में लालन छायी
 कबीर ने भांग पिलायी अंखियों में लालन छायी

saahib tamaari saahibee sab ghaT rahee samaae
jyon mehendi ke paat mein laalee lakhee naheen jaae

laalee mere laal kee aur jit dekhoon ut laal
laalee dekhan main gayee toh main bhee ho gayee laal

saahib ne bhaang pilaayee akhiyon me laalan chhaayee
peekar pyaala huaa divaanaa ghaum rahaa jaise matavaalaa
janam janam kaa taalaa khul gayaa
merey jot lagee ghaT maanhee
      saahib ne bhaang pilaayee ankhiyon mein laalan chhaayee

jhaaD bind aur jeev charaachar mein
phool rahaa hai saanyee
tahaan dekhoon vahaan reetaa naaheen
tahaan dekhoon vahaan khaalee naaheen
sab ghaT rahaa samaaee
      saahib ne bhaang pilaayee ankhiyon mein laalan chhaayee

guru raamaanand tumharee balihaaree
sir par Thokar aisee deenii
saahib kabeer baksees kar lo
ya agam baaNii gaayee
      kabeer ne bhaang pilaayee ankhiyon mein laalan chhaayee

My lord, your majesty is everywhere
It floods every shore, it's here, it's there
The henna looks green
Its remnant redness unseen
Your love is the only harness
It comes bearing a red redness

The redness of my love has spread
Wherever I turn it is red
When I went to see my beloved
I was coloured the same red

The guru has got me high on cannabis
He has shown me the path to bliss
My eyes have turned rose-red
This the truelove of my beloved
    He got me high on his brew
    He's my love, my true guru

Just a cupful and it's gone to my head
Dancing with joy, I paint the town red
All the locks of my life have been broken
A lamp has been lit, I've awoken
    The guru has got me high on cannabis
    I'm singing the song of bliss

In water and on land, in all forms of life
My beloved blooms and a redness is rife
Wherever I see there's no end in sight
This love keeps me up day and night
    The guru has got me high
    Now I laugh and now I cry

Guru Ramanand, you did the right thing
It's your kick to my head that got me going
Do accept my small thanksgiving
This wordless word, this song of awakening
    Kabir has got me high on his brew
    He's my love, my true guru

Prahlad Tipaniya—a teetotaller—inserts Kabir into this schema as the guru. Bhaang is just a metaphor it seems, and we can take that with a pinch of the good stuff. Crucially, there's no talk of revenge against a wicked ungiving guru who lacks benevolence. He is forgiven, he is incorporated, appropriated, renewed, transformed, and born again, blessed by the kind of love and shelter Kabir and his community of song-poetry offer.

I choose to read the retention of the Ramanand story radically: 'It's your kick to my head that got me going'. For herein lies the dialectic of knowledge. The rejection by Ramanand creates the consciousness of a more universal, emancipatory subject. It is the unfortunate experience of untouchability that elicits the most profound Ambedkarite concept of Dalit subjectivity—the norm of equality. Quite like capitalism evokes the revolutionary subject of the proletariat. Lenin: 'The Capitalists will sell us the rope with which we will hang them.'

Kabir or Ambedkar would not wish to hang their caste or class enemies though. They would rather transform the 'enemy', and burn the rope. So a graceless Brahmin-guru is saved from the disgrace he visits upon himself. He is at once destroyed, renewed and rescued. Such is the grace of the fabric of equality. It wraps everyone in its folds.

The master of light and shade
गुरुजी जहां बैठूं वहां छाया जी

गुरुजी जहां बैठूं वहां छाया जी
सोहि तो मालक म्हारी नजराना/ नजरां आया जी

गेरा गेरा झाड़ झाड़ी शीतल छाया म्हारा हो
हम सतगुरु बैठन/ देखन आया जी
सोहि तो मालक म्हारी नजरां आया जी
       गुरुजी गुरुजी
       गुरुजी जहां बैठूं वहां छाया जी
कुम्हारया जो घर से कलस्या मंगाया म्हाने
म्हारे सतगुरु जी ने भेंट चढ़ाया जी
सोहि तो मालक म्हारी नजरां आया जी
       गुरुजी गुरुजी
       गुरुजी जहां बैठूं वहां छाया जी
तन भर ताला सबद भर कुंजी म्हाने सतगुरु जी ने खोल बताया जी
सोहि तो मालक म्हारी नजरां आया जी
       गुरुजी गुरुजी
       गुरुजी जहां बैठूं वहां छाया जी
जीव नगर में हाट भराणो म्हारे सतगुरु जी ने सौदे लाया जी
सोहि तो मालक म्हारी नजरां आया जी

गुरुजी गुरुजी

गुरुजी जहां बैठूं वहां छाया जी

दोई कर जोड़ देवानाथ बोल्या म्हाने केसर तिलक चढ़ाया जी

सोहि तो मालक म्हारी नजरां आया जी

गुरुजी गुरुजी

गुरुजी जहां बैठूं वहां छाया जी

gurujee jahaan baiThoon vahaan chhaayaa jee
sohi toh maalak mhaaree najaraanaa/ najaraan aayaa jee

geraa geraa jhaaD jhaaDee sheetal chhaayaa mhaaraa ho
ham sataguru baiThan/ dekhan aayaa jee
sohi toh maalak mhaaree najaraan aayaa jee
    gurujee gurujee
    gurujee jahaan baiThoon vahaan chhaaya jee

kumhaaraya jo ghar se kalasyaa mangaayaa mhaane
mhaare satguru jee ne bhenT chaDhaayaa jee
sohi toh maalak mhaaree najaraan aayaa jee
    gurujee gurujee
    gurujee jahaan baiThoon vahaan chhaayaa jee

tan bhar taalaa sabad bhar kunjee
mhaane sataguru jee ne khol bataayaa jee
sohi toh maalak mhaaree najaraan aayaa jee
    gurujee gurujee
    gurujee jahaan baiThoon vahaan chhaayaa jee

jeev nagar mein haaT bharaaNo
mhaare sataguru jee ne saude laayaa jee
sohi toh maalak mhaaree najaraan aayaa jee

gurujee gurujee
gurujee jahaan baiThoon vahaan chhaayaa jee

doii kar joD devanaath bolyaa
mhaane kesar tilak chaDhaayaa jee
sohi toh maalak mhaaree najaraan aayaa jee
    gurujee gurujee
    gurujee jahaan baiThoon vahaan chhaayaa jee

Master, wherever I sit, a shade tends to me
Master, you're the sight that helps me see
Master, wherever you sit, I find sweet shade
And there my master you bestow your grace

Under the dense weave of green, light condenses
Wearing the garment of light, he enchants the senses
He sits still and teaches stillness becoming still
He stills me, distilling light, willing me to be still
    Master, wherever I sit, a shade tends to me
    And there my master you bestow grace on me

The master bids a potter home to fetch a pot
In it my master fills up an offering of naught
He drinks nothing from it, he gifts us everything
Wearing the garment of light, my master sings
    Master, wherever you sit, I find sweet shade
    And my master you are the sight of my eyes

The body is a city of locks, the key is the word
The master punches into me the song he's heard
The master opens the place beyond locks and keys

He sits still and teaches stillness, the ease of ease
    Master, wherever I sit, a shade tends to me
    And there my master you bestow grace on me

In the city of life, the dazzling market of wares
The master, a radiant radius, delivers the goods with flair
Striking the right bargain, he frees freedom with care
He stills me, distilling light, willing me to be aware
    Master, wherever you sit, sweet shade finds me
    Master, wherever I sit, your gaze tends to me

Hands folded, Devanath says, I'm emblazoned by your blaze
My guru streaks me red, a reddened redness reddens my face
Plugging in earphones, My Ustad locks me in an embrace
Showing me the many ways in, there's no way out, he says
    Master, wherever you sit, there's sweet shade
    Master, wherever I sit, I'm tended by your grace

Master, wherever you sit, I find sweet shade
And there my master you bestow your grace

Into this nirguni song, "Gurujee jahan baiThoon vahaan chhaayaa jee", Kumar Gandharva empties himself. The tune, and the odd–even three–four rupak taal, are in step with another song for the 'beloved guru ji' that beloved Kumar ji sings, featured as "A spotless spot, a spot of you" (p.201). With both these songs, Kumar ji, his own master that he is, walks at an angle with the early morning raga Bhairav, sung to the waking sun, joyously and judiciously inviting other variants of the raga to join the play of light and shade. Devanath—not quite Kabir but someone who can be more Kabir than Kabir while walking this path/ panth—is the signature, offering us the mastery of nothing. After Covid-19 and the lockdowns, Ustad Faiyaz Wasifuddin Dagar taught me and scores of his students 'online'. Wherever I sat, I found sweet shade.

My own god am I
काची छे काया थारी

काची छे काया थारी झूठड़ी छे माया राम
झूठड़ा सा लेख लिखया राम राम राम राम

काची हो कौन घड़ेली थारि काया जी जी जी
  काची छे काया थारी
घट ही में गंगा राम घट ही में यमुना राम
घट ही में तीरथ न्हाया राम राम राम राम
  काची छे काया थारी
घट ही में ताला राम घट ही में कुंजी राम
घट ही में खोलनहारा राम राम राम राम
  काची छे काया थारी
घट ही में अम्बा राम घट ही में अम्बुलि राम
घट ही में चाकनहारा राम राम राम राम
  काची छे काया थारी
मच्छिंदर प्रताप जति गोरख बोले राम राम
समझा सोई नर पाया राम राम राम राम
  काची छे काया थारी

kaachee chhe kaayaa thaaree jhooThaDee chhe maayaa raam
jhooThaDaa saa lekh likhayaa raam raam raam raam

kaachee ho kaun ghaDelee thaaree kaayaa jee jee jee
    kaachee chhe kaayaa thaaree

ghaT hee mein gangaa raam ghaT hee mein yamunaa raam
ghaT hee mein teerath nhaayaa raam raam raam raam
    kaachee chhe kaayaa thaaree

ghaT hee mein taalaa raam ghaT hee mein kunjee raam
ghaT hee mein kholanahaaraa raam raam raam raam
    kaachee chhe kaayaa thaaree

ghaT hee mein ambaa raam ghaT hee mein ambulee raam
ghaT hee mein chaakanahaaraa raam raam raam raam
    kaachee chhe kaayaa thaaree

machhindar prataap jatee gorakh boley raam raam
samajhaa soi nar paayaa raam raam raam raam
    kaachee chhe kaayaa thaaree

Your body is a wet claypot
    even this illusion is not
        by god
Your writing saying
    all writing comes to nothing
        shall come to nothing, oh god
Who made this raw vessel
    so fragile and subtle
        who my god
In this vessel flows the Ganga
    here flows the Jamuna
        I swear on god

I've bathed within this body
    I've been bathed without
        dear god
In this body the lock
    in this body the key
        by the grace of god
And in this body lies the one
    that will break it open
        so help me god
In this body the mango raw
    in this body the mango ripe
        good god
In this body the one who tastes it
    and he's got a taste for himself
        thank god
When Gorakh
    holding everything in nothing, speaks
        it's an act of god
The one who gets this is as boundless as I
    who am my own god
        my own god

I found the lyric for "Kaachee chhe kaayaa thaaree" in Linda Hess's *Singing Emptiness: Kumar Gandharva Performs the Poetry of Kabir*. I have not heard Gandharva or others sing it though. It does not bear Kabir's signature but Gorakh's. The issue of signature, as always, is amenable, and this lyric figures in a modern book that bears Kabir's name. In our frame, Kabir is indeed less an actual person than the aspiration for the nirgun, formless. After I translated this verse, I tuned it in the late-night raga Malkauns in

Ranikhet in 2017. I have since wondered how I manage to sing this lyric with gusto and joy despite my discomfort with the name Ram—the chant and refrain here that I translate as 'god' uttered with many variations (repeated countless times during the singing). Arguably, the song both mocks and celebrates 'Ram'. And Ram, as we are often told by both Kabir singers and scholars, is an allegory. It is not the specific protagonist–god of the epic Ramayana but a term for the abstraction called god. Kabir does mock the fiction of Ram (do turn and return to Fariduddin Ayaz and company's garland of songs offered earlier in this book as "Things that do not know their name", p.64). Why is god then given the burden of a name?

My turn to Kabir—both singing and translating him—has happened parallel to exercises in annotating the writings of B.R. Ambedkar, and working on books that revolve around him. One among these is **"The Riddle of Rama and Krishna"** in *Riddles in Hinduism*, where Ambedkar says Rama is 'no better than a brute'. Recall, Ambedkar was raised by his father, Ramji Sakpal, who had converted to Kabirpanth. Ramji Sakpal's father Maloji Sakpal was a renegade Hindu too, and had embraced the Ramanandi cult—formed around the very guru Ramanand who rejects–kicks Kabir, and is very popular among the subordinated castes of north India since the seventeenth century. Each of the last three generations in Ambedkar's patrilineal ancestry had found their own way and reinvented their relationship to tradition. Each of them converted. But Ambedkar breaks free of all this, of all modes of bhakti, giving up on Hinduism or a version of it by another name. He does not seek surrender to god but a release for all of humanity from this god business, which in various manifestations of Hinduism is also the business of reifying and justifying inequality.

Be that as it may, what is the riddle of Ram in Kabir when Kabir's songs are riddled with Ram? In 2018, ahead of the publication of the annotated edition of Ambedkar's writings on beef and its connection to untouchability (*Beef, Brahmins and Broken Men*), during a singing session, I ended up breaking into a chant of 'Jai Bhim' in the raga Malkauns. The session ended with "Kaachi chhe kaayaa thaaree". When nirgun, or formless abstraction, takes a form, becomes *sagun*, when something is named, politics begins. After an hour-long abstract *alaap*, words and names come into play. The time of timelessness is divided. A beat is set. A rhythm is worked up. I shared my anxieties over the guilty pleasures of going into a late-night trance over 'Ram Ram Ram Ram' in this song, and the inherent inescapable beauty of formulations like Taala Ram, Amba Ram, Ambali Ram and such with my fellow-worker, fellow-annotator and friend Alex. He casually suggested I add Kanshi Ram to this list. Since then, I have strung the name of the founder of the Bahujan Samaj Party to the string of names. I once vainly and quietly (not quite quietly) added Anand Ram to it. 'The past and present wilt—I have fill'd them, emptied them./ And proceed to fill my next fold of the future.'

They call me life
जारो गरव करे सो गिवारा

हीरो नाम ईसांसरो है—ये सांस की कीमत एक एक हीरे के समान है

साध कहे सगराम हाथ में हीरो आयो
दियो मूरख के हाथ बंदे ऐड़ो गंवायो
गमावत गमावत गंवा दिया जद हीरो रहियो एक
आयो हीरां से पारखूं जद रोयो माथो टेक
रोयो माथो टेक ऐड़ा मैं घणै गमाया
साध कहे सगराम हाथ में हीरो आया

जारो गरव करे सो गिवारा
जौबन धन पावना दिन चारा
(अरे) पांच तत्व का बन्या पूतला भीतर भरया भंगारा
ऊपर रंग सुरंग चढ़ाया कारीगर किरतारा

जारो गरव करे सो गिवारा पावना दिन चारा

पशु चाम का बनत पनय्या नौबत बनत नगारा
नर तेरो चाम काम नहीं आवे पड़ जल हो जावे खारा

जारो गरय करे सो गिवारा जौबन धन पावना दिन चारा

दस मस्तक ज्यरे बीस भुजा है बहु पुत्तर परिवारा
ऐसे ऐसे मरद गरद में मिल गये लंकापती सरदारा

जारो गरव करे सो गिवारा जौबन धन पावना दिन चारा

यो संसार ओस को मोती बिन सत लगे नहीं यारा
केहत कबीर सुनो भाई साधो हर भज उतरो पारा

जारो गरव करे सो गिवारा जौबन धन पावना दिन चारा

heero naam eesaansaro hai—ye saans ki keemat ek ek heere ke samaan hai

saadh kahe sagaraam haath mein heero aayo
diyo moorakh ke haath bande aiDo ganvaayo
gamaavat gamaavat ganva diyaa jad heero rahiyo ek
aayo heeraan se paarakhoon jad royo maatho Tek
royo maatho Tek aiDaa main ghaNai gamaayaa
saadh kahe sagaraam haath mein heero aayaa

jaaro garav kare so givaaraa
jauban dhan paavanas din chaaraa
(arey) paanch tatv kaa banyaa pootalaa bheetar bharayaa bhangaaraa
oopara rang surang chaDhaayaa kaareegar kirataaraa
jaaro garav kare so givaaraa jauban dhan paavanaa din chaaraa

pashu chaam kaa banat panayyaa naubat banat nagaaraa
nar tero chaam kaam naheen aave paD jal ho jaave khaaraa
jaaro garav kare so givaaraa jauban dhan paavanaa din chaaraa

das mastak jyare bees bhujaa hai bahu puttar parivaaraa
aise aise marad garad mein mil gaye lankaapatee saradaaraa
jaaro garav kare so givaaraa jauban dhan paavanaa din chaaraa

yo sansaar os ko motee bin sat lage naheen yaaraa
kehat kabeer suno bhaaii saadho har bhaj utaro paaraa
jaaro garav kare so givaaraa jauban dhan paavanaa din chaaraa

The name of this jewel is life
Each breath is worth a diamond

That's a jewel in your hands, says Sagram the wise
Give it to a fool and he'd lose it in a trice

He drops one gem after another till he's left with just one
He weeps, knowing each breath is singular as the sun

O the jewel of a moment is the one slipping away
Sagram's the wise fool who has been this way

O why puff with pride, youth is a fast-footed guest
You're a doll of five elements, a bag made of dust
Painted bright on the outside by the artist who knows best

With the hide of a beast you can make a bag, fashion a drum
Man, your skin's good for nothing, it has no use for anyone

Ten heads and twenty arms, mighty sons and a big clan
He may be the king of Lanka, but he dies like any man

The whole world is a dewdrop but you've an ocean to cross
Says Kabir, the truth of these songs will help you get across

Mukhtiyar Ali sings "Jaaro garav kare so givaaraa" (in
"The Kabir Project"). The signature here is Sagram's, not
Kabir's, yet it is a Kabir song. The jewel of a poem, like
breath, is in everyone. Now mine, now yours.

In the eye of an eye
मुरशिद नैनों बीच नबी है

मुरशिद नैनों बीच नबी है
स्याह सफ़ेद तिलों बिच तारा
अविगत अलख रबी है
मुरशिद नैनों बीच नबी है
नबी है नबी है
    मुरशिद नैनों बीच नबी है
आँखि मढ़े पांखी चमके चमके
पांखी मढ़े द्वारा
तेही द्वारा दूरबीन लगाके लगाके
उतरे भवजल पारा
    मुरशिद नैनों बीच नबी है
    नबी है नबी है
सुन्न सहर में बास हमारा
तहुं सरवंगी जावै
साहेब कबीरा सदा के संगी
सबद महल ले आवै
    मुरशिद नैनों बीच नबी है
    मुरशिद नैनों बीच नबी है

murashid nainon beech nabee hai
syaah safed tilon bich taaraa

avigat alakh rabee hai
murashid nainon beech nabee hai
nabee hai nabee hai
    murashid nainon beech nabee hai

aankhi maddhe paankhee chamake chamake
paankhee maddhe dvaaraa
tehee dvaaraa doorbeen lagaake lagaake
utare bhavajal paaraa
    murashid nainon beech nabee hai

nabee hai nabee hai
sunn sahar me baas hamaaraa
tahun saravangee jaavai
saaheb kabeeraa sadaa ke sangee
sabad mahal le aavai
    murashid nainon beech nabee hai
    murashid nainon beech nabee hai

My master, the prophet, the eye between eyes
In the middle of blacks, between pools of white
The pupil, the eye, my master, the sight
The eye, the master, the pupil, the light
My prophet, the eye of an eye, the third eye
My master an insight lodged in plain sight
Between the two eyes, the prophet, a star in sight
Unseen unknown, the god who eludes sight
The prophet, the opening, the eye of an eye
The shut-eyed sight, the opening, the insight
The opening insight, the closing outsight
    My master, the prophet, the eye between eyes

Between the eyes, a bird, twinkling
In the heart of the bird, a door, beckoning
In the middle of the door, a scope, zooming
Through the eye of the scope, this life, passing
The master, the insight, the sight of seeing
    The eye between eyes, the eye of an eye

The twinkle in the eye of an eye of an eye
My master, the prophet, the eye between eyes
The house of song in the city of emptiness
I'm headed there with all my senses
Kabir and his master are lovers of verse
What they call home is a palace of words
Kabir and Anand are comrades forever
They share a cabin of words, here and after
    My master, the prophet, the eye between eyes

The pupil of the eye, the master of sight
The prophet between the eyes, the inlight
In the twinkle of the eye, a star in plain sight
    My master, the prophet, the eye between eyes

The contemporary Khayal singer Madhup Mudgal finds himself at home in this Kabir song he says he gleaned and gathered from his guru Kumar Gandharva's notebook when the latter was away. An offering not given to his guru is granted to us. 'I set it to music but was not audacious or foolish enough to present it to him,' he tells Shabnam Virmani, who gets the best out of him. Reading this, a friend from Chennai promptly asked, 'Would Kabir have known of telescopes? What's the Hindi for telescope?' It is *door-been*, and in the fifteenth–sixteenth century there's little chance the historical Kabir had encountered one. But that's not the point. I told her trains and airplanes are also found in the living Kabir. Linda Hess, who offers us a song which features a 'rifle-shot' and a 'bullet' that metaphorically effect the Wound of the Word, cites the work of Monika Horstmann in her 2015 *Bodies of Song*:

> The historical point of view … has no meaning for the Kabir devotees; to them Kabir was a seer and therefore … he could, quite naturally, have spoken with Mira or with Gorakhnath. … He could also have foreseen the arrival of rail technology and composed a song where the body is the engine, and the soul–passenger is advised not to lose her ticket.

You don't have to be a devotee or a believer to get this. You just need the love of the Word. And the Word must love you too. You get the word, and the word gets you.

I gather all rapture in me
धुन सुन के

धुन सुन के मनवा मगन हुआ जी

लागी समाधी गुरु चरणा जी अंत सखा दुख दूर हुआ जी
　　धुन सुन के मनवा मगन हुआ जी
सार शबद इक डोरी लागी ते चढ़ हंसा पार हुआ जी
　　धुन सुन के मनवा मगन हुआ जी
शुन्न शिखर पर झालर झलके बरसत अमिरत प्रेम चुआ जी
　　धुन सुन के मनवा मगन हुआ जी
कहे कबीरा सुनो भाई सधो चाख चाख अलमस्त हुआ जी
　　धुन सुन के मनवा मगन हुआ जी

dhun sun ke manavaa magan huaa jee

laagee samaadhee guru charaNaa jee ant sakhaa dukh door huaa jee
　　dhun sun ke manavaa magan huaa jee
saar shabad ik Doree laagee te chaDh hansaa paar huaa jee
　　dhun sun ke manavaa magan huaa jee
shunn shikhar par jhaalar jhalake barasat amirat prem chuaa jee
　　dhun sun ke manavaa magan huaa jee
kahe kabeeraa suno bhaaii sadho chaakh chaakh almast huaa jee
　　dhun sun ke manavaa magan huaa jee

I hear the song and my heart breaks into dance
I hear the song and love lifts me in its arms
I hear the song and float a little above myself
    With my ear to the song, I find bliss

The fell-fall of the sweet hum in my ears
My heart held free by a song, I smile tears

        My being centered on one thing
        My heart caught in the song I sing
        My body tuned to but one sound
        My face turned to but one face
        The sweet thrum of the one I hum
        The turning of zero into the only one

I bury my freedom in the guru's bosom
        Friend, I'm free from every grief
I still my mind by the lotus of the guru's feet
    Friend, I'm free from every grief

        I hear the song and my heart breaks into song
        I hear the song and the arms of love lift me up
        I hear the song and float a little above myself

All words held by one thread
All meaning held in one string
All worlds held by one word

The meaning of all words is tied to one string
    the swan holds it with a deep knowing

The juice of the Word is held in a drop
        the swan drinks it and flies across
All the world is held in one breath
        holding this thread the swan flies to its death

Struck by the song, I don't know head from heel
Struck by the song, I taste victory in defeat
Struck by the song, I fall between meaning and word
Struck by the song, I'm raised by what fells me
Struck by the song, I gather all rapture in me

At the apex of the void, the shimmer of cymbals
        It's raining amrit, it's pouring love
        O it takes but a drop to wash me clean
        It's showering nectar, it's pelting love
        O it takes but a drop to quell my thirst
        It's a storm of sweetness, a flood of love
        O just one wave will take me under

The fell–fall of the sweet hum in my ears
My heart held free by a song, I smile tears
Says Kabir to those who'd listen
        each taste of the song is rhapsody
        each lick of the song gives bliss
        each kiss the taste of the last kiss
        each taste each lick each kiss
        it's bliss it's bliss it's bliss it's bliss

Reading or reciting the five lines of the original poem, sans the refrain, takes less than a minute. But when a singer plumbs the depth of its words, the song's being expands. There's repetition, a chant, a jive, a pulse, an explosion of meanings that comes to mean something after the song ends. I found this lyric in Linda Hess's *Singing Emptiness* but have not come across a Kumar Gandharva recording of it. Seeing this as an invitation, I set this song to the raga Bhairavi over a week in July 2018. One day, as I concluded a session, the opening line that is also the refrain—धुन सुन के मनवा मगन हुआ जी/ *dhun sun ke manavaa magan huaa jee/* With my ear to the song, I found bliss—turned itself around playfully to come to mean this:

मन सुन के धुनवा मगन हुआ जी

man sun ke dhunavaa magan huaa jee

With its ear to my heart, the song got blissed

The sound sound
सूर चराचर छायो

सूर चराचर छायो
एक सूर चराचर छायो

घट घट तुम्बा बना उसीका
ऐसा नाद जगायो
    एक सूर चराचर छायो
तार अखंड अभेद हुए सब
जब यह सूर लगायो
    एक सूर चराचर छायो
ताल काल से रहयो अभाजित
सम से सम समझायो जी
    एक सूर चराचर छायो
किसे सुनाना किसे सुनना
सूर कहाँ से आयो
    एक सूर चराचर छायो
सुनने वाला कोई न था
जब अलख निरंजन गायो जी
    एक सूर चराचर छायो

soor charaachar chhaayo
ek soor charaachar chhaayo

ghaT ghaT tumbaa banaa useekaa
aisaa naad jagaayo
    ek soor charaachar chhaayo
taar akhanD abhed huey sab
jab yah soor lagaayo
    ek soor charaachar chhaayo
taal kaal se rahayo abhaajit
sam se sam samajhaayo jee
    ek soor charaachar chhaayo
kise sunaana kise sunanaa
soor kahaan se aayo
    ek soor charaachar chhaayo
sunne vaalaa koii naa thaa
jab alakh niranjan gaayo jee
    ek soor charaachar chhaayo

sound spreading stillness
the still spread of sound
sound still quivering spreading
sound, still, quivering, spreading
the sound of awareness, wavering
the awareness of sound, spreading
stilled sound, soundstill
sound surrounding sound
sound around sound
one sound all around
sound around sound
sound sound sound
just one sound
just one, sound
    sound, still, quivering, spreading
 one sound

sounding re
sounding
sound
    sound, still, quivering, spreading

every body a gourd
the hollow of resonance
the sonic in every one
a resonant gourd everyone
in every hollow one sound
the sound in everyone
the sound sound
    sound, still, quivering, spreading

strings infinite, each bound in one
strings infinite, each finite
the sound of sounds
when this sound is struck
a symphony of strings
sighing as one
when this sound is struck
when you reach this sound
you're one with sound
the song I sing now
fragrant with silence
a fine sound
one fine sound
a sound sound
    sound, still, quivering, spreading

beat and time can't cleave this sound
it teaches all to be one with all

freed of time and beat, undivided by division
the one dividing one into one with one
the sorrow of life can't wound this sound
the sound that sounds like one in all sound
    sound, still, quivering, spreading
the light that hears sound
the sound that sees light
    sound, still, quivering, spreading

whom do I sing for? what's to listen?
where does this sound come from?
where would such sound go?
this vibe this throb this thrum
    sound, still, quivering, spreading

there was no one to listen
when I became one with one
singing the one without ends
that's in everyone
the sound of sounds
    sound, still, quivering, spreading
    sound, quivering, spreading, still

On listening to Jitendra Abhisheki becoming the sound
that's one with all sound, thanks to Phalguni from
Mumbai sending a YouTube link to "Ek soor charaachar
chhaayo". This is a nirguni song in the Kabiru tradition
that like many does not bear a signature. Abhisheki (1929–
1998) was one of the finest singers of Khayal music of the
twentieth century.

Spot less ness
सम भीम निरंजन न्यारा रे

सम भीम निरंजन न्यारा रे अंजन सकल पसारा रे (भाई)
सम भीम निरंजन न्यारा रे

अंजन उतपत्ति ओ ओंकारा अंजन मांड्या सब बिस्तारा
अंजन ब्रह्म शंकर इन्द अंजन गोपीसंगी गोविन्द रे
सम भीम निरंजन न्यारा रे
अंजन वाणी अंजन वेद अंजन किया नाना भेद
अंजन विद्या पाठ पुराण अंजन फोकट कतही गियान रे
सम भीम निरंजन न्यारा रे
अंजन पाती अंजन देव अंजन की करे अंजन सेव
अंजन नाचे अंजन गावे अंजन भेद अनंत दिखावे रे
सम भीम निरंजन न्यारा रे
अंजन कहौं कहां लग केता दान पुनी तप तीरथ जेता
कहे कबीरा कोई बिरला जागे अंजन छाड़ी निरंजन लागे रे
भीम निरंजन न्यारा रे

~~raam~~ bheem niranjan nyaaraa re anjan sakal pasaara re (bhaaii)
~~raam~~ bheem niranjan nyaaraa re

anjan utapatti o onkaaraa anjan maanDya sab bistaaraa
anjan brahma shankar indh anjan gopeesangi govind re
    ~~raam~~ bheem niranjan nyaaraa re

anjan vaaNii anjan ved anjan kiyaa naanaa bhed
anjan vidyaa paaTh puraaN anjan phokaT katahee giyaan re
    ~~raam~~ bheem niranjan nyaara re

anjan paati anjan dev anjan kee kare anjan sev
anjan naache anjan gaave anjan bhed anant dikhaave re
    ~~raam~~ bheem niranjan nyaaraa re

anjan kahaun kahaan lag ketaa daan punii tap teerath jetaa
kahe kabeeraa koii biralaa jaage anjan chhaaDee niranjan laage re
    bheem niranjan nyaaraa re

Love is a spotless light, all else, my love, is shadow of the eye
The spotless is the subtle spot, you're in the wink of its eye

From this spot all forms rise and unform, it is atom it is om
It is you it is I, the spread before us is shadow of the eye

Creator Preserver Destroyer—the trinity is nonsense
Eye shadow Govind and his million girlfriends

Here even poetry comes to an end, the Vedas make no sense
All distinctions come to nothing, at once subtle and dense

All science is a lie, all history is someone else's story
This parade of wisdom bears the grace of sorcery

All this greenery just colour, god just bestselling fiction
All worship is pretence, rituals mere addiction

In the spot where I dance losing all sense, I'm spotless
Singing the song of songness I become songlessness

How much can be said of nothing without being said
Why fake charity, austerity, pilgrimage—no cheating death

Being endless in the moment, I shine in the spotless spot
Only some get it when Kabir leaves his spot for what is not

I found "Raam niranjan nyaaraa re" in Linda Hess's *Singing Emptiness* but had not heard Kumar Gandharva sing it, so I set it to the morning raga Ahir Bhairav.

Consider the ways in which a proper noun, Ram, can be rendered, reworded, translated, moved from one place to another, carried over, without it ever being Ram or even god (like we saw with "Kaachi chhe kaayaa thaaree"/ "My own god am I", p.262). In time, while singing, I came to substitute 'Ram' (राम) with 'Bhim' (भीम)—converting the song, so to say. Wouldn't Kabir raise a 'Jai Bhim' if he were around now? But that's not even the spot to linger on here, even if every utterance is a matchstrike of meaning. If you listen well, अंजन/ anjan is the one spot, the spotless spot, the one shadow, the one word-sound cluster that dances all through the song-poem imploding with palettes of meanings, melding with every other sound and its echo, teasing every word and its shadow. Notice how this Kabir song forsakes the heavy Sanskrit-leaning formal pompous self-important ज्ञान/ gnyaan and even the slightly respectable ग्यान/ gyaan to offer us some plebeian proletarian working caste गियान/ giyaan. Likewise, the common-tongued Indh/ इन्द and not Indra/ इन्द्र in the third line of the Hindi. Kabir does this with and to every word he strings to a song. He offers us the spoken word, moistened by a million tongues. And he has the last word.

I, eye shadow, pretending to understand, stand under the shadow of the spot that is not.

Easy like a song
बेर चल्या मेरे भाई

बेर चल्या मेरे भाई मगन हुईं बेर चल्या मेरे भाई (अब)
राम [भीम] रे नाम रो गेलो रे पकड़ी छोड़ी नी मूरखाई
    बेर चल्या मेरे भाई

पेहले तो गुरुजी हम जन्म्या पीछे बड़ा भाई
धूम धाम से पिता रे जन्म्या सब से पीछे माई
    बेर चल्या मेरे भाई
पेहले तो गुरुजी दूध जमाई पी छे गाय नो दोई
बछड़ा उनरे रमे पेट मा धुरत बेचता गयी
    बेर चल्या मेरे भाई
कीड़ी चाली सासरे नौ मन सुरमो साथ
हाथी उपरे हाथ में ऊँट लपेटा जाई
    बेर चल्या मेरे भाई
इंडा हता बोलता बछिया बोल्या नाई
कहत कबीर सुण भाई साधो मूरख समझे नांहि
    बेर चल्या मेरे भाई

ber chalyaa merey bhaaii magan hueen ber chalyaa merey bhaaii (ab)
raam [bheem] re naam ro gelo re pakaDee chhoDee nii moorakhaaii
    ber chalyaa merey bhaaii

pehale toh gurujee ham janmyaa peechhe baDaa bhaaii
dhoom dhaam se pitaa re janmyaa sab se peechhe maaii
    ber chalyaa merey bhaaii

pehale toh gurujee doodh jamaaii peechhe gaay no doii
bachhaDaa unare ramey peT maa dhurat bechataa gayee
    ber chalyaa merey bhaaii

keeDee chaalee saasare nau man suramo saath
haathee upare haath mein oonT lapeTaa jaaii
    ber chalyaa merey bhaaii

inDaa hataa bolataa bachhiyaa bolyaa naaii
kahat kabeer suN bhaaii saadho moorakh samajhe naanhi
    ber chalyaa merey bhaaii

Time's flitting fast, my friend
It doesn't begin, it doesn't end
Take joy in the nameless one
Shed your sense of self, it's fun
    Time's flitting fast, my friend

There blows time, come catch its wind
Let it simply blow your mind
Take the name of the nameless one
Step outside your self and it's done
    Time's fast-footing, my friend

First among firsts, I was born first
My elder brother, he came next

My father followed, with drums and trumpets
My mother came last, she's the youngest
      Time's updowning, my friend

First, the guru taught us to set the curd
Then to milk the cow of dreams
The calf in the womb plays with the herd
Off she goes then to sell the cream
      Time's beating time, my friend

Eyes rimmed with tons of lamp-black
An ant sets off after a grand wedding
On its head an elephant is dancing
And a camel's mounted on its back
      Time's marching past, my friend

The child in the womb finds speech
Born, she falls into a deep silence
Says Kabir, this lesson is for one and each
It's not for fools, transcendence
      There's no time to lose, my friend

Transcendence is not for fools? Then what am I doing here?
And you? Why does the popularity of the word 'buddhu',
the fool, antonymously equal and rival the word 'buddha',
the wise and awakened one? Does one actually mean the
other, completing and complementing the other? That we
are all equal to nothing. (Well, that's for another book.)
      It could well be that it, transcendence, is for fools.
Doesn't the song say, in the previous line, that this lesson
is for one and each, which could mean to be wise is to

be a fool? But the truth is we are none the wiser either way. There goes Kabir, and that is no Kabir. So Kabir, says Kabir.

Mahesha Ram's "Ber chalyaa merey bhaaii" had eluded me for years. This a song that underwent a gentle yet forceful conversion when I sang it, with the change of just one key word. The refrain of the original has the cry, 'Cry the name of Ram, shed your foolishness'. In my first draft of 9 May 2020, I had turned Ram into the Nameless One. Somehow, when I learnt to sing it in August 2022, the word–idea–conceit 'Ram' did not sit well on my tongue nor in my ears. The entire song embraces ulaTbansi—an upside-downness, and I had to mar Ram by turning it anew. So the cry 'Ram' underwent a conversion into a cry for the god-slayer Bhim. And adding rhyme to reason, Bhim echoed well with bhaaii, brother, the addressee and object of the song—the listening public. This realization unfolded as I was rehearsing for a performance called "Bhim Gaan" on 14 October 2022 at The Community Library Project in Khirki, Delhi, to commemorate the 66th anniversary of Babasaheb Ambedkar's Day of Decision (to embrace Buddhism formally with half a million followers). Earlier, in "In the bustling market, stand empty" (p.205) and "My own god am I" (p.262), consider how we come to terms with the ubiquitous word Ram, both a god and not.

I am the one, the swarm is me
युगन युगन हम योगी

अवधूता युगन युगन हम योगी
आवै ना जाय मिटै ना कबहूं
सबद अनाहत भोगी
    अवधूता युगन युगन हम योगी
सभी ठौर जमात हमरी
सब ही ठौर पर मेला
हम सब माय सब है हम माय
हम है बहुरी अकेला
    अवधूता युगन युगन हम योगी
हम ही सिद्ध समाधि हम ही
हम मौनी हम बोले
रूप सरुप अरूप दिखा के
हम ही हम तो खेलें
    अवधूता युगन युगन हम योगी
कहे कबीर जो सुनो भाई साधो
नाहीं न कोई इच्छा
अपनी मढ़ी में आप मैं डोलूं
खेलूं सहज स्वेच्छा
    अवधूता युगन युगन हम योगी

avadhootaa yugan yugan ham yogee
aavai naa jaay miTai naa kabahoon
sabad anaahat bhogee
avadhootaa yugan yugan ham yogee

sabhee Thaur jamaat hamaree
sab hee Thaur par melaa
ham sab maay sab hai ham maay
ham hai bahuree akelaa
    avadhootaa yugan yugan ham yogee

ham hee siddh samaadhee ham hee
ham maunii ham boley
roop saroop aroop dikhaa ke
ham hee ham toh khelen
    avadhootaa yugan yugan ham yogee

kahe kabeeraa jo suno bhaii saadho
naaheen naa koii ichchhaa
apanii maDhee mein aap main Doloon
kheloon sahaj svechchhaa
    avadhootaa yugan yugan ham yogee

I'm time's ghost wandering amongst us as us
In every moment momentless and momentous

I'm the breath of time in all times
A migrant peddling easy rhymes

Comings and goings are not me, not one nor zero
The savour of unuttered sound, the void, the echo

I'm in every resistance, at every protest I'm the song
Every throng gathers in me, I'm gathered at every throng

The allness of the world is me, its smallness is me
I am the one, the swarm is me

I am the trance, I am transcendence
I am speech, I am silence

Formness, formless, a different sameness—I dabble in all
This is a game of one, and I'm having a ball

Kabir says, listen up comrades, I swear on my poetry
I signed no book deals, lit-fests are not for me

I sway on the swing of the self, my home my kingdom
Until I may free myself from my freedom

Kumar Gandharva and Vasundhara Komkali breeze through "Avadhootaa yugan yugan ham yogee" with joyous innocence. It is a little too beautiful. I've heard it countless times. Listening to it on a loop during the Covid lockdowns, I heard in it the menace of the momentous and momentless present. I, standing where I am, alone and in a throng, where we all stand now, heeded the words a little differently than the great Gandharva allows for.

In Kabir's time and now, pundits might frown and correct much of what they have seen as a standard form of language (the word 'Hindi' we use today is a sweeping, post-facto generalization like the word 'Hindu' that erases a million different ways of being and knowing). Kabir today would be the one that has been failed at school early, the one made to sweep the yard or clean the toilet by the teacher (Drona–Guru Ramanand) as happens often with Dalit students. He is forced out—'dropout' becoming another word for exclusion.

Yet, language stands at once at the edge and at the dead centre of consciousness in Kabir.

Many among those who are considered a part apart from the very society they serve, 'migrant labourers', know their Kabir. His distichs are popular across the subcontinent. It is not just that 'labourers', those plying donkey-carts or sweeping the streets know their Kabir or nirguni poetry better than university professors, professional musicians and translators, as Comrade Fariduddin Ayaz, the qawwal from Karachi, says in Shabnam Virmani's documentary film *Had Anhad*. It is that they *are* Kabir. Kabir's *boli* is not just the tongue of the people, it is people. He is one, he is all, one in all.

हम सब माय सब है हम माय
हम है बहुरी अकेला

ham sab maay sab hai ham maay
ham hai bahuree akelaa

The allness of the world is me, its smallness is me
I am the one, the swarm is me

Covid or not, he's not working from home. He's out there, wandering. Neither mysterious nor mystical.

I'm an odd bird
हम परदेसी पंछी बाबा

हम परदेसी पंछी बाबा अणी देसरा नाही हो जी
अणी देसरा लोग अचेता पल पल पर पछताई भाई संतो
     अणी देसरा नाही
मुख बिन गाना पग बिन चलना बिन पंख उड जाई हो जी
बिना मोह की सुरत हमारी अनहद मे रम जाई भाई संतो
     अणी देसरा नाही
छाया बैठू अगनी व्यापे धूप अधिक सितलाई हो जी
छाया धूप से सतगुरु न्यारा हम सतगुरु के माहीं भाई संतो
     अणी देसरा नाही
आठो पहर अडग रहे आसन कदे न उतरे साई हो जी
मन पवन दोनो नही पहुंचे उन्ही देस के माही भाई संतो
     अणी देसरा नाही
निरगुण रूप है मेरे दाता सरगुण नाम धराई हो जी
कहे कबीर सुनो भाई साधो साहब है घट माही भाई संतो
     अणी देसरा नाही

ham paradesee panchhee baabaa aNii desaraa naahee ho jee
aNii desaraa log achetaa pal pal par pachhtaaii bhaaii santo
     aNii desaraa naahee

mukh bin gaanaa pag bin chalanaa bin pankh uDa jaaii ho jee
binaa moh kee surat hamaaree anahad mein ram jaaii bhaaii santo
    aNii desaraa naahee

chhaayaa baithoo aganii vyaape dhoop adhik sitalaaii ho jee
chhaayaa dhoop se sataguru nyaaraa ham sataguru ke maahin bhaaii santo
    aNii desaraa naahee

aaTho pahar aDag rahe aasan kade na utare saaii ho jee
man pavan dono nahee pahunche unhee des ke maahee bhaaii santo
    aNii desaraa naahee

niraguNa roop hai mere daataa saraguNa naam dharaaii ho jee
kahe kabeer suno bhaaii saadho saahab hai ghaT maahee bhaaii santo
    aNii desaraa naahee

I'm a bird from nowhere near
I'm here but not from here
People here lack light but burn
They rue and regret at every turn
    Oho I'm a bird flying far from home

Song without mouth, walk without legs
I'm the flight without wings, no less
I'm but one and I'm boundless
It knows no address, my awareness
    Oho I'm a bird singing far from home

A fire rises when I sit in the shade
A chill spreads when I'm in the sun
The true guru isn't bright, doesn't fade

And I bide in my guru, the only one
    Oho I'm a bird flying far from home

Hold your posture, practice and preach
But the good lord always eludes
Where the mind and wind have no reach
That be my country, sing along dudes
    Oho I'm a bird singing far from home

The formless in form is my maker
He takes the form of a guru
Says Kabir, listen up, brother
The lord turns right inside you
    Ohno I'm not a bird from this land
    Aiyo I'm an odd bird from not this span

Sujata, whom I met after this *Notbook* had been submitted to the publisher, asked me casually if I sing "Ham paradesee panchhee baabaa". I said I didn't and wondered why. I heard it afresh, learnt to sing it, and found the words for it. It was set to music by Kumar Gandharva and many of the Malwa singers he had become friends with sang it during his cremation in 1992.

पत्ते एक पेड़ के
Words to a tree

Music expands the breath of song
Love fills the heart with light
The tree knows breeze-kissed space

Keep the eye ready for the sun
Walk in the shade beneath words
Shift the shape of meanings to come

Stand still in the eye of the song
Sleep now in the bed of my ear
Let go of all that draws close

Water remembers it was once air
Earth feels the weight of every seed
These words, for Kabir, leaves to a tree

राग से शबद का साँस फुले
प्यार से मन का जोत जले
पवन को चूम के पेड़ हिले

नज़र जो भान से आन मिले
शबद के छाँव में सैर करे
तत्थ के रूप अरूप सजे

कान के खाट पे सुरत बसे
धुन के नैन में अचल चले
पास जो आवे दूर रखे

पवन रूप जल याद करे
हर बीज का भार भव जो सहे
ये शबद कबीर अनूप कहे

raag se shabad ka saans fhule
pyaar se man kaa jot jale
pavan ko choom ke peD hile

nazar jo bhaan se aan miley
shabad ke chhaanv mein sair kare
tatth ke roop aroop saje

kaan ke khaaT pe surat basey
dhun ke nain mein achal chale
paas jo aave door rakhe

pavan roop jal yaad kare
har beej kaa bhaar bhav jo sahe
ye shabad kabeer anoop kahe

I found this song lying somewhere between Delhi's Neb Sarai and Mehrauli and set it to the raga Bhairav.

The world in a trice
धीरे धीरे रे मना

I

धीरे धीरे रे मना धीरे सब कुछ होय
माली सींचे सौ घड़ा रितु आये फल होय

dheere dheere re manaa dheere sab kuchh hoy
maali seenche sau ghaDaa ritu aaye phal hoy

Take it slow, my love, let love come slowly
A hundred pitchers won't bring spring early

It's slow, a slow unfolding of things that happen
    like the finding of words without reason
The gardener may water the plant too often
    it will fruit only in the right season

II

पोथी पढ़ पढ़ जग मुआ पंडित भया न कोय
ढाई आखर प्रेम का पढ़े सो पंडित होय

pothee paDh paDh jag muaa panDit bhayaa na koy
Dhaaii aakhar prem kaa paDhe so panDit hoy

The rut of reading won't make a pundit
If you can't love, you just won't get it

All the reading in the world can't make a Brahmin wise
The one who can spell love gets the world in a trice

III

बुरा जो देखन मैं चला बुरा न मिल्या कोय
अन्दर खोजा आपणा तो मुझसे बुरा न कोय

buraa jo dekhan main chalaa buraa na milyaa koy
andar khojaa aapaNaa toh mujhse buraa na koy

I went looking for evil, for the detail in the devil
When I searched within, I ceased to cavil

IV

कबीरा ये घर प्रेम का ख़ाला का घर नाहीं
सीस उतारे भुंइया धरो तब पैठे घर माहिं

kabeeraa ye ghar prem kaa khaalaa kaa ghar naaheen
sees utaare bhunyaa dharo tab paiThe ghar maahin

This is the house of love, Kabir, don't saunter
Lower your swollen head and enter

V

बामन से गदह भला आन जात से कुत्ता
मुल्ला से मुर्गा भला रात जगावे सूता

baaman se gadah bhalaa aan jaat se kuttaa
mullaa se murgaa bhalaa raat jagaave sootaa

A donkey's better than a baaman, a dog bests other castes
A rooster's better than a mullah to tell us the night is past

VI

कबीरा खड़ा बाजार में माँगे सब की खैर
ना काऊ से दोसती ना काऊ से बैर

kabeeraa khadaa bazaar mein maange sab kee khair
naa kaau se dosatee naa kaau se bair

Kabir stands at the square, wishing y'all well
He's no one's friend, he bears no one ill-will

VII

कबीरा खड़ा बाजार में लिए लुकाठी हाथ
जो घर फूंके आपनौ चले हमारे साथ

kabeeraa khadaa bazaar mein liye lukaaThee haath
jo ghar phoonke aapano chale hamare saath

Kabir stands at the square, flambeau in hand
Burn your house down first, then join my band

Save for these fragments, I have not paid much attention in
The Notbook to the standalone dohas or couplets credited
to Kabir. They are legion. They often preface many songs,

including several featured in *The Notbook*, and are invoked from memory depending on the singer's mood and disposition. The fifth distich is rendered by the late scholar and friend Gail Omvedt in her work, which I published in 2008, *Seeking Begumpura: The Social Vision of Anticaste Intellectuals*. Her vision, in a way, set me on this course.

देख शेरनी चरवे घास
A tigress chewing grass

There, a tigress chewing grass
Here, a cow relishing steak
What it is is not what it was
There's no meaning here at stake
　　A tigress chewing grass

देख शेरनी चरवे घास
इधर गाय जो चूसे मास
देखा था जो वो नहीं है
मतलब से कुछ भी नहीं है
　　देख शेरनी चरवे घास

dekh shernii charave ghaas
idhar gaay jo choosey maas
dekha jo thaa woh naheen hai
matalab se kuchh bhee naheen hai
　　dekh shernii charve ghaas

iss jangal mein papeel raajaa
(bas) maanus maane aapano khaajaa
raag vahee hal zabaan hamare
aap ho sunn samaan hamare
　　dekh shernii charave ghaas

इस जंगल में पपील राजा
(बस) मानुस माने आपनो खाजा
राग वही है ज़बान हमरे
आप हो सुन्न समान हमरे
　　देख शेरनी चरवे घास

In this forest, the ant is king
Only man thinks he is wise
It is the same song that I sing
I make it mine, I make it nice
    Me and you, equal to nothing

सब ही ठौर पर जमा है मेला
हम सब माय सब है हम माय
हम में सब सब हम माय
हम है बहुरी हम अकेला
    देख शेरनी चरवे घास

The allness of the world is me
The smallness of the world is me
I am the one, the swarm is me
I am gathered at every throng
    A tigress chewing grass

sab hi Thaur par jamaa hai melaa
ham sab maay sab hai ham maay
ham mein sab sab ham maay
ham hai bahuree ham akelaa
    dekh shernii charave ghaasaa

kahe aanand kabeer jee suniye
sabad ye hamare aap bhee raTiye
dekho apane laash fakeeraa
ab kaun hai poora kaun adhauraa
    dekh shernii charave ghaasaa

कहे आनंद कबीर जी सुनिये
सबद ये हमरे आप भी रटिये
देखो अपने लाश फ़कीरा
अब कौन है पूरा कौन अधौरा
    देख शेरनी चरवे घास

Here's Anand asking Kabir
To sing these songs, learn them well
See your own corpse, my fakir
Who sings whose song, you can't tell
    A tigress chewing grass

... everything that has been read here in his name, in the final analysis, is nothing more than a free version and adaptation of a text which probably has little in common with this one and that as far as we can foresee, will be kept back until the very last line, and out of reach ...

José Saramago, *The History of the Siege of Lisbon*

We're trying to find Kabir in words and languages. But Kabir is not wearing the garb of language. Kabir is the name of a theme ... a concept ... who wears different garbs in different places. You can't get Kabir's knowledge from universities, scholars or professors. For that you'll have to go to Kabir himself. You'll have to break free of your shackles and go. To enter his country, you need Kabir's visa. And you'll get it when he decides to give it to you.

Fariduddin Ayaz, interviewed by Shabnam Virmani in the film *Had Anhad*, 2008

Notes on Sources
स्रोत के बारे में

Despite Kabir rubbishing books, and this book rubbishing the idea of gathering Kabir in a *Notbook*, my writing is the sum of my readings. And I read precious little. I devote more time to listening. This book has come from listening. Working as a publisher and editor for twenty years, I have necessarily and always come between the author and the reader—as I have done here with Kabir, the author who authors authors, who's turned me into a poet unlike me.

Here's a list of songs, books, essays, articles, images and other (re)sources that I refer to in *The Notbook*. They are not in alphabetical order but in the sequence in which they appear in the book, where the relevant phrases are highlighted in **semibold**. Here, the corresponding page numbers are provided in square parentheses to loop back to the main text. Those reading paperless will thumb this differently.

Many of the songs I have translated here—those rendered by Mukhtiyar Ali, Fariduddin Ayaz and party, Prahlad Tipaniya, Mahesha Ram, Kaluram Bamaniya and Madhup Mudgal—feature in "The Kabir Project" anchored by Shabnam Virmani.

A first-line YouTube search for most Kabiri songs featured here, many of them not covered by "The Kabir Project", should land you with the singer and the song. You may find versions I have not heard. You will be led to other songs.

To listen to most of the songs featured in the *The Notbook*, go to the playlist on my YouTube channel, Raga N Bhim:

https://t.ly/-VNS2 or click the QR code at the end of this book.

Unless otherwise stated, all etymological references are from Etymonline.com overseen by the self-styled 'sciolist' Douglas Harper.

1. On **takhallus** [p.18] and its origins, the Urdu linguist Rauf Parekh says that it must not be confused with a pseudonym or nom de plume where the writer seeks to conceal his or her identity. 'A poet may use takhallus in the last verse in a ghazal, or any other poetic expression, to refer to him or herself. The practice of taking takhallus began in Iran when some Persian poets felt that their couplets could be plagiarised or attributed to other poets and mentioning their name in poetry would lessen the threat.' However, in the modern period, many female writers in Urdu used the takhallus not to assert their distinctiveness but to conceal their identity owing to social taboos. See his essay, "Ghostwriting, pseudonyms and concealed identities in Urdu literature" in *Dawn*, 10 April 2023. **Bhanita**, literally something spoken or uttered, has a similar charge in Pali and Sanskrit, and it refers to the signature line in a poem.

2. **Roland Barthes** [p.24], "The Death of the Author", in *Images-Music-Text*, trans. Stephen Heath (New York: Hill & Wang, 1977), 142–48.

3. *One Hundred Poems of Kabir* translated by **Rabindranath Tagore** [p.24] appeared in 1915 (London: Macmillan). Evelyn Underhill was credited with assistance and wrote the Introduction, which says: 'It has been based upon the printed Hindi text with Bengali translation of Mr Kshiti Mohan Sen; who has gathered from many sources sometimes from books and manuscripts, sometimes

from the lips of wandering ascetics and minstrels a large collection of poems and hymns to which Kabir's name is attached, and carefully sifted the authentic songs from the many spurious works now attributed to him' (xlii).

4. **Christian Lee Novetzke** [p.26], currently a professor at Washington University, has worked on Namdev, the preeminent thirteenth-century Marathi poet, calico printer/ tailor by occupation, regarded as the founder of the abhang form of song-poetry (along with Jnandev, a Brahmin child prodigy). In his 2008 work, *Religion and Public Memory: A Cultural History of Saint Namdev in India* (New York: Columbia University Press), he devotes a chapter to this idea, saying 'authorial anamnesis' is a 'mnemonic system based on repetition, imitation and similarity' (xiv) which enables 'the recollection of the past through imitation and repetition' (159). Here, authorship becomes 'a process not tied to faithfully preserving a set of songs created by a single author but, rather, of maintaining a performance tradition that involves several kinds of authors operating at once in a chain of anamnesis, of remembering through imitation with variation. ... The later composers used "Nama" [Namdev's signature] in their names in some way, and they wrote on themes and in styles associated with Namdev. There was no attempt to disguise a distinct identity, yet there was no desire to have an entirely separate identity, either' (137–8). Novetzke, who also uses the term 'corporate authorship', concludes that this 'complex, multifaceted and historically interconnected notion of authorship' (138) started sometime in the sixteenth century. We see this happening with Kabir too, well into our times.

5. *Adi Granth*, meaning The First Book [p.28], also known as the *Guru Granth Sahib*, was compiled and edited in 1604 CE by the fifth guru Arjan Dev (1564–1606). Seen

as the embodiment of the wisdom of ten gurus, it is the primary object of worship among the Sikhs. Since Sikhism is an aniconic religion, the wisdom of the gurus, their shabad, their Word, is worshipped. Placed on a *takht* or throne in a gurdwara (literally the door to the wisdom of the gurus), the *Adi Granth* is fanned with a fly-whisk, known as Chaur Sahib (made of yak hair). The holy book features over six thousand hymns, sung in prescribed ragas, including between three and five hundred credited to Kabir, and many to Namdev and Raidas. There are also over a hundred verses by the Punjabi Sufi, Baba Sheikh Farid of the thirteenth century. Despite it being a relatively modern religion, no women poets are featured. To listen to recitations, called *kirtan*, from this book, visit a nearby gurdwara or there's always YouTube.

6. **Linda Hess** [p.28] is a scholar who has been working on Kabir and the bhakti tradition since the 1980s. *Bodies of Song: Kabir Oral Traditions and Performative Worlds in Northern India*, her 2015 work (New York: Oxford University Press), is the culmination of years of engagement with Kabir. Here, Hess sheds her academic persona and becomes a participating observer, coming happily close to her subjects—the Kabir singers of the Malwa region. She often turns those she studies into brothers and friends. The objective of her book is stated elegantly at the outset: 'This book is about Kabir; about oral tradition and the oral-performative lives of texts; about poetry and music; and about communities that coalesce around Kabir, his poetry and music. Widening the lens, we could also say that it is about religion, literature, society and expressive culture in north and central India—particularly in the Malwa region of Madhya Pradesh—in the early twenty-first century, as revealed by the study of Kabir oral traditions' (1). Her

work, read along with Novetzke's ideas around anamnesis, blurs the distance between authentic and inauthentic Kabirs. *The Notbook* also engages with another key book by her, *Singing Emptiness: Kumar Gandharva Performs the Poetry of Kabir* (Kolkata: Seagull, 2009). *Singing Emptiness* throws light on how, where, when and why one of the finest raga musicians of the twentieth century turned to Kabir, and how he arrived at this Kabir through a range of sources. Her book includes prefatory essays, translations of thirty nirguni lyrics, and a CD of five nirgun bhajans rendered by Gandharva at private gatherings. Hess has been working on Kabir since the 1980s and her first book of translations, done with Sukhadeo Singh, *The Bijak of Kabir*, was published in 1983 and reissued in 2002 (New York: Oxford University Press).

7. **"The Kabir Project"** [p.30] was initiated and incubated since 2002 at the Srishti Institute of Art, Design and Technology in Bangalore, and anchored by the filmmaker and singer Shabnam Virmani. Most of the content of this ongoing project, including ten music CDs-cum-books, two 'folk music' videos and four roadshow documentary films called *Kabira Khada Bazaar Mein*, *Had Anhad*, *Chalo Hamara Des* and *Koi Sunta Hai*, are hosted on ajabshahar. com. There's also a dedicated YouTube channel, youtube. com/@Kabirproject-ajabshahar. Both the website and channel are often updated. To view the part where **Kashi Ba** is interviewed and this quote appears in the film *Koi Sunta Hai: Journeys with Kumar and Kabir*, see this four-minute excerpt https://www.youtube.com/watch?v=oMeOg7zPXzA

8. **B.R. Ambedkar's opus *The Buddha and His Dhamma*** [p.43] was first published posthumously in 1957 by Siddharth College, Mumbai. The quotations on **sunnya-**

vad here are taken from pages 240–41 of volume 11 of *Dr Babasaheb Ambedkar:Writings and Speeches* series, known by the acronym BAWS, published by the Education Department of the Maharashtra government. Seventeen volumes of BAWS are available online as PDFs at mea.gov.in/books-writings-of-ambedkar.htm

9. Kumar Gandharva's **prejudice about the Islamic influence** [p.43] on what's come to be called Hindustani music of north India has become almost the default view among several savarna musicians of post-independence India. Gandharva's case has been discussed in passing by Janaki Bakhle in her scholarly work, *Two Men and Music: Nationalism in the Making of an Indian Classical Tradition* (New York: Oxford University Press, 2005, 170). Focusing on the preeminent nationalist figures Vishnu Narayan Bhatkhande (1860–1936) and Vishnu Digambar Paluskar (1872–1931), Bakhle discusses how the emergence of an 'Indian' classical music tradition in the nationalist period reflected colonial and exclusionary practices, particularly the exclusion of Muslims by the Brahmanic elite, and how this occurred despite Muslims being the major practitioners of raga music that was installed as a 'Hindu' national tradition. The late Omkarnath Thakur, Kumar Gandharva, Kishori Amonkar and several eminent singers partook in this view. For an overview of such communalization, see "Music, the Media, and Communal Relations in North India: Past and Present" by Peter L. Manuel (1996, CUNY Academic Works, 119–39). The scholar Katherine Butler Schofield, in what is one of the finest histories of raga music and its rather modern and cosmopolitan evolution, *Music and Musicians in Late Mughal India: Histories of the Ephemeral, 1748–1858* (New Delhi: Cambridge University Press, 2024), shows us how the Hindustani raga idiom emerged out of both the praxis

and the scores of theoretical treatises on music written often by Muslim ustads during the Mughal period. Her work offers a corrective to the standard and foundational textbook narrative led by Bhatkhande who had the biggest influence on modern-day Hindustani music. Bhatkhande dismissed hereditary Muslim ustads as illiterate and ignorant of theory and sought to revive an aesthetic based on 'our old Sanskrit granthas'. Kumar Gandharva, his musical genius and love of Kabir notwithstanding, participated in this Islamophobic narrative.

10. **Eleanor Zelliot** [p.44] is a pioneering American scholar of Ambedkar and the Marathi saint-poets of the medieval period. She was the first to do a PhD on Ambedkar and the movement among the Untouchables of western India that led to his emergence. Her 1969 thesis remained unpublished till 2004 when it was issued by the now-defunct Blumoon Books of Delhi. A revised, edited version was published by me at Navayana in 2013 as *Ambedkar's World: The Making of Babasaheb and the Dalit Movement*. The vows that Ambedkar administered to nearly half a million Dalits on 14 October 1956 are cited from this edition (170).

11. **Ambedkar's** *Riddles in Hinduism: An Exposition to Enlighten the Masses* [p.45] was written in the early 1950s. The manuscript remained unpublished in his lifetime. It was first published in 1987 in volume 4 of the BAWS series. At Navayana, I annotated selections from this work and published it in 2016 with an introduction by the anti-caste intellectual Kancha Ilaiah Shepherd. The quotation here appears on p.56 of the Navayana edition and p.8 of BAWS 4.

12. **Thanissaro Bhikkhu** [p.47], born Geoffrey DeGraff, is an American Buddhist monk. He's known for his translations of the *Dhammapada* and the *Sutta Pitaka*. His works are

available for free online. I have cited his 1994 translation of the Bahiya Sutta from accesstoinsight.org (also available on the updated dhammatalks.org/suttas/KN/Ud/ ud1_10.html).

13. That canonical **Buddhism did not allow for chandalas or women to be bodhisattas** [p.49] has been studied and commented upon by scholars. The pioneering C.A.F. Rhys Davids in her 1901 paper, "Notes on Early Economic Conditions in Northern India" (in *The Journal of the Royal Asiatic Society of Great Britain and Ireland*, 859–88) says the Jataka depicts Kshatriyas, Brahmins and Vaishyas (Savarnas) having meals and learning together, and intermarrying. However, the chandalas are despised. The scholar Y. Krishan in his paper "Buddhism and the Caste System" (*Journal of the International Association of Buddhist Studies*, Vol 9. No. 1, 1986, 71–84), documents the following events in the Jatakas: 'In the Setaketu Jataka (no. 377), brahmana Setaketu, on seeing a candala fears that "the wind, after striking the candala's body, might touch his own body" and thereby pollute him. He calls the candala ill-omened. In the Matanga Jataka (no. 497), Dittha-mangalika, on seeing a candala, says "Bah, I have seen something that brings bad luck" and washes her eyes with scented water. This is repeated in the Citta Sambhutta Jataka (no. 498). In the same Jataka a man describes a candala as "the blot in the blood" (*jatiya doso*). The dwellings of the candalas were outside the towns.' The Orientalist French scholar Eugène Burnouf (1801–1852), in his 1844 work translated by Katia Buffetrille and Donald S. Lopez Jr. as *Introduction to the History of Indian Buddhism* (Chicago: University of Chicago Press, 2010), says of the Buddhist suttas: 'The brahmans are those whose name occurs most often; they figure in almost all the sutras, and their superiority over the

other castes is always uncontested' (168–9). In Lalitavistara Sutra of Mahayana Buddhism dated to the third century CE, it is explicitly said that 'bodhisattvas are not born into the womb of abject families, like those of the candalas, of flute players, of cart makers, and of the puskasas. There are only two races into which they are born, the race of the brahmans and that of the ksatriyas. When it is principally to the brahmans that the world shows respect, it is in a family of brahmans that bodhisattvas descend to earth. When, on the contrary, it is principally to the ksatriyas that the world shows respect, then they are born into a family of ksatriyas. Today, O monks, the ksatriyas obtain all the respect of the people: it is for this that bodhisattvas are born among the ksatriyas' (173). Ambedkar of course rejects all this and formulates a new Buddhism by writing a new book toward the end of his life (*The Buddha and His Dhamma*, 1957) where he rejects the stories that 'do not appeal to reason', stopping often to ask, 'Do they form part of the original teachings of the Buddha?' (13–4). Rejecting texts and stories often written three to five hundred years after Siddhartha Gautama's passing, he contends that the Buddha 'was the strongest opponent of caste and the earliest and staunchest upholder of equality' and 'there is no argument in favour of caste and inequality which he [Buddha] did not refute' (301–2).

14. **David Lorenzen** [p.103] is an American scholar of bhakti, religion and South Asian history, and the author of, among several books, *Praises to a Formless God: Nirguni Texts from North India* (New York: SUNY Press, 1996). The cited passage is from p.6.

15. The Pali text of the **Tittha Sutta** [p.117], listed as *Jaccandhavaggo, 6-4: Pathamananatitthiyasuttam (54)*, "The First Discourse about the Various Sectarians", is sourced

from ancient-buddhist-texts.net/Texts-and-Translations/ Udana/6-Jaccandhavaggo-04.htm. The text of the Buddha's discourse, 'Monks, the wanderers of other sects are blind and eyeless…' is from Thanissaro Bhikkhu's translation accessed from dhammatalks.org

16. **William Rockhill's** [p.118] *Udanavarga: Collection of Verses from the Buddhist Canon* was first published in 1883 (London: Trübner and Co) and accessed from archive.org. The quotation is from the Introduction (vii–viii).

17. **Fa-Hsien's** [p.119] *A Record of Buddhistic Kingdoms* has been accessed from archive.org

18. The etymology of *Tittha/ teertha* has been accessed from wisdomlib.org

19. **Farrukh Dhondy** [p.122], *Rumi: A New Translation of Selected Poems* (Delhi: Harper Perennial, 2011).

20. The idea of how the Persian alphabet is used to make sense of the elephant is obtained from **E.H. Whinfield's** 1898 translation [p.122] accessed from sacred-texts.com/isl/ masnavi/msn03.htm

21. **"Buddha or Karl Marx"** [p.128] is the speech given by Ambedkar at the fourth general conference of the World Fellowship of Buddhists in Kathmandu on 15 November 1956, three weeks before he died. It features in BAWS 3 (1987). The quotation is from p.452.

22. The **many recensions of the Tittha Sutta** [p.118] verse listed here are taken from ancient-buddhist-texts. net/Buddhist-Texts/C2-Udana-Parallels/Udana-Parallels-6.htm

23. *Finding My Way* [p.139], a large format hardback with expansive artwork in colour was published in 2016 in two editions—a trade edition was issued by Juggernaut, and a limited collector's edition by Navayana. Both editions are

out of print. In 2019, a new graphic edition, sans colour, was published as *Ganja–Mahua Chronicles*, by Navayana.

24. The story of the **flautist T. Viswanathan** [p.164] citing **Venkatamakhin**'s *Chaturdandiprakashika* is retold by V.N. Muthukumar and M.V. Ramana (2002) with the title "Kalyani" in Rajan Parrikar's online music archive, accessible at parrikar.org/carnatic/kalyani/. The primary source is T. Viswanathan, *Raga Alapana in South Indian Music* (Ph.D. dissertation, Wesleyan University, 1974).

25. **"Waiting for a Visa"** [p.176] is the title Ambedkar gave to a set of six 'illustrations' (as he called them) covering a period of twenty years (1917 to 1938). In a short preface, he says that this text is meant for 'foreigners' to understand the nature and scope of untouchability. Running to about ten thousand words, it was first published in English in 1990, and appeared again in the BAWS series in Volume 12 (663–91) in 1993, with this brief editorial note by Vasant Moon: 'Here are some of the reminiscences drawn by Dr Ambedkar in his own handwriting. The MSS traced in the collection of the People's Education Society were published by the society as a booklet on 19th March 1990.—ed.' Some of these incidents had been recounted by Ambedkar at various public meetings during his lifetime and had been reported at length in the newspaper *Janata* (which he founded in 1929) in the issue dated 23 May 1936. At Navayana, one of the first books in 2003 was a reissue of this text with the title *Ambedkar: Autobiographical Notes*. In 2010, this was reimagined as a graphic book, *Bhimayana: Experiences of Untouchability*, with Durgabai Vyam and Subhash Vyam's art.

26. Published in 2001, **Raghava R. Menon**'s [p.188] slender work, simply called *Kumar Gandharva*, has been out of print for years. It is more a work of appreciation of the

musical persona than a biography. Earlier made available as a Word document on arvindguptatoys.com, it can now also be accessed at archive.org/details/KumarGandharva-English-RaghavaR.Menon

27. The *Gautama Dharma Sutra* [p.208] is cited here from the edition that Ambedkar consulted in his scholarly expositions: Georg Bühler's *The Sacred Laws of the Aryas: As Taught in the Schools of Apastamba, Gautama, Vasishtha and Baudhayana* (New York: The Christian Literature Company). First published in 1879, it is available on archive.org.

28. **Ambedkar's narration of how Rama murders Shambuka** [p.209] is from "The Riddle of Rama and Krishna" in *Riddles in Hinduism.*This is from p.332 of BAWS 4 (1987), and p.231 of Navayana's annotated edition discussed in Note 11.

29. According to the biography written by Ashok Gopal (*A Part Apart: The Life and Thought of B.R. Ambedkar*, New Delhi: Navayana, 2023), Ambedkar is believed to have written **"Away from the Hindus"** [p.214] in 1936 soon after *Annihilation of Caste* was published on 15 May 1936. The essay remained unpublished in his life. It features in BAWS 5 (1989, 403–21) as a chapter under the same title. The quotation here is from p.419.

30. Ambedkar's **"Castes in India: Their Mechanism, Genesis and Development"** [p.215] was first presented on 9 May 1916 at a seminar on 'primitive versus modern society' organized by Alexander Goldenweiser, lecturer of anthropology at Columbia University. Ambedkar, twenty-five then, speculated on the origins of caste. Seeing caste primarily as a divisive force, he argued that it was more as a 'System of Castes', where alongside endogamy (marrying within a clan or community), exogamy (marrying outside)

also played its part. A slightly modified version of the paper was published in *Indian Antiquary* in Mumbai in May 1917. This version is reproduced in BAWS 1 (1979, 3–21). Despite it being a pioneering work of scholarship, generations of Indian sociologists and historians did not engage with it or with other works by Ambedkar. It is only since the 1990s, after Dalits made some inroads into academia, that some of Ambedkar's works are taught and discussed.

31. On **beef-eating** [p.217] being almost the norm for the Vedic brahmans, see the historian D.N. Jha's classic work *The Myth of the Holy Cow* (New Delhi: Navayana 2009). Jha, however, does not engage with or acknowledge Ambedkar who makes similar points in his 1948 work, *The Untouchables: Who Were They and Why They Became Untouchable*. At Navayana, in 2019, we published selections from *The Untouchables* as *Beef, Brahmins, and Broken Men: An Annotated Critical Selection from "The Untouchables"* with an introduction by Kancha Ilaiah Shepherd. It was co-published by Columbia University Press.

32. See **Stephanie Jamison and Joel Brereton**: [p.217] *The Rigveda: The Earliest Religious Poetry of India, Vol. 1, 2 and 3* (New York: Oxford University Press, 2014). Here's a telling passage: 'Beginning with the Vedic prose texts, one of the most enduring mythological structures is the perpetual conflict between Devas (deva being the Sanskrit word for "god") and Asuras, with the two (almost) balanced groups contending with each other in numerous myths and myth fragments in all sorts of situations. The Asuras are, as it were, the anti-Devas, with negative traits exactly corresponding to the positive ones possessed by the Devas. In the various combats depicted, the Devas always prevail, but only barely. This conflict continues to be prominent in the post-Vedic religious landscape, as in the well-known

story of the churning of the ocean of milk in which the two moieties fight over the treasures churned up' (37).

33. Jamison and Brereton (2014) underscore the centrality of memorization rather than commiting the Rig Veda to a **script** [p.218]: 'Up to the creation of the recensions of the *Rig Veda* and long afterward, the transmission of the *Rig Veda* was oral. At some point, however, the Rig Vedic schools did produce **manuscripts** of the text. It is difficult to say when this occurred, but the transmission of the text likely remained exclusively oral at least until around 1000 CE.The oldest manuscript in the collection of the Bhandarkar Oriental Research Institute collection dates only to 1464; the Sampurnanand Sanskrit University in Varanasi has an older *Rig Veda* manuscript from the fourteenth century—thus a gap of considerably over two millennia between the fixation of the text and our earliest written evidence for it. Even when these activities did begin to occur, copying and preserving manuscripts never displaced memorization of the text as the primary means of transmission of the *Rig Veda* until quite modern times' (18).

34. **Ralph Griffith's** [p.219] translation of the *Rig Veda*, which Ambedkar also cited, can be accessed as an e-text at sacred-texts.com/hin/rigveda/index.htm. The citation I have used, to illustrate **dasa** and **dasyu**, is from Book X, verse 22 on the Vedic god Indra.

35. **A.K. Ramanujan** [p.229] writes this in his prefatory note (p.12) in *Speaking of Siva* (Harmondsworth: Penguin, 1972), his translation of a selection of vachanas from Kannada. It remains in print as a Penguin Classic.

36. **H.S. Shivaprakash's** [p.230] translation *I Keep Vigil of Rudra: The Vachanas* (New Delhi: Penguin, 2010), although lacking lyricism, is far more inclusive and expansive than

Ramanujan's. He makes a conscious effort to feature Dalit and women poets. The vachana by Madara Dhoolaiah features on p.90.

37. **Gail Omvedt** [p.234], who followed in Eleanor Zelliot's footsteps to chronicle the anti-caste movement in India, went on to become a part of the movements that she observed and wrote about. Her lifelong study of anti-caste thought led to the work *Seeking Begumpura*: *The Social Vision of Anticaste Intellectuals* (New Delhi: Navayana, 2008), where she linked the earliest anti-caste voices such as Namdev and Kabir to Ambedkar. In the chapter on the poet Namdev, she discusses the possible feminine origins of the divinised figure of Vitthal (86).

38. **Jayant Lele** [p.234], in an important but neglected essay, "The Bhakti Movement in India: A Critical Introduction" (*Journal of Asian and African Studies* 1980, 15: 1–2), says that bhakti's origins stem from Buddhism, and there are even perhaps 'pre-Vedic tribal origins of bhakti'. Crucially for us, he says: 'Dalit intellectuals in Maharashtra, not unlike their savarna counterparts, are, it seems to me, exercising two faculties at the same time but in isolation from each other. They are correctly suspicious and critical of bhakti. They see Chokhamela as well as his followers of today as being taken for a ride by the hegemonic classes, and perhaps rightly so. But they also fail to examine the source of the potency of the Warkari message and practice for most non-Mahar Dalits. In this, they act out of an arrogant elitism which makes them indistinguishable from savarna intellectuals whose hegemony they reject. While they show a willingness to suspect the legitimacy of Warkari symbolism—for it has done nothing but legitimize oppression—they also show a willingness to listen without suspicion to the symbolism of Marxism or Buddhism.'

39. **Ambedkar's dismissal** [p.235] of the bhakti saints is discussed in passing in Ashok Gopal's work, *A Part Apart: The Life and Thought of B.R. Ambedkar* (New Delhi: Navayana, 2023), p.83–84.

40. For an engrossing narrative on how the god Vitthal has likely Buddhist origins and a discussion of Chokhamela's **Abhang 283** [p.235] among others, see this episode on the popular Marathi YouTube channel, Buddh Vitevari (बुद्ध विटेवरी): https://www.youtube.com/watch?v=UrAhaW_ sUuw. Run by a farmer and local historian called Sriranga Panduranga Paval of Karmala village (Solapur district, Maharashtra), it is dedicated to a Buddhist reclamation of the history of the sainted Marathi poets. Over a phone call in April 2024, Dalit History Month, during a round of edits on this book, Paval told me: 'What you call Buddhist bhikkhus were the ones who became our sants and gave us all this poetry.' For the likely Buddhist and even nomadic origins of the cult of Vitthal, see the scholar Ramchandra Chintaman Dhere's *Sri Vitthal: Ek Mahasamnvay* (Lord Vitthal: A Great Confluence or Syncretization, 1984 in Marathi; translated into English by Anne Feldhaus in 2001 as *Rise of a Folk God Vitthal of Pandharpur*, New Delhi: Oxford University Press), and the chapters on Namdev and Tukaram in Gail Omvedt's *Seeking Begumpura* (Note 34).

41. *Annihilation of Caste* [p.236] is perhaps Ambedkar's most read work, and has spawned hundreds of editions in many Indian languages. Ambedkar self-published it in 1936 after the Jat-Pat-Todak Mandal of Lahore (Forum for Break-up of Caste), a radical offshoot of the reformist Arya Samaj, invited and then disinvited him from delivering the presidential address at their annual conference. The Mandal asked for and received the text of the speech in advance, and found the contents 'unbearable'. Realizing

that Ambedkar intended to use its platform not just to criticize the practice of caste, but to denounce Hinduism itself, the invitation was withdrawn. The speech-text dared to imagine a society without caste at a time when caste and varna had champion defenders. On 15 May 1936, Ambedkar printed 1500 copies of *Annihilation of Caste* at his own expense. It was soon translated into six languages. Ignored by most of the intellectuals and the media of the time, only M.K. Gandhi came up with a tepid response in *Harijan*, which Ambedkar rebutted. In the third edition, issued in 1944, Ambedkar says he hoped to produce a combined edition of "Castes in India" (Note 30) and *Annihilation of Caste*, but 'as I could not find time, and as there is very little prospect of my being able to do so ... I am content to let this be a mere reprint of the Second Edition.' In 2014, I annotated and published a critical edition of *Annihilation of Caste* at Navayana with an introduction by the writer Arundhati Roy. This invited scathing criticism from several Dalits and anti-caste writers, academics and activists who wondered how a Savarna duo like Roy and I could appropriate and repackage a foundational text of the Dalit movement. A selection of these critiques was compiled and published as *Hatred in the Belly: Politics Behind the Appropriation of Dr Ambedkar's Writings*, described by its publisher as 'a collection of essays by writers, academics, students and activists, who are referred to as the Ambedkar Age Collective' (Hyderabad: The Shared Mirror, 2015).

42. **Dhananjay Keer**'s [p.237] biography, *Dr Babasaheb Ambedkar: Life and Mission*, was first published in 1954 (Mumbai: Popular Prakashan). I am citing from the 2002 reprint of the third edition, p.482.

43. I chanced upon this **unpublished, rare, handwritten essay by Ambedkar, "Who is Pandurang?"** [p.238], in 2013

in the private collection of Ramesh Tukaram Shinde, the octogenarian mnemonist and archivist of Ambedkariana in Mumbai. I was allowed to click photographs of the brittle papers on my phone. Ambedkar here is referring to G.H. Khare's 1953 work *Sri Vitthala ani Pandharpur* (published from Pune). Ambedkar likely wrote this just a few years before he formally embraced Buddhism. In this essay, he proposes that Vitthal is yet another Vishnuized form of the Buddha.

44. According to Ashok Gopal, author of *A Part Apart: The Life and Thought of B.R. Ambedkar* (New Delhi: Navayana, 2023), on **13 October 1935**, addressing thousands of his supporters in **Yeola** [p.238], a small town near Nashik, Ambedkar declared that he was going to renounce the Hindu religion. Gopal translates from a report dated 20 October 1935 in the Marathi weekly *Vividh Vritta*, that quoted Ambedkar as saying: 'I had the misfortune of being born with the "Untouchable Hindu" stain; that was not in my hands. Nevertheless, I can shake off this degrading status and improve my condition. I do not have the slightest doubt that I will do that. Let me make it clear: I will not die as a person who calls himself a Hindu!' (37).

45. **Parita Mukta**'s essay [p.240] "Mirabai in Rajasthan" appeared in the journal *Manushi: A Journal about Women and Society* in January–June 1989 (94–99). Mukta went on to publish the ground-breaking *Upholding the Common Life: The Community of Mirabai* (New Delhi: Oxford University Press, 1984), where she shows us how Mira, cast out and reviled by the Rajputs, was adopted by a range of labouring castes, and how her songs and life are remembered among members of these communities in Rajasthan and Gujarat. Mukta distinguishes the domesticated 'Mirabai' manufactured by nationalistic forces from the radical

untamed Mira who lives and thrives among the so-called lower castes. In these stories and histories, the Rajput-born Mira is often the chief disciple of the poet Raidas (also spelt Ravidas, Rohidas), born a Chamar and a native of Benares, who's said to have met her when he was on a pilgrimage with Kabir's daughter, Kamali. (This speculative history inspired the Kabiri poem—"देखन देखत हो/ It is seeing"—in this *Notbook*.) Mukta writes, 'Though the "historical" claim to the relationship between Mira and Rohidas is open to question there are strong indications that on the ground Mira was widely revered as the disciple of Rohidas. So much so that by AD 1693 the linking of Mira's name to Rohidas had spread to the Punjab, and had been accepted in the hagiographical literature there' (79).

46. **Kazimir Malevich** (1878–1935) [p.242] was a Russian avant-garde artist who espoused non-objective art through an abstract form of painting of geometric figures that he called Suprematism. He advocated and practised an art of pure form, where colour, line and shape reigned supreme over subject matter and narrative. This, he believed, was universally comprehensible. In "The Non-Objective World: The Manifesto of Suprematism" (1926), he wrote, 'To the Suprematist the visual phenomena of the objective world are, in themselves, meaningless; the significant thing is feeling.' See britannica.com/biography/Kazimir-Malevich

47. See the **online Britannica** [p.243] entry: britannica.com/topic/guru-Hinduism

48. **Georg Bühler's** [p.244] 1886 translation, *The Laws of Manu*, first featured as volume 25 in the 50-volume series "Sacred Books of the East" edited by Max Müller and published by the Oxford University Press between 1879 and 1910. It can be accessed on archive.org.

49. **Charlotte Vaudeville** (1918–2006) [p.248] was a French Indologist who was well versed in Hindi and Avadhi and studied various bhakti poets of the north: Mira, Surdas, Malik Muhmmad Jayasi and Kabir. *A Weaver Named Kabir: Selected Verses with a Detailed Biographical and Historical Introduction*, published in 1993 by Oxford University Press (Delhi), is a revised edition of *Kabir: Vol 1*, originally published by the Clarendon Press, Oxford, in 1974. The 1993 edition, which remains in print, gives us the context and milieu in which Kabir emerged, and discusses his many predecessors and contemporaries. The first half of the book comprises introductory essays, and the latter half contains translations of selected verses from various 'standard' editions of Kabir published in the twentieth century, and also select verses of his forerunners and coevals.

50. See the philosopher **Slavoj Žižek**'s [p.248] short essay (2004) "A Cup of Decaf Reality", accessed at lacan.com/zizekdecaf.htm. He repeats this point in many of his works.

51. It was through **Coleman Barks**'s [p.248] bestselling translation of Rumi that I was introduced to Rumi in my twenties, in the 1990s. Barks's Rumi—with over twenty volumes in thirty years—tops the charts in poetry across the world with a host of celebrities (Coldplay's Chris Martin to Tilda Swinton, Madonna to Brad Pitt) courting this version of the thirteenth-century Sufi poet. Recently, there's been some pushback. A *New Yorker* article (5 January 2017), "The Erasure of Islam from the Poetry of Rumi" by Rozina Ali, takes issue with this anodyne approach. She points to efforts to look for mystical poetry from the Arab world sans Islam since the Victorian era, and how Barks, steeped in this tradition, vastly expanded Rumi's readership. 'He is not a translator so much as an interpreter: he does not read or write Persian. Instead, he transforms

nineteenth-century translations into American verse. ... Fatemeh Keshavarz, a professor of Persian studies at the University of Maryland, told me that Rumi probably had the Koran memorized, given how often he drew from it in his poetry. Rumi himself described the "Masnavi" as "the roots of the roots of the roots of religion"—meaning Islam—"and the explainer of the Koran." And yet little trace of the religion exists in the translations that sell so well in the United States. "The Rumi that people love is very beautiful in English, and the price you pay is to cut the culture and religion," Jawid Mojaddedi, a scholar of early Sufism at Rutgers, told me recently.'

52. **John Stratton Hawley** [p.251], professor of religion at Columbia University, has extensively worked on bhakti traditions in north India. This passage on Kabir and Ramanand is from his 2005 work, *Three Bhakti Voices: Mirabai, Surdas, and Kabir in Their Times and Ours* (Delhi: Oxford University Press), p.272. He also uses the same passage in his introduction to the American poet Robert Bly's bestselling 2004 edition of Kabir's poems, *Kabir: Ecstatic Poems* (New York: Beacon Press). Bly calls his work, originally published in 1976, 'versions' of Kabir, which are quite like Coleman Barks doing Rumi. It was Bly who introduced the idea of working on Rumi to Barks in 1976.

53. **"The Riddle of Rama and Krishna"** [p.265] features in Ambedkar's *Riddles in Hinduism* discussed earlier in Note 11. Besides berating Rama for murdering Shambuka, Ambedkar also says: 'The murder of Vali is the greatest blot on the character of Rama. It was a crime which was thoroughly unprovoked, for Vali had no quarrel with Rama. It was most cowardly act for Vali was unarmed. It was a planned and premeditated murder.' When *Riddles in Hinduism* was published in 1987 under BAWS Volume

4, protests broke out in Maharashtra. Copies of the book were burnt in public at a Maratha Mahamandal meeting in Amravati in January 1988. The state government withdrew the book when the Shiv Sena rioted in Mumbai for the removal of the chapter, "The Riddle of Rama and Krishna". After thousands of Dalits staged counter-protests across the state, the chapter was reinstated but with a caveat: 'The government does not concur with views expressed in this chapter.' The government edition carries this disclaimer till date.

54. *Beef, Brahmins and Broken Men* (2019) [p.266] is an annotated critical edition of selections from Ambedkar's 1948 work *The Untouchables: Who were they and why they became Untouchables?* See also Note 30.

55. For the riveting 18-min excerpt focused on Ayaz from Virmani's documentary *Had Anhad* [p.293], see "Episode 6", youtube.com/watch?v=EWH3vxIYZcA

Acknowledgements
आभार

Over the years I have learnt much from the artists I first discovered through Shabnam Virmani and "The Kabir Project" she oversees. I owe a special thanks to her and Fariduddin Ayaz–Abu Mohammed and their qawwal troupe, and to Kaluram Bamaniya, Mukhtiyar Ali, Prahlad Tipaniya, Mahesha Ram, Shafi Mohammed Faqir, Kashi Ba and the many wayfarers on this many-forked road, most of whose work is now shared generously online on ajabshahar.com and YouTube. I am indebted to Kumar Gandharva and his song-poetry of Kabir, to which I began paying fresh attention only into my fortieth year. I thank Linda Hess for her work. The meticulous scholarship of Charlotte Vaudeville remains unsurpassed. Each of these Kabirs is distinct and yet they are all undergirded by one immortal idea: the liberties Kabir lovingly allows us to take. All the other artists whose singing helps me fathom the fathomlessness of Kabir are mentioned in the body of this book. I have not met most of these artists, scholars and translators. I have corresponded over texts and a few calls with Kaluram ji. After work on this book was almost complete, I had a joyous meeting with Ustad Mukhtiyar Ali in August 2022 in Jaipur at a baithak. It was listening to him and singing with him that made me return to this script, which I had set aside. This book owes to all those named and not, invoked by the sign Kabir. It is in this sense a shared effort—and yet I string my name to it.

First among friends, Venkat, who stirred both the Kabir and the music I had stilled within me. Over the years many friends have put up with my writing, some with my singing too, and some sent Kabir my way: Sowmya, Akila, Anushiya, Mini, Amit, Arif, Alex, Sharmi, Rama, Sheela ji, Gitanjali, Salim, Manisha, Rahul, Saumya, Juli, Asad, Ankit, Sucheta, and the late Faruqi saab. Shomo and Bhanwar have left their imprint on this book, as has Douglas Harper of etymonline.com. Gail is not around to see this, but her re-envisioning of Raidas's Beghampura shaped my thinking. My Amma, who set me on the course of music. To Pushpesh Pant and Sangam House, I owe the time spent in Ranikhet (Jayanti Residency) that has left its impress on this *Notbook*. Reyazul Haque went through the manuscript, especially the Nagari sections, and corrected it with care and love. Swati Singh made her point.

The role Alex George has played as an editor goes beyond duty. Possessed by the spirit of Kabir, the Kabir in him came to life. He has pushed me to be better than I am. In the guise of editing one Kabiri poem, देखन देखत हो, he threaded his way in. Now, he owns this doha:

कहे अलेक्सा सुनो सब कामरेड   Kahe Alexa suno sab comrade
I'm the edit you can't evade   में वो हूं जो समझे सब भेद

In other words: Says Alex, listen up comrade/ I know your secrets, you've been made.

Jerry Pinto read the final draft with a generous heart and a critical eye that are unique to him—his suggestions and comments helped me sharpen some lines. The feedback

Linda Hess offered, sifting each verse and line, was both jheenii and nyaaraa. I thank both of them, and all those who read *The Notbook* and have said kind things about it so that readers may kindly take my Kabir home.

Agent Kanishka Gupta has championed the book. His reader Janani Ganesan's questions and responses helped me arrive at the title. Without Neelini Sarkar's careful eye, this might have been a Nitbook. At Penguin, I thank and bow to everyone.

The labours of Rukmini and Dharmender subsidized my ill-earned leisure at Hilltop Apartments, Neb Sarai—home for ten years in Dilli—where much of this book got cooked.

Priya, my saans, told me what to cut, what to let go: she is *The Notbook*'s fragrance.

To my Ustad, Faiyaz Wasifuddin Dagar, I owe my sa.

Scan QR code to access the
curated YouTube playlist of songs from
The Notbook of Kabir

Scan QR code to access the
Penguin Random House India website